Objective Approaches
to Personality Assessment

THE UNIVERSITY SERIES IN PSYCHOLOGY

Editor

DAVID C. McCLELLAND
Harvard University

Objective Approaches
to Personality Assessment

Edited by

BERNARD M. BASS AND IRWIN A. BERG

Department of Psychology
Louisiana State University

D. VAN NOSTRAND COMPANY, INC.

PRINCETON, NEW JERSEY

TORONTO   LONDON

NEW YORK

D. VAN NOSTRAND COMPANY, INC.
120 Alexander St., Princeton, New Jersey (*Principal office*)
257 Fourth Avenue, New York 10, New York

D. VAN NOSTRAND COMPANY, LTD.
358, Kensington High Street, London, W.14, England

D. VAN NOSTRAND COMPANY (Canada), LTD.
25 Hollinger Road, Toronto 16, Canada

Published simultaneously in Canada by
D. VAN NOSTRAND COMPANY (Canada), LTD.

Library of Congress Catalogue Card No. 59-9762

PRINTED IN THE UNITED STATES OF AMERICA

Preface

T HE PRESENT BOOK comprises a collection of hitherto unpublished papers which were read in Baton Rouge at a Louisiana State University Psychology Symposium, February 1958, the aim of which was to present the most recent concepts and developments in objective personality assessment. Accordingly, nationally known experts from virtually every section of the country were invited to read papers concerned with their current thinking about problems of objective personality measurement, together with a description of some of their present research and its background.

The final result is considered to be an accurate representation of what leaders in the field of objective personality testing are now doing. This volume tells what many of the personality tests of tomorrow will look like and what the rationale behind them will be. There was, of course, no general agreement about personality measurement among the authors. About the only point of real agreement was that personality testing should be objective. Even here, the historian of the symposium, Robert I. Watson, a clinician of note though not a dedicated objective measurement psychologist, was moved to protest when the clinical usefulness of the *Rorschach* and other projective devices was seriously questioned during one of the discussion periods.

Each of the contributors has developed a definite approach to measuring one or more facets of personality; and he acknowledges, at least by implication, a serene confidence in his methodology. He sees room for improvement, of course, in what he is doing and he is willing to discuss it. He sees even greater room for improvement in what his colleagues are doing, at least as they revealed their professional activities at the symposium.

It is impossible to capture in print the total atmosphere of a symposium where oral exchanges are many, where gestures and expressions often convey as much meaning as the words used. Yet, if one were to describe the general flavor of the meetings, it would be that one distinctly felt that the speakers knew what they were doing and that they enjoyed doing it. This was reflected in the willingness, almost eagerness of each speaker, to reply to all questions raised by members of a sizeable audience and to answer without cavil.

Thus far, the present editors have been referring to the invited speakers who assembled to present their papers. Each of the speakers, it is true, exerted some form of catalytic effect upon the others; yet there was more. There was the audience, of course, and there were several people who were invited because the editors, in planning the symposium, believed these persons would contribute directly to the atmosphere of scholarly enthusiasm. There was, for instance, H. Max Houtchens of the Veterans Administration Central Office in Washington. He has a trick of quietly asking some of the most pointed questions in the kindliest way imaginable and serves, thereby, as a first-order clarifier of cloudy issues.

Out of the informal interchange several points appeared. The speakers had nothing against projective tests as such but they liked objective tests better, at least, as they conceived of them. As may be noted in the first chapter, the conceptions of *objective* vary somewhat, even among a group of experts such as the authors of this book. But objective in their fashion, the speakers at the symposium liked objective tests for reasons which may be summarized as follows:

1. They are usually easier to administer (often requiring little training of test examiners).

2. They are more easily evaluated. It is usually much easier to gauge the reliability and validity of objective than subjective tests. It is thus easier to discover the errors in one's measurements which is less often true in the case of subjective assessment.

3. Objective testing is more likely to contribute to constructing a body of theory and generalization about human behavior. If there is to be a true "science of personality," a body of integrated constructs anchored by operational definitions to observables, the observables will have to be measured objectively.

The present symposium is part of the graduate training program in psychology at Louisiana State University. It would have been much smaller in scope were it not for the broad professional vision of the administrators of the Louisiana State Department of Hospitals. This state agency supplies funds for training and research in psychiatry, psychiatric social work, psychiatric nursing, and clinical psychology, with provision for visiting lecturers being typically included in such grants. This is one product of the firm conviction of the Department of Hospital administrators that those who serve the State should have the best training possible. Therefore it is a pleasure to thank Mr. Jesse H. Bankston, Director of the Department of Hospitals, and his program directors, Mr. Winborn E. Davis and Mr. E. R. Rogillio, for their encouragement and for their uncompromising stand on quality in professional training. The present symposium is but one product of their far-sightedness.

Manuscript preparation is always a chore and sometimes irksome. The present task was less irksome than usual because Mr. Arthur Kaufman checked the references, while Mrs. Vera Foil and Mrs. Floy Brown did the final typing of the manuscript. Mrs. Sylvia Berg is to be thanked heartily for her work with the Author Index; Mrs. June T. Bradford for her completion of the Subject Index.

BERNARD M. BASS
IRWIN A. BERG

Baton Rouge, Louisiana

Contents

Historical Review of Objective Personality Testing: The Search for Objectivity

Robert I. Watson
Northwestern University

The NOTED philosopher of science, Herbert Feigl, considers a major standard of science to be inter-subjective testability. Concerning intersubjective testability he writes:

This is only a more adequate formulation of what is generally meant by the "objectivity" of science. What is here involved is not only the freedom from personal or cultural bias or partiality, but—even more fundamentally—the requirement that the knowledge claims of science be in principle capable of test (confirmation or disconfirmation, at least indirectly and to some degree) on the part of any person properly equipped with intelligence and the technical devices of observation or experimentation. The term *intersubjective* stresses the social nature of the scientific enterprise. If there be any "truths" that are accessible only to privileged individuals, such as mystics or visionaries—that is, knowledge-claims which by their very nature cannot independently be checked by anyone else—then such "truths" are not of the kind that we seek in the sciences. The criterion of intersubjective testability thus delimits the scientific from the nonscientific activities of man. (15, p. 11).

I would add that objectivity is a goal of science, not a prerequisite for scientific endeavors. Objectivity is not absolute, but relative. It is not unusual in science for basic phenomena to be first described in a qualitative way. Objective methods emerge only upon more intensive study. Our efforts are in the direction of increasing objectivity whenever possible, but this does not mean that we can neglect problems simply because they are not yet objective. At least some of us select problems which we feel are capable of being rendered more objective and make our research task this search for increasing objectivity. For example, in Chapter 9 by Hunt, we shall find that a demonstration of the reliability of clinical judgment is a means whereby the clinician, himself, becomes a more objective instrument. In the present chapter, a major theme is the search for objectivity in personality testing.

Of necessity, my topic must be considered in a somewhat narrower framework than the entire scope of personality theory. A major omission in the consideration of objectivity in personality evaluation is the argument as to why one should go beyond the objective approach, as advanced by philosophical and phenomenological characterologists. This, otherwise, serious omission is tempered somewhat by the fact that the characterologists have not been particularly interested in psychological testing, despite the fact that many projective tests can be shown to be interpretable on phenomenological principles.

In order to place objective personality testing in historical perspective, it is necessary to say something about objective psychological testing in general. We cannot ignore early mental testing in our search for the beginnings of personality testing, for to do so would be to ignore a truism of historical research—that the beginnings of attention to a topic may not be referred to in the same manner as it is referred to in later years. Personality, as our various conceptions now regard it, was not a systematic rubric in the earlier psychological traditions. Lack of specific reference, however, does not prevent us from seeing in the perspective of the present-day, some of the aspects of what we now call personality. So we begin with the history of testing, not the history of personality testing, narrowly regarded.

BEGINNINGS OF OBJECTIVE TESTING

At the time the history of objective psychological testing begins, in about 1880-1890, the mind was still the subject matter of psychology. For our purposes, we can turn to a classification of tests adopted by Whipple in his 1910 publication, *Manual of Mental and Physical Tests* (37).[1] Mental tests served the purpose of determin-

[1] Numerals in parentheses refer to bibliographical references at the end of each chapter.

ing and measuring some phase of mental capacity or trait. I would like to add parenthetically that even in 1910 he could plead that what was needed was not new tests, but an exhaustive investigation of those already available. But to return to his classification of mental tests, the major heading (disregarding the anthropometric) were physical and motor capacity, sensory capacity, attention and perception, description and report, association learning and memory, suggestibility, imagination and invention, and intelligence. Note, there is no mention of personality. However, the tests of suggestibility and imagination and invention could be called personality tests in today's perspective. It would also be possible to include description and report in the scope of personality. Note also that tests for emotion were not mentioned, for measures of emotion came later. Many of the personality questionnaires of the twenties were called measures of emotionality. So, too, were more objective efforts, such as the X-O, or cross-out tests of Pressey, in which the number of words found to be unpleasant was the affectivity score. With this justification of what is included in the discussion to follow, we may now turn to the history of mental tests.

Sir Francis Galton shares with James McKeen Cattell, the founding of psychological testing. As early as 1882, Galton had established a small laboratory in London where, for a small fee, individuals could take a series of physical measurements and tests of reaction time and sensory acuity. (One might ask in passing whether this payment meant that he was the first psychological practitioner.) The very fact that he thought people would be interested in their standing on these measures shows their test-orientation.

Galton was primarily interested in no less than an inventory of human abilities. He related these to his evolutionary views and to his studies of inheritance, but the fact remains, that he conceived of his various measures as tapping as broad a spectrum of psychological characteristics as was possible. If the term, personality, had been used as it is now, I believe he would not have hesitated to use it to describe some of his efforts.

In a paper published in 1890, in which he coined the term, mental tests, Cattell proposed a standard series of tests to be applied for "discovering the constancy of mental processes, their interdependence, and their variation under different circumstances" (6, p. 373). He offered both a select list of ten tests then being used in the Psychological Laboratory of the University of Pennsylvania, and a longer list of 50 others proposed for further consideration. The ten tests were dynamometer pressure, rate of movement, two-point threshold, pain sensitivity, least noticeable difference in weight, reaction time for sound, time for naming colors, bisection of a 50 cm. line, judgment of ten seconds time, and those numbers of letters repeated on once hearing. The list of 50 was essentially similar. The fact that Galton (6) contributed a number of comments at the end of this article gives unequivocal evidence of the connection between Galton's interest in individual differences and the mental-test movement.

Earlier, in 1883, with his already formed interests in individual differences and in reaction time as a measure of intelligence, Cattell had gone to Wundt's laboratory. Here he had completed his doctoral dissertation on his own problem of individual differences in reaction times, which Wundt, it might be added, had viewed dubiously as a suitable problem for a psychologist to undertake.

After Cattell's sojourn at the University of Pennsylvania, he moved to Columbia University, where he continued his testing program with essentially the same battery of tests. After several years' data had been collected, a monograph by Clark Wissler (39) appeared in 1901 reporting the findings. Correlation between results from the various tests and academic class standing was negligible. Moreover, the tests were no more intercorrelated among themselves than they were related to class standing. This was in sharp contrast to the substantial correlations found between standing on the various college subjects. These disappointing results, plus another negative trial made in Titchener's laboratory by Sharp (29), probably did much to make psychologists lose interest in the topic. Certainly, other students of Titchener and Cattell did not follow up these matters with laboratory devices. These two men were training the majority of psychologists who did not receive their training in Europe. On the continent Wundt's emphasis upon the generalized human mind, a view which was shared by most other European psychologists, did nothing to encourage further exploration.

The interest in simple sensory and motor tests during this period was theoretical and was laboratory-bound. Interest in individual differences was central. Measuring devices were single tests, not organized into scales. The now usual checks on reliability were missing, and standardization, aside from a certain similarity of instruction, was lacking. The first period of objective testing, then, is that of the laboratory. After these negative findings, the enthusiasm for, and interest in them was much less.

So we have seen that initial enthusiasm for mental tests in the

United States was met by negative results and this particular line of development lapsed, in what may be, for convenience, referred to as the laboratory period in psychological testing.

EARLY LACK OF CONCERN FOR OBJECTIVE TESTING

It is pertinent to pause to consider psychologists' views in relation to this search for objectivity. It is probable that the question of objectivity did not concern them because of the origins of test materials in the laboratory. Reaction time devices measure reaction time; learning nonsense syllables is learning. The process measured was defined by the material, just as in the laboratory today one does not ask, "Are we really measuring learning?" when serial learning lists are exposed or maze paths are threaded. These measures had what we now would call content validity. Content validity is the degree to which the test samples the universe of content specified, as in an achievement test and in the usual measures for the experiments in learning. The step from measuring reaction time to using it for the measurement of intelligence "because intelligence calls for speedy reaction," seemed plausible but of no great theoretical moment. It was not then seen that it was a great leap from observed behavior to construct.

By and large, the question of objectivity was not verbalized during these years. Psychology, after all, was still the study of mental structures or functions, and introspection the method for advancement of psychological knowledge. For example, Whipple, (37) in his 1910 authoritative and widely used test manual, does not mention objectivity. He does, however, speak of standardization of conditions, which is conducive to objectivity. Familiarity with instructions and their clarity were also stressed. General knowledge of the literature and an inspection of some of the textbooks of the period, however, did not reveal discussion of objectivity as a topic. After all, psychologists could not use "objective" in referring to a subjective science. But this does not mean they were unaware of the problem. In fact, the centuries-old question of the personal equation which, years later, Wundt's students and others investigated, is a recognition of precisely this point. So, too, is the psychologist's fallacy of James, the confusion of the personal standpoint with the mental facts. Training of introspectors served the same function of increasing what we could call objectivity.

INTELLIGENCE TESTING

It is tempting, but not particularly germane to the major issue, to turn now to the work of Binet who, after working with similar sensory and motor tests with similarly unproductive results, eventually found in more complex or higher mental functions the means to measure intelligence. But this is part of the history of intelligence testing of 1900-1920. In the United States this history of intelligence testing was not closely bound to personality testing, for various reasons. Interest in and research on intelligence testing were directly related to Binet's efforts but the others who came after him did not continue his systematic analytic interests. Those who followed Binet were pragmatic and interested in the application of intelligence tests to social matters, such as mental retardation, school placement, and the like. But they were so absorbed with their instruments of measurement that they were not very much interested in problems beyond these instruments.

As the well-known definition would have it, psychologists of that day, and for some years to come, tended to consider intelligence to be whatever intelligence tests measured. So, in this sense, interest was in intelligence as a global concept. And yet, what Spearman called the anarchic theory of mental structure, a theory of extreme specificity of mental structure and function, was the prevailing view. The studies of William James, Thorndike, and others on transfer of training had fostered the view that abilities were highly specific. The results of sensory-motor testing, described earlier, had much the same effect. Thus, we had the practical pragmatic interests in intelligence testing, on the one hand, and, on the other, even larger segments of the psychological field in which abilities and traits were viewed as highly specific.

This lack of relevance of developments in the specific areas of intelligence testing, during these years in the United States, curiously enough, does not seem to have a counterpart in Britain. In a sense, the British psychologists continued more closely the tradition of the laboratory that has been described. In part, this was due to the impetus of Galton and a continued stress on the part of his students on individual difference. In part, it was due to the statistical advances in England, first under Galton and Pearson, and later under Spearman and Burt.

Many of the tests used in Britain at the turn of the century were the logical derivatives of earlier sensory and motor tests, but they also included as measures, association tests, such as retention measures, target aiming, card-sorting, and the like.

In an important paper published in 1904, Spearman (30) criticized the previous methodological efforts on statistical grounds. For example, many earlier workers had failed to use quantitatively precise statements of the degree of correlation between tests, they did not calculate the probable error, and they did not allow for errors of observation. In addition, based upon his correlation between sensory tests and estimates of intelligence, Spearman arrived at the conclusion that "all branches of intellectual activity have in common one fundamental function . . . (30, p. 284). Thus was launched the beginnings of the thinking from which, a few years later, came factor analysis. The British psychologists saw more clearly than their American contemporaries the reasons that early attempts at testing had failed.

Above all, they had something positive and challenging to work with in factor analysis. Their general associationist background was conducive to continuing this tradition. They continued an interest in these measures, gradually including more and more material relevant to the higher mental processes.

Factor analysis is a tool, by the very nature of which you cannot in advance tell what factors will emerge. True, the material was so selected as to get at intellectual function, but the nature of the technique required an analytic attitude. Nor were nonintellectual factors entirely neglected. The pioneering factor analytic study of Webb (36) in 1915 was based on ratings and yielded a factor which seemed to be strength of character or will, called *w*. Burt (4), the same year, briefly reported on the interrelation of ratings of emotions. But now we must return to developments taking place in the United States in 1910's and 1920's.

BEHAVIORISM AND OBJECTIVITY OF MEASUREMENT

The appearance of Behaviorism, with its militant espousal of an objective approach, had a profound effect on psychological thinking. For our purposes, it may be dated by the appearance of the work of John B. Watson, beginning in 1913 with his articles and culminating in his 1919 publication, *Psychology from the Standpoint of a Behaviorist*. Mentalistic terms, including, "subjective" became epithets. The Russian reflexology, which came into being in the immediately preceding years, is sometimes referred to as, "Objective

Psychology," after the book by that name published in 1910 by Bekhterev.

Psychologists then found in objectivity a standard of science. No longer did they have to struggle with mediate and immediate experience, dependent and independent experience, and the differences between the objective science of physics, and the subjective science of psychology. They could then use "objectivity" proudly, as we do to this very day. In the recently received copy of the supplement to the *Psychological Review*, there was a "Glossary of Some Terms Used in the Objective Science of Behavior," by Verplanck (34), who did not even find it necessary to define objective among the many, many terms covered.

The spirit of the times or the *Zeitgeist*, a term popularized by E. G. Boring, had prepared the way for the appearance of an interest in performance tests. An interesting example is the Will-Temperament Test, a behavior measure, which fitted in with the times. In 1919, June Downey (11) introduced a test for the measurement of what she called will-temperament. Its nature was intriguing, consisting largely as it did of handwriting samples under different conditions and, thus, behavioral in nature. A sample of writing was obtained at "ordinary" speed (for a baseline), as rapidly as possible (to get a comparison with ordinary speed on the theory that those writing much slower than they can are subject to a load or inhibition), in a different style (to measure flexibility), as slowly as possible (to measure motor inhibition or control), and so on. The test appealed to the desire for objectivity; so it was met with enthusiasm. It was given trial after trial until about fifty studies were performed, despite almost uniformly negative results from the beginning. It was as if such a behavioral test as this could not fail to work, just because it was a behavioral approach. The test is also important as the first major performance measure of personality.

Another of the earlier performance measures of personality was that used in 1921 in the study by Voelker (35) of "moral reactions to conduct." This was followed in 1923 by the Character Education Inquiry, with which we associate the names of Hartshorne and May, and which produced well-known performance tests for honesty, trustworthiness, helpfulness, inhibition, and persistence. The nature of these tests is too well known to pause over them. Their findings of the low correlation between specific measures helped to accentuate an era of considerable skepticism about tests as measures of personality, or that Spearman referred to as the anarchic view.

Behaviorism, itself, with its emphasis upon S-R bonds and personality as a bundle of habits, had helped to bring about this skepticism concerning tests on the part of many psychologists. The results of Hartshorne and May, even though behavioral, however, were another invitation akin to that furnished by the earlier results of Wissler and Sharp, to see testing in a skeptical light.

Performance tests are logically and chronologically related to assessment procedures of the miniature life situation sort. They, too, have a long past despite their short history. The earliest statement of the potentials of this method is probably that of Galton (19). In 1884 he wrote:

Emergencies need not be waited for, they can be extemporized; traps, as it were, can be laid. Thus, a great ruler whose word can make or mar a subject's fortune, wants a secret agent and tests his character during a single interview. He contrives by a few minutes' questioning, temptation, and show of displeasure, to turn his character inside out, exciting in turns his hopes, fear, zeal, loyalty, ambition, and so forth. Ordinary observers who stand on a far lower pedestal, cannot hope to excite the same tension and outburst of feeling in those whom they examine, but they can obtain good data in a more leisurely way. If they are unable to note a man's conduct under great trials for want of opportunity, they may do it in small ones, and it is well that those small occasions should be such as are of frequent occurrence, that the statistics of men's conduct under like conditions may be compared. After fixing upon some particular class of persons of similar age, sex, and social conditions, we have to find out what common incidents in their lives are most apt to make them betray their character. We may then take note as often as we can, of what they do on these occasions, so as to arrive at their statistics of conduct in a limited number of well-defined small trials (30, p. 182).

He goes on to offer specific suggestions, such as the following:

The poetical metaphors of ordinary language suggest many possibilities of measurement. Thus when two persons have an "inclination" to one another, they visibly incline or slope together when sitting side by side, as at a dinner-table, and they then throw the stress of their weights on the near legs of their chairs. It does not require much ingenuity to arrange a pressure gauge with an index and dial to indicate changes in stress, but it is difficult to devise an arrangement that shall fulfill the threefold condition of being effective, not attracting notice, and being applicable to ordinary furniture. I made some rude experiments, but being busy with other matters, have not carried them on, as I had hoped (30, p. 184).

In view of the date in which this was published, 1884, it would be possible to argue that this was the first proposal for an objective personality measure.

MODERN ASSESSMENT METHODS

Modern assessment procedures, as in the stress interview, the OSS procedures, and the Michigan VA trainee study, are apparently moving out of a period in which they were enthusiastically accepted and tried, to a period of skepticism about them. If there is to be a period of synthesis, it is too early to predict its nature.

Personality Questionnaire

I shall now turn to personality questionnaires in this search for objectivity. During World War I, Woodworth's *Personal Data Sheet,* or, as it was later called, the *Psychoneurotic Inventory,* was developed. It contained 116 items derived from descriptions of symptoms of neurotic patients (18). "Yes" or "no" responses were called for and were scored by simple counting to arrive at a total. Because the Armistice intervened, this inventory was not used extensively in the military setting. It became, over the years, the form to which to turn to select and develop items.

We have had since that time a phenomenal growth in the development and application of personality questionnaires. Macfarlane (22), in a critique of projective testing, spoke of the rapidity of appearance of projective instruments as partaking of the nature of a virulent infection. This remark can be applied with equal force to the self-report personality questionnaire. I would roughly estimate from the Buros reviews of mental measurements and other sources that either as single short questionnaires or in multiple capsule form, at least 500 commercially available personality questionnaires have appeared. A tremendous number of psychologists (including the present writer) helped to develop these get-knowl-edge-quick devices.

There is no question that personality questionnaires had their period of enthusiastic acceptance. Their appeal was to be found in their partial objectivity; a score could be derived on which independent scorers could agree. Scoring, did not then, nor does it now, ordinarily involve subjective judgment. Nevertheless, several very important sources of subjectivity were present which, at first, were obscured by scoring objectivity. Customarily, they are not independent of the motivation of the person completing the questionnaire; there is conscious deception, and there is unconscious distortion. It is to another subjective factor, however, to which detailed illustrative attention will be given. These questionnaires are subjective in that they require interpretation of the meaning of the questions asked by the tester.

Interpretive subjectivity for the person taking them is rampant in most personality questionnaires. Consider an early study of Benton (3). He interviewed subjects after completion of questionnaire items, as to what they thought was meant by the items. He found, for example, that the item, "Do you take pride in your physical appearance?" was answered as if the question meant, do you always feel proud, sometimes feel proud, are you always careful, and are you sometimes careful of your physical appearance? Similar results have been found by others.

Instead of dealing with other more detailed and significant findings, let me indulge in an anecdote from personal experience. The psychological interview on the receiving line in a Naval Recruit Training Center during World War II partook of the quality of a verbally administered personality questionnaire, since sheer press of time did not allow using that distinctive characteristic of the interview, the follow-through probing of replies. Enuresis was a rather common and disturbing symptom and, consequently, precious time was taken to inquire about it. An affirmative or a negative reply to the question "Do you wet the bed at night?" had to be checked, since "Yes" might mean, "Yes, because fifteen years ago at the age of six I had an accident," while "No," might mean "No, I haven't for two nights in a row." Wording "When did you last wet the bed?" was found to increase objectivity in that a better understanding of the intent of the question followed. In this pedestrian, minute improvement we can see how objectivity improves.

Sometimes personality questionnaires are criticized as if objectivity were an absolute. In view of Thurstone's work with the personality questionnaire, it is of interest to note that this is the position he took. He asserts flatly that such questionnaires are not tests in any strict sense since tests are ". . . objective procedures" (321, p. 353) with the implication that questionnaires are not. One may sharply separate tests from questionnaires, as Cattell does, without denying questionnaires some objective status. To Thurstone's position, one may take exception, as I have tried to do in arguing that objectivity is a relative matter.

Most personality questionnaires, in my opinion, have proven to be unsuccessful in their tasks as scientific instruments. The indictments by Ellis (12) and Ellis and Conrad (13) in large measure seem justified. One may, however, argue on certain points, such as, classifying all questionnaires together, when a breakdown by the particular instrument may show more encouraging results. The *Minnesota Multiphasic Personality Inventory,* for example, fared considerably better in its reviews than other instruments.

Certain measures, particularly the MMPI, probably owe their continuing use and expanded value, despite the general failure in part, to the development of specific means of increasing objectivity. The Lie Scale is one such device. In addition to indices of increasing objectivity with the MMPI, there is the intimately related fact that it is a more complete, complex, and intricate instrument than many of the other personality measures.

Psychology is a broad subject and other influences, perhaps running counter to the prevailing *Zeitgeist* (perhaps, representing still another trend), which appeared in some measure in the late twenties reached a considerably higher peak of visibility in the mid-thirties. I refer, of course, to projective testing.

Projective Techniques

At first, it might seem that the present concern does not call for direct attention to projective techniques. Nevertheless, in our search for objectivity some reminder of the beginning of projective testing is necessary to place its developing influence upon objectivity.

Rorschach worked with his inkblots in Switzerland during the decade 1910-1920. Studies with the Rorschach Test in the United States can be dated from about 1930 with the appearance of Beck's monograph (2). He, in turn, had been trained in *Rorschach* by David Levy. The Rorschach was not deliberately planned to test projection, despite its preeminence today as a projective test.

Inkblots, themselves, are nothing new or startling. Indeed, Leonardo da Vinci (8) proposed for the training of painters throwing a sponge full of various colors against the wall, for the perceptions one might see and significantly, he added, provided one wants to. So far as psychological research in the narrow sense is concerned, inkblots were proposed as a measure of visual imagination in 1895 by Binet and Henri (36). Dearborn (9, 10), two years later, published material on the use of inkblots with a small group of Harvard professors and students.

The recognition of projection as a method of testing arose more or less simultaneously and independently. In 1935 Murray (23) published with Morgan his first paper on the Thematic Apperception Test. Sears (28) published the first of his papers on experimental studies of projection in 1936. In Britain, in the same year, Cattell (7) published his *Guide to Mental Testing,* including a description of a projection test. Since it is probably not too well known to American audiences, it will be described briefly. He called it a "projection test," which, I believe, is the first time the term was applied directly to a test. It consists of 74 items in which each item has three alternatives as in the following instance (33, p. 71):

John strained every nerve to beat the others because:
he was determined to be top
his father wished him to succeed
he needed the scholarship.

The most appropriate of the three endings was to be checked on the assumption that one person will project his own chief impulses onto the ending chosen. If self-assertive, he would be likely to choose the first; if submissive, he would prefer the second. The items were developed so as to give scores on Self-Assertive *versus* Submissive, Cautious *versus* Bold, Acquisitive, Gregarious, Curious and Dependent tendencies, adapted from McDougall's list of instincts. Standardization was not carried out and not too much use has been made of the test. In today's perspective, it could be called a multiple-choice, sentence-completion test. It is pertinent to my theme to indicate that, if standardized, this could have been an objective test in the sense that scoring was objective. The more detailed and explicit formulation of the projective hypothesis of L. K. Frank (16), appeared in 1939. This was the first major source of knowledge of projection which became well known to psychologists.

Thurstone considered the projective procedures "the nearest approach to personality tests" in revealing personal idiosyncracies. He asked only that it be unstructured for the subject but well structured for the psychologists since with this structure it could be objectively scored. However, he went on to add, if the interpretation were as unstructured as the test, it would be useless for scientific inquiry. Structure, from the point of view of the examiner, may be equated with objectivity. Rorschach inkblots seem highly subjective, but experts can prepare independent interpretations which agree on essential particulars. This form of objectivity is one of the grounds on which the Rorschach is defended.

The influence of projective techniques upon objective personality testing, involves diametrically opposed influences. Undoubtedly, this kind of measurement increased subjective, impressionistic, intuitive trends in psychology. The heady wine of its multi-dimensional character; its relation to dynamic theory, particularly psychoanalysis; its enthusiastic reception by psychiatric colleagues;

and its usefulness in clinical settings all contributed to this anti-objective trend. Yet, without its challenge to objectivity, psychologists would probably not have seen the possibilities of increasing the scope of objectivity to include improving the objectivity of the psychologist himself. In considerable measure, whether viewing the use of projective techniques sympathetically or as irritants, it has forced us to re-evaluate and broaden our meaning of objectivity.

The many validity studies of the Rorschach that have produced negative results have given for the third time in the last fifty years an excuse to be skeptical of testing, this time of projective personality testing. Since this is a current skepticism, no one can say "what happened next." But something will happen, and I would suggest that it will be further objectification of projective techniques, but without disregard of the complexity and subtlety these devices permit. In one of the later chapters of this book, Holtzman focuses attention on the problems of objective scoring of projective techniques, while preserving their underlying purpose.

What Is an Objective Test?

Now that the historical survey has been completed, I would like to consider present-day thinking about objective personality testing.

In order to be able to present a cross-section of present-day conceptions of objective personality testing, the authors of this symposium indicated what they considered to be the meaning of "Objective Approaches to Personality Assessment," with special emphasis upon the qualifying term, "Objective."

Bass considered objectivity to be complete independence from examiner effects, or as he also put it, zero variance due to the examiner. Berg referred to scorable, fairly clearly structured tests for which scoring would be identical if performed by competent persons. Edwards emphasized the rigorously defined method of scoring. McQuitty considered it to mean the isolation of consistent individual differences in a manner such that numbers can be applied, resulting in a similar classification or measurement of behavior by different users of the approach. Pepinsky, in relating objectivity to an approach to personality testing, disclaimed use of the term but believed what is meant is two-fold: (1) minimization of errors of observing and recording, and (2) minimization of variability in the task conditions on separate occasions (not, he adds, in minimizing stimulus ambiguity or uncertainty for the subject).

In varying degrees and either implicitly or explicitly, many of these statements stressed not the test alone, but objectivity as a matter of *interaction* of test material and examiner. Objectivity is localized not only in the material, but also in the examiner. Objectivity is not the same as numerical scores or impersonal records, although it is the one way objectivity is expressed. Blood-pressure records are numerical and x-ray photographs are objective, but both are open to subjectivity of interpretation.

It must be remembered that these were succinct replies to a question. It does not follow that the respondents would not agree in some instances with expansion of the meanings they specify, or even agreement with other, more extended ways of putting the matter. I will also add that they reserve the right to disagree, violently or otherwise, with later remarks, either of my own, or of the other participants. I shall now proceed to summarize the somewhat more lengthy statements.

Cattell gives a more specific meaning than do the others, drawing upon his glossary to *Personality and Motivation Structure and Measurements,* wherein he defines an objective test as follows: "A test in which the subject's behavior is measured, for inferring personality, without his being aware in what ways his behavior is likely to affect the interpretation." To leave no doubt about their differentiation from questionnaires and the like, he further expands in the text as follows. "It is a portable, exactly reproducible, stimulus situation, with an exactly prescribed mode of scoring the response, *of which the subject is not informed.* All objective tests are also *experimental measurements,* but not all experimental measurements are tests. The difference of T data from Q data resides in the last clause, for "the *response* cannot be deliberately self-evaluative and self-revelatory if the subject is not told how his response is going to be evaluated." Cattell would, thereby, rule out personality questionnaires as tests, but not, of course, as personality measures.

Super goes beyond this discussion, to speak of a test as objective in any one or more of three ways: "(1) its stimulus, (2) the response which it permits, and (3) the scoring method used." He continues:

The quality of objectivity is one of clarity of structure; in this sense the objectivity-subjectivity continuum is equivalent to the clarity-ambiguity dimension and the structured-unstructured dimension. This means that a truly, completely, objective test is one in which the stimulus has the same significance to all subjects, the responses which he may make are limited in number and clear in meaning, and the scoring leaves no room for judgment by the scorer. By this definition, the tests we actually use are scattered along a continuum, and any judgment as to whether a particular test is objective or otherwise is somewhat arbitrary.

As I see it, Super is saying that objectivity is either clarity or structure, suggesting that these terms are more clear in the present context than is objectivity, though not denying meaning to objectivity. His personal preference, he goes on to state, is the structured-unstructured continuum, so far as classification of tests are concerned.

Hunt, as might be expected from his present interests in objectification of clinical impression, does not limit himself to test settings. He writes:

I interpret "objective" as pertaining to "public" rather than "private" information. Thus the data of introspection are private until turned into some form of report when they thus become public, since the forms of report, language or behavioral, can be handled as public, verifiable (by others) phenomena. "Objective" has many parameters, loosely the clarity and specificity of definition of the phenomena, its duplicability, its control for experimental observation, its statistical amenability, etc.

This is a still broader definition, and very close in spirit to Feigl's account of intersubjective testability.

Hathaway gives the most detailed analysis, but I am taking the liberty of quoting him verbatim.

I believe I am correct in placing our local emphasis in definition of the word "objective" upon the qualities of reproducibility and most of all upon the absence of an intervening interpretation between behavior of the subject and the material available to a third person. Data are objective when they are transmitted directly from the subject to others who may then interpret them. The verbatim responses to Rorschach cards are objective items, but they become something else (loosely, improperly called subjective) when they are classified or in any other way characterized by the examiner. The MMPI items checked by a subject constitute objective information, and these remain objective when put into scales. Discussion of the meaning of the scales or profiles is no longer objective. A TAT story is an objective item when presented verbatim but loses objectivity as soon as any interpretation or condensation or expansion occurs on the part of the examiner. There are intermediate situations. A series of experiments may establish that certain Rorschach responses occur with a greater frequency than others. Preserving objectivity, one could then classify a given response or set of responses as having a certain degree of frequency. The frequency score becomes, therefore, an objective item. It is to be noted, however, that responses frequently occur in slightly unusual form, although elements of the responses are frequent. The examiner could exercise freedom and call a response either a frequent one or an infrequent one. When such examiner freedom enters the situation, the resulting score loses objectivity. Similarly, an MMPI administered under special deviant conditions that may not be mentioned in presentation of the objective data from the responses also loses objectivity. One ordinarily has the right to expect of an objective test that roughly standard administration was used.

I have not developed the idea of reproducibility, but it is inherent in what I have been saying. One does not require that the objective score be reproducible in exactly the usual sense of reliability but rather, that there be possible a hypothetical construct representing a reproducible element in the subject. This construct is not possible if the product of the situation represents some interaction of the examiner with the subject or some aspect of the examiner's psyche.

Most projective devices (and I tend to use "test" as almost completely implying objectivity) have traditionally been much less objective than devices that permit the patient to make responses that can be treated by clerical means. It is unfortunate that objectivity has been tied to "paper and pencil" and to the idea of formulated items such as in the MMPI. I believe that we would benefit from the attempt to extend objective measurement to include not only the objective aspects of projective devices, which has been partly developed, but also objective ways of treating interview material and free behavior as this may be observed by others.

Projective and Objective Tests are not Dichotomous

Interest in searching for objectivity is by no means confined to the authors of this book. A considerable variety of opinion has been expressed elsewhere. One that I consider especially pernicious, when the distinction is made without qualification or explanation, is that between objective and projective tests, treating them as if they were mutually exclusive. One rather widespread systematic error has been to contrast projective tests with all other tests to which, unfortunately, we have sometimes applied the undeserved label, of objective tests. For example, in some of our *Annual Review of Psychology,* two of the major sections on diagnostic testing have been labelled *projective* and *objective.* Many "objective" tests are not objective in any of the senses we find the world to have been used, and projective test materials may be treated objectively. If we must have only projective tests and something else, which I do not believe is the case, the lame category of nonprojective is a shade better, because, at least, it does make an invidious comparison.

There has been some involvement, spurious in my opinion, in the question of objective *versus* projective, in relation to the nomothetic and idiographic approaches. Beck (2) has asserted that objective tests are limited to the "subpersonality" in the course of discussing the question, or pseudo-question if you will, of the idiographic and nomothetic approaches. It may be, that projective tests have more adherents from those with an idiographic approach and objective tests have more from the nomothetic camp, but it does not follow that objective tests cannot be used as measures of personality. To be sure, single objective tests or test items will certainly fail in this task. Factor and pattern analyses, as in the Cattell and McQuitty approaches, are surely approaches to the total personality, although with the inevitable loss of individuality or uniqueness that accompanies any theoretical formulation of personality, *including* that in projective formulations.

What is Tested?

White's discussion (38) of what is tested by psychological tests is pertinent. He points out the psychological tests can no longer be regarded as inducing specimens or samples of performance of restricted functions. The samples may be conceived of as inducing, say, problem-solving capacity, but many other characteristics of personality also contribute. He argues that we can never arrange a situation on which one variable alone is tested. For example, the problem-solving measure may also tap frustration tolerance, anxiety control, and level of aspiration. Tests consequently supply overlapping information. In line with this, White goes on to propose we must use test batteries since we can no longer pin our faith on single tests. By use of a test battery, there is an increase in knowledge, not merely in an additive fashion, but in geometric progression. In the same vein he proposes multiple examiners. He speaks, in this connection, of psychological tests not yet being so objective as to dispense with this safeguard. In a sense, then, the whole discussion is a plea for objectivity, but objectivity at a high enough level of complexity so as not to do violence to the complexity of personality.

This point of view can be seen in contrast with the position of factoring psychologists who are interested in purifying their measures so they are free of what could be called contamination. But one man's contamination is another man's extra premium of subtlety. A not inconsiderable group of psychologists accept this position, considering that it is not only futile to try to purify their existing instruments, but also that it is quite valuable, especially in clinical settings, to have these additional premiums of information.

Some Classifications

There has been some interest expressed in the classification of tests and personality measures. Rosenzweig (27) has classified personality measures into objective or overt, subjective or covert and projective or implicit levels of reference. He, however, explicitly indicates that they are not too exclusively associated with one or another of the diagnostic methods. In fact, the same instrument may supply information at all three levels. They are not defined so as to give objectivity to only one level. Campbell (5) has developed a classification of tests based on three dichotomies. In the first dichotomy he contrasts objective tests for which the subjects understand there are correct responses, and voluntary tests in which, in one fashion or another, the subjects are informed that there are no right or wrong answers. The other dichotomies are direct *versus* indirect, having to do with the subject's understanding of the purpose of the test, and free-response *versus* structured, having to do with the usual distinction made between them, but from the point of view of the subject. He would classify tests in terms of these three dimensions simultaneously, as in the voluntary, indirect, free response type, which would include the *Rorschach* and the TAT, and the voluntary, direct, structured type which would include the MMPI, and so on. His use of objective runs counter to several of the meanings of objective we have considered. In large measure, this arises from his use of objective in a phenomenological orientation—the phenomenologically objective environment. Accuracy and error, as he says, are in the subject's mind. Rosenzweig, in contrast, refers to the psychologist's orientation, not the subject's. Perhaps some classification uniting both, the subject's and the examiner's frames of reference will give us an even more adequate classification than do Campbell's and Rosenzweig's when considered separately. I am reminded in this connection of George Kelly's witty remark that, "When the subject is asked to guess what the examiner is thinking, we call it an objective test; when the examiner tries to guess what the subject is thinking, we call it a projective device" (20).

Space limitation makes impossible an exhaustive survey of the remainder of modern literature relevant to the question of objectivity in personality testing. Certain other selected references might be mentioned. Frank (17) contrasts the psychometric and projective approach. In the context of norms for the TAT, Rosenzweig (26) has offered a discussion of how they help in the process of objectification. Levinson (21) compares and contrasts projective and ability tests. Rapaport (24) discusses the principles underlying nonprojective tests of personality. Allport (1) considers the advantages of straightforward, direct methods over projective techniques. Among his various publications, Eysenck deals more directly with what he means by objective personality tests in a review (14); Stephenson (31) has devoted considerable effort to demonstrating the objectivity of his variety of Q-technique.

References

1. Allport, G. W. The trend in motivational theory. *Amer. J. Orthopsychiat.*, 1953, 23, 107-119.
2. Beck, S. J. The science of personality: nomothetic or idiographic? *Psychol. Rev.*, 1953, 60, 353-359.
3. Benton, A. L. The interpretation of questionnaire items in a personality schedule. *Arch. Psychol., N.Y.*, 1953, No. 190.
4. Burt, C. L. General and specific factors underlying the primary emotions. Rep. Brit. Assoc., 1915, 694.
5. Campbell, D. T. A typology of tests, projective and otherwise. *J. consult. Psychol.*, 1957, 21, 207-210.
6. Cattell, J. M. Mental tests and measurements. *Mind*, 1890, 15, 373-381.
7. Cattell, R. B. *A guide to mental testing.* London: University of London Press, 1936.
8. da Vinci, L. *Treatise on painting.* In L. da Vinci, *Buch von der Malerei.* Nach dem Codex Vaticanus (Urbinas), 1270. Vienna: W. Braumuller, 1882.
9. Dearborn, G. Blots of ink in experimental psychology. *Psychol. Rev.*, 1897, 4, 390-391.
10. Dearborn, G. A study of imagination. *Amer. J. Psychol.*, 1898, 9, 183-190.
11. Downey, June E. The Will-Profile. *Univ. Wyoming Dept. Psychol. Bull.*, 1919, No. 3.
12. Ellis, A. The validity of personality questionnaires. *Psychol. Bull.*, 1946, 43, 385-440.
13. Ellis, A., and Conrad, H. S. The validity of personality inventories in military practice. *Psychol. Bull.*, 1948, 45, 385-426.
14. Eysenck, H. Personality tests 1944-49. In G. W. T. H. Fleming (Ed.), *Recent progress in psychiatry.* London: Churchill, 1950.
15. Feigl, H. The scientific outlook: naturalism and humanism. In H. Feigl and May Brodbeck (eds.), *Readings in the philosophy of science.* New York: Appleton-Century-Crofts, 1953, 8-18.

16. Frank, L. K. Projective methods of the study of personality. *J. Psychol.*, 1939, 8, 389-413.
17. Frank, L. K. *Projective methods.* Springfield, Ill.: Thomas, 1948.
18. Franz, S. I. *Handbook of mental examination methods.* New York: Macmillan, 1919.
19. Galton, F. Measurements of character. *Fortnightly Rev.*, 1884, 36, 179-185.
20. Kelly, G. A. The theory and technique of assessment. *Annual Review of Psychology, Vol.* 9, Palo Alto: Annual Reviews, 1958, 323-352.
21. Levinson, D. J. A note on the similarities and differences between projective tests and ability tests. *Psychol. Rev.*, 1946, 53, 189-194.
22. Macfarlane, Jean W. Problems of validation inherent in projective methods. *Amer. J. Orthopsychiat.*, 1942, 12, 405-410.
23. Morgan, Christina D., and Murray, H. A. A method for investigating phantasies: the thematic apperception test. *Arch. Neurol. Psychiatr., Chicago*, 1935, 34, 289-306.
24. Rapaport, D. Principles underlying non-projective tests of personality. *Ann. N. Y. Acad. Sci.*, 1946, 46, 643-652.
25. Rorschach, H., and Oberholzer, E. The application of the form interpretation test. In H. Rorschach *Psychodiagnostics.* Bern, Switzerland: Herber, 1942.
26. Rosenzweig, S. Apperceptive norms for the Thematic Apperception Test. I. The problem of norms in projective methods. *J. Personality*, 1949, 17, 475-482.
27. Rosenzweig, S. Levels of behavior in psychodiagnosis with special reference to the Picture-Frustration Study. *Amer. J. Orthopsychiat.*, 1950, 20, 63-72.
28. Sears, R. R. Experimental studies of projection: I. Attribution of traits. *J. soc. Psychol.*, 1936, 7, 151-163.
29. Sharp, Stella, E. Individual psychology: a study in psychological method. *Amer. J. Psychol.*, 1899, 10, 329-391.
30. Spearman, C. "General intelligence," objectively determined and measured. *Amer. J. Psychol.*, 1904, 15, 201-293.
31. Stephenson, W. *The study of behavior: Q-technique and its methodology.* Chicago: University of Chicago Press, 1953.
32. Thurstone, L. L. The criterion problem in personality research. *Educ. psychol. Measmt.*, 1955, 15, 353-361.
33. Vernon, P. E. *The assessment of psychological qualities by verbal methods.* London: HMS Stationery Office, 1938.
34. Verplanck, W. S. A glossary of some terms used in the objective science of behavior. *Psychol., Rev. Suppl.*, 1957, 64, 1-42.
35. Voelker, P. F. An account of certain methods of testing of normal reactions in conduct. *Relig. Educ.*, 1921, 16, 81-83.
36. Webb, E. Character and intelligence. *Brit. J. Psychol. Monogr. Suppl.*, 1915, 1, No. 3.

37. Whipple, G. M. *Manual of mental and physical tests.* Baltimore: Warwick & York, 1910.

38. White, R. W. What is tested by psychological tests? In P. H. Hoch and J. Zubin, (Eds.), *Relation of psychological tests to psychiatry.* New York: Grune and Stratton, 1952, 3-14.

39. Wissler, C. The correlation of mental and physical tests. *Psychol. Rev. Monogr. Suppl.,* 1901, 3, No. 16.

II

Theories and Assumptions Underlying Approaches to Personality Assessment

Donald E. Super

Teachers College, Columbia University

"Theories in psychology," writes Jensen in the 1958 edition of the *Annual Review of Psychology* (17, p. 295) "are seldom disproved: they just fade away." The thought is rather humbling, suggesting a paraphrase of the poet's "where are the snows of yesteryear?" And it is particularly so, since this thought seems to occur to the writers of the *Annual Review* chapters on personality and assessment almost annually. In the 1956 *Review* the fads appeared to McClelland (25) to be empathy and rigidity, in the 1957 edition Eriksen (8) identified them as need-in-perception and the authoritarian personality, and in the 1958 edition Jensen saw them as motivation and anxiety. Of course, some of these fads are not quite as ephemeral as the brevity or the biases of the respective authors suggest, for rigidity is still not unfashionable and the authoritarian personality is still with us, and anxiety has been driving us for more than the year preceding 1958. I need only mention the successive but now subsided waves of ascendance-submission, introversion-extraversion, and expressive movement, which once inundated our journals, in order to make clear the validity of the notion that the theories of personality that underlie our tools and techniques, and the instruments themselves, tend to have some

24

of the enthusiastic and transient support of fads. In fact, Jensen (17, p. 306) was moved to write a formula for a psychological fad, which consists of "making available an easy-to-use measuring device with a significant label and fascinating content." The reasons for this seem clear: a readily used and fascinating tool prompts people to make use of it. When it has some bearing on a current theory, this use becomes not only interesting but academically respectable and even, perhaps, prestigeful.

Perhaps one reason why theories take on something of the nature of the fad is that the instruments used in studying them at first seem relatively simple, suggesting that one can readily test the underlying theory. In due course, research proves that neither the instrument nor the theory is as simple and straightforward as it seemed, and the fringe researchers drop them, moving on to a newer theory and a newer test. And so, as Jensen says, the theory does not die, it fades away. That the fading process is only relative, but not complete, is shown by the emphasis put on introversion-extraversion in Eysenck's current work (9). An historical example is the revival of interest in the expressive movement, resulting from Allport and Vernon's work twenty-five years ago (2), about ten years after Downey's work with it (7) had actually faded.

I feel humble in dealing with theories for another reason, for I work, not as a theorist, but as an empiricist. As an empiricist, however, I feel the need to organize facts, to see what they add up to, and to be guided in planning my further work by the perspective thus gained. This, I have found to my surprise, makes me, in the true sense of the term, a theorist. For theory, so I am informed by theoretical theorists, is nothing more than the attempt to explain the relationships between sets of facts. I do that, and so do all of us, more or less consciously and in more or less sophisticated ways. The result is a rationale, a set of assumptions, underlying every instrument we use, every technique we employ. These may not be integrated into theoretical systems, but they constitute theories. Perhaps here is the difference between the theorist as we generally conceive of him and the empiricist: the former constructs a system, the latter does not build nor adopt a system but gets along with a less well organized body of related facts.

In preparing this paper, then, I found that I was dealing, not with theoretical systems, but with the limited theories, with the more specific assumptions and hypotheses underlying methods of assessing personality. Most test authors have not consciously developed their tests in terms of a systematic theory of personality; rather, they have developed their instruments on the basis of more specific hypotheses concerning the ways in which personality manifests itself. Underlying these hypotheses, of course, there have been theories as to both the structure of personality and its dimensions. The structure issues have generally been those of the organismic whole versus the atomistic constellation of traits; the dimension issues have been questions concerning the traits that make up the organism or the constellation.

Since our concern is with the measurement of personality, rather than with personality theory as such, and since I am perhaps a measurement practitioner but certainly not a personality theorist, I shall address myself to the first type of theory, that is, the lower order theories and hypotheses governing the development of personality measures. And, since our focus here is on objective approaches, I shall deal at greater length with that end of the continuum, treating the more subjective or unstructured methods only enough to place all of these approaches in perspective.

The Observation Approach

Performance. One approach to personality assessment is through observation of performance, of the personality in action. It assumes that people are what they do. The medium in which the personality characteristics manifest themselves in thus overt, observable behavior; the *method of assessment* is observation; the *measure* resulting is a characterization or a rating. Let us look briefly at each of these categories.

Media. The medium in which the performance takes place may be either of two types: a life situation, or a miniature, that is an artificial or manufactured, situation. In the *life situation test* the basic assumption is that significant personality traits manifest themselves in everyday behavior, and that observations of this behavior may be recorded to obtain a meaningful picture of personality functioning. In the *miniature situation test* the assumption is that one can set up situations that bring out important traits more quickly and more completely than in everyday life, for closer observation by more highly trained observers.

Method. The method of measurement, *recorded observation,* makes assumptions concerning the observer and the situation. Basic among these is the assumption that observers can identify significant behavior, noting it, classifying it, and even judging its strength.

Measures. These observations may be recorded in several ways.

In *sociometrics,* participants in the situation record their choices of friends or companions for real or fictitious activities, thus in effect summing up their observations; it is assumed that people are aware of their differential preferences and are willing to express them under appropriate conditions. In *nominations,* participants name the persons whom they believe fit each of a series of labels, roles, or personality descriptions; here, too, they in effect summarize observations of performance. The assumption is that people notice individual differences, particularly differences in roles played in social groups, and are willing to share these observations. In *ratings,* either participants or observers rate participants in the situation for characteristics that are believed to be important and that are considered likely to manifest themselves in such a situation. The assumption is that the rater will be able to identify the trait or behavior in question, and be able to make a judgment concerning the frequency or degree to which the subject manifests it. In *behavior frequency counts,* the observer records the incidence of types of behavior or actions which are expected to have significance, the assumption being that the frequency of types of behavior in that situation is indicative of behavior tendencies in other situations and reflects underlying personality dimensions.

Evaluation. It would be worthwhile, but this is neither the time nor the place, to evaluate in detail the construct and predictive validity of each of the types of measures and media used in assessing personality through performance. At the risk of overgeneralizing, and without citing evidence which has been well summarized by Heyns and Lippitt (14), by Bass (4), Lindsay and Borgatta (24), Flanagan and others (11), and by Hollander (15), I shall nevertheless express in a few brief statements my understanding of the status of each of the measures and media used, of the method (observation), and of performance tests of personality in general.

First, the *measures.* Behavior frequency counts have generally proved useful when appropriate dimensions of behavior have been identified for personality assessment as pointed out by Bass (4), the Ohio State group (31) and others working on the initiation of structure. Ratings have proved useful as global measures, but not as measures of specific traits, for global measures seem to reflect either the success of or liking for the subject. Nominating and sociometric techniques (15, 24) have stood the test of experimentation rather well, the former for the assessment of social roles and the latter, like ratings, for the assessment of social acceptance.

Secondly, the *method.* Observation puts a premium on the person doing the observing if little structure is provided, on rationale and training if much structuring is done (14). In this method, the person is the instrument more than the devices which he uses to record his observations when structure is minimal, less than his devices when his procedural directions are so refined as to make a machine of him. The question has typically been that of the clinician as a tool (28), a topic of considerable current interest with which others will deal later in this book. Heyns and Lippitt point out in the *Handbook of Social Psychology* (14, p. 403), making the clinician rather than his procedures central is a mistake in the use of observational methods.

Finally, in this brief evaluation of observation of performance in the assessment of personality, we come to the *media,* the life situation and the miniature situation. The former has the advantage of realism, for here the test is life itself; but it has the disadvantages arising from the psychologist's inability to control the situation. The sampling of behavior may be poor, and conditions may make the recording of observations difficult, as exemplified in studies made of personality factors in survival. In those studies observations of any one air crew in the Strategic Air Command living under survival conditions could be made under either winter or summer conditions, but not under both. Observers could watch all of the crew some of the time and some of the crew all of the time, but not all of the crew all of the time. The miniature situation test, on the other hand, tends to lose verisimilitude both in content and in the motivation of participants for some purposes, although for others verisimilitude can be achieved. The leaderless group discussion can, for example, capture both the content and the spirit of many executive situations.

PERSONALITY PROJECTION

Projection

The second major approach to personality assessment is through unstructured or semi-structured materials, as contrasted with situations into which the examinee is asked to inject meaning. These are, of course, the *media* of projection; the *method* of assessment is one of test scoring and interpretation, which varies considerably in degree of structure; and the *measure* is either a trait score or a personality description, with varying degrees of structure.

Media. Let us consider, first, the media of projection. They are basically three, and each type has its devotees, so much so, in fact, that we might follow George Kelly (20, p. 335) in describing them as the fluid-blot people, the human-picture people, and the disjunctive-sentence people. The media differ in two ways. They differ in the amount of structure provided, as in the amorphousness of an inkblot and the focus provided by the sentence-stem, as well as in the use of stimuli which may evoke either impersonal or personal content. Inkblots, for example, are more likely to elicit impersonal responses than are the cartoons of the Rosenzweig PF test.

Method. The method of test scoring and interpretation used in this kind of assessment may be contrasted with the recorded observation method used in situation tests. The observer, we have seen, is a cross between a clinical instrument and a machine because he collects, sorts, and records data; in projective testing, on the other hand, it is the medium, the test, that collects, sorts, and provides a record of responses. Since important further sorting of data takes place later in both types of testing, it may be important to illustrate what I mean here. In situation testing, the observer makes decisions as to what behavior to record, sorting out responses such as sneezing as "not-to-be-recorded," and others, such as asking a neighbor a question, as "to-be-recorded." In projective testing, the test, not the examiner, does the first sorting for the directions ask the examinee what the inkblot might be and the examiner merely records the responses to that stimulus; this is even clearer in the case of incomplete sentences tests, in which the examinee reads each question and writes his response himself. Here the examiner makes no decisions as to what behavior to evoke or to record. The examiner plays his important part in analyzing the recorded data, both in the inquiry of a Rorschach examination and in the scoring of Rorschach, TAT, and Incomplete Sentence Test protocols. This may or may not be done by the observer in a situation test, but the scoring processes are basically similar in both situational and projective tests once the data have been recorded. They may be quite objective, as in the identification and counting of forms or of structure-initiating responses, or they may be very subjective, as in the making of a global rating of leadership promise. Scoring may use a Gestalt approach and focus on stimuli to which responses are made, as in scoring form and color responses in the Rorschach, or it may use a psychoanalytic approach and deal with the content of responses, as in determining sex identification in the TAT.

Measures. This leads to the question of the measures derived from projective techniques of assessment, and to theories that have been much debated in the literature. One theory is the organismic, which is used to justify a global interpretation of the projective protocol. Several other types of theory, ranging from neobehaviorism to psychoanalysis, are used to support the objective scoring of the protocol through the identification and counting of well-defined responses. These scores are in turn interpreted in terms of their hypothesized, or occasionally their demonstrated, significance. It would be possible to dwell on these theories at some length, but that is not the purpose of this paper.

Evaluation. Perhaps the best way to evaluate briefly is to see what the evaluators say rather than by looking at each medium, method, and measure. We can do so by glancing at the *Annual Reviews* for three recent years. In 1954 Lowell Kelly wrote (18, p. 288): "The curious state of affairs wherein the most widely (and confidently) used techniques are those for which there is little or no evidence of predictive validity is indeed a phenomenon appropriate for study by social psychologists."

In 1956 Cronbach wrote (6, p. 173) that "Assessment in the OSS style has now been proved a failure," and he cites, among other studies, the Holtzman-Sells analysis of the predictive value of clinical analyses of projective protocols (16). He concluded that, "Assessment encounters trouble because it involves hazardous inferences," in which assessors go considerably beyond known relationships between predictor and criterion variables. He quotes Symonds and other students of projective methods, to the effect that there is little theoretical basis for expecting fantasy, as revealed by projective techniques, to be directly related to overt manifestations of personality such as academic success or work proficiency.

In the 1958 *Annual Review* (20) George Kelly is cautious, but the impression resulting from the specific studies that he cites but refrains from synthesizing is not good. Cronbach's earlier conclusions seem to hold, and even if it does in due course develop that projective techniques have construct validity, we must ask of what value the constructs are if they do not help predict behavior.

A few years ago someone suggested that if we were honest we would cease using projective techniques in assessment, since they have not been shown to have predictive validity. After a review of the research with the Rorschach (29) which led to the conclusion that it has no validity for differential diagnosis, for understanding conflicts or fantasies for psychotherapy, personality description, the prediction of behavior, or evaluating or predicting the outcome of psychotherapy, Eysenck reported in 1955 (10, p. 233) that the Rorschach was abandoned as a clinical tool at the Maudsley Hospital.

Although we have considered dropping the skill course in projectives in my own institution, we still require that all clinical, counseling, most people in personnel, and all school psychologists devote a large block of time to acquiring some competence with these projective techniques, the utility of which is unknown. We have agreed that they have no validity, but we retain the requirement. We do this for three reasons: 1) the unsatisfactory but practical consideration that such psychologists are expected to have these skills and are likely to both feel and be handicapped if they do not, 2) the fact that they can learn something useful about clinical interaction by studying these procedures, and, 3) the hope that familiarity with these methods may yet provide psychologists with a basis for some major break-through in the field of personality assessment.

SELF-DESCRIPTION

We come now to our third and last type of personality assessment procedure, self-description. George Kelly (20, p. 332) describes this type of method as the one in which "the subject is asked to guess what the examiner is thinking," as contrasted with projective techniques in which "the examiner tries to guess what the subject is thinking." This is the oldest of our three types of approaches, and that which has most readily lent itself to experimentation and research. It best qualifies as an objective approach to personality assessment, being near the upper end of the structured-unstructured continuum. By some definitions of that term I might legitimately have confined my paper to this type of device. While it seemed wiser to try to gain perspective by reviewing all three types, I have saved this type for the last with the aim of dealing with it in somewhat more detail, under two headings: trait lists and biographical inventories.

Media: I. Trait Lists

The media for self-description in assessment work have typically been behavior or trait lists in the form of the personality inventory, the check-list, and the rating scale. These, according to such diverse students of personality as Gordon Allport (1) and Frederick Wyatt (35), are appropriately used because of the importance of conscious motivation in normally well-integrated people. They are direct methods, in that they ask the individual to describe himself as he sees himself. George Kelly (19) and Leary (22) have recently, with quite different approaches, made considerable use of self-descriptions. The various underlying theories of personality are too numerous and too diverse for discussion here, but it is relevant and possible to comment on the general theoretical acceptability of these methods.

Because self-description was found, in Woodworth's work in World War I, to work reasonably well, this medium was widely exploited during the pragmatic, empirical, behavioristic period that followed. With greater sophistication in assessment and personality theory, self-descriptive methods came into disfavor among psychologists. The devices developed by Woodworth, Allport, Laird, Bernreuter, Bell, and others were still used, for lack of better methods of personality appraisal, but generally with recognition of their weaknesses and with some apology for not having something better. Thus in 1944 Maller wrote, in Hunt's symposium on personality (27, p. 180), "It is the psychologist's dilemma to choose between the standardized questionnaire which is broad in scope but of doubtful validity and the performance record which is obviously valid but of narrow scope."

The dissatisfaction with the self-descriptive inventories which resulted from the unbridled empiricism of the 1920's led not only to work with other methods but also to better empirical work with, and better theorizing, about self-description. Thus Guilford embarked upon the twenty-year long program of refinement of personality inventories through factor analysis, which has taken current form in the Guilford-Zimmerman Temperament Survey. Hathaway built on Rosanoff's theory of personality as well as on the Minnesota empiricism in selecting items for, and for ascertaining the concurrent validity of, the Minnesota Multiphasic Personality Inventory. Edwards developed the Personal Preference Schedule by combining Murray's need theory with psychometric improvements such as the equating of items for social desirability, and Bills developed his Index of Adjustment and Values with the help of self theory both in devising his scoring system and in designing validation experiments.

Method. Early work with personality inventories relied on a combination of *content and construct* validities. Items were written or selected because they described symptoms which were believed to characterize various types of adjustment; this was content validity as defined by the APA Committee on Test Standards (3). Items were retained or rejected on the basis of internal consistency, of agreement with the total score for the scale in question: this was construct validity as now understood. It was generally assumed that if the item described a symptom that had been observed to characterize a type of maladjustment, such as neuroticism, and if answers to it tended to agree with total score for that trait, then validity was demonstrated. It is interesting to note that these two types of procedure fell into some disrepute until the APA Committee gave them a name, and that their new respectability was not much dimmed by the greater stress put by that Committee on predictive validity!

Experience and experiment showed, however, that construct validity is merely suggested, not proved, by item-score correlations and item inspection and that it is not equivalent to empirical validity. Scales purporting to measure neuroticism, for example, were found by Landis and Katz (21) to contain some items which were answered by neurotics in the normal way, and by normals in the neurotic way, more often than in the expected manner. And the scales were found not to have appreciable concurrent or predictive validity, in that they failed to differentiate effectively among groups of people who were known at the time of testing or later to differ in significant and presumably relevant respects, such as neuroticism, type of psychosis, social role on a college campus, or occupation. This led to the decline of interest in the content and construct method of developing self-descriptive instruments which characterized the 1940's, and to less emphasis on the assumption that people can and will accurately describe their own traits.

One of the further outcomes has already been mentioned: it was a greater interest in *empirical validation,* in both concurrent validity and predictive validity as now understood. The best example of this approach is the MMPI, in which McKinley and Hathaway set out to devise a self-descriptive inventory that would differentiate between various types of maladjusted and disturbed patients, and between these persons and normals. But, it was recognized, in the first writing or selection of items that it was important to have some kind of guide, that is a theory which would generate hypotheses concerning differences.

A second outcome, also mentioned, was thus an emphasis on a *higher order of theory.* Theory of a very low level had been tapped in earlier work: lists of symptoms characterizing each group were examined for suggestions as to items. A higher order of theory was now brought into play, however, by the demonstrated weakness of the symptom method: it was the use of a theory of personality organization. In the case of the MMPI it was Rosanoff's theory that provided a framework for the inclusion or exclusion of existing items, and for suggestions as to additional types and traits and of behavior which might be included. Item-score correlations are obtained, or items are factor analyzed, by some investigators in order to establish internal consistency or to validate theories concerning personality structure. But the ability of total scores to differentiate between criterion groups is also checked, and in addition item-criterion correlations are often obtained in order further to purify the scales.

A third outcome was a recognition of the fact that *self-description cannot and need not always be taken at face value.* Empirical validation can be used to strengthen construct validity, as in the MMPI, but it can also be used to avoid construct validity as an issue, as in Strong's Vocational Interest Blank. The success of purely empirical self-descriptive instruments, unlike that of those having a theoretical basis for item selection, left unanswered questions concerning the reason for the success of the empirical approach.

And hence the fourth and, so far, final refinement in the development of self-descriptive methods. Referring specifically to Strong's Blank, but making a point more broadly applicable, Bordin suggested (5) that the reason for the *validity of self-descriptions lies in the fact that a self-description reflects a self-concept*, and that self-concepts have a directive effect on behavior. Thus the man who describes himself as friendly may not actually be friendly, but his behavior does tend to resemble that of other persons whose constellations of self-ascribed traits are like his. The man who sees himself as friendly, active, and alert may not actually be friendly, active, and alert, but he is likely to act in the same way as others who see themselves thus. His self concept is similar, and the associated behavior tends to be similar.

Measures. The measures derived from these various self-descriptive devices fall into three categories: they are scores for traits, for nosological or other groups, or for self-acceptance. Most of the self-descriptive instruments we have are of the first type, yielding scores for traits such as dominance-submission, introversion-extraversion, need achievement, or emotional stability.

The MMPI has changed from the second type to a cross between the first two types, for while it yields scores derived from nosological groups, these scores are translated by many users into traits which tend to characterize those groups, a practice which Gough has carried further in developing the California Psychological Inventory from the MMPI.

In the third group we find the Bills Index, Gough's Adjective Checklist, and other less well-known derivatives of Sweet's 30-year-old self-other-ideal technique (34). In these, self ratings are contrasted with ideal ratings, or favorable self descriptions are compared to unfavorable self descriptions, in order to obtain a measure of discrepancy between self and ideal or of self acceptance.

Some work has been done with still another type of measure derived from self descriptions, a measure of self consistency or integration such as McQuitty (26) sought to derive by analyzing the congruence of self-attributed traits. The reasoning is that the integrated, self consistent person tends to attribute to himself only traits or behaviors that tend to be associated or that are compatible with each other, whereas the conflicted or unintegrated person will attribute to himself traits that are incompatible with each other.

Evaluation. In evaluating the measures, methods, and media that have been used to obtain self descriptions, it seems safe to say that we have finally developed two approaches that lead to valid results. One might be called *the group difference method,* as used by Hathaway with the MMPI. It consists of starting with a well-defined group, be it clinical or occupational; of developing a theoretical model of that group from whatever data are already available, a model that serves as a guide in item selection or item writing; of purifying the scales to which items are assigned by internal consistency or factor analysis methods; and of empirically validating the self-descriptions against concurrent or predictive criteria. The second method might be called the *generalized model method,* and is illustrated by Cattell's work with the 16 PF Test. The person who uses this method starts with a theory as to the significant dimensions of personality, which may be quite empirical in its origins, selects or writes items according to this theory, establishes the internal consistency of the scales to which these items are assigned, and validates them empirically by establishing the existence of hypothesized differences in selected nosological or other groups. When one or more of the steps has been omitted, one may well be suspicious of the validity of a self-descriptive instrument. Some of the contemporary personality inventories and adjective checklists have been developed by these methods, with results which appear much more promising than those of the less systematic and less thoroughgoing approaches used prior to World War II.

Media: II. Biographical Inventories

The second type of self-descriptive technique, as distinguished from the trait list, is the biographical inventory. The basic assumption here is that one's past behavior is a good predictor of his future behavior. In his discussion of personality in terms of associative learning Guthrie (13, p. 66) says, a person's "past affiliations . . . offer better and more specific predictions of his future than any of the traits that we usually think of as personality traits. But it is just this predictive value that is required of a personality trait and *nothing else.*"

Method. The method with which we are most familiar in connection with the biographical inventory is that of the Aptitude Index used by many life insurance companies since the birth of applied psychology, and applied with signal success to the selection of aircraft pilots by Kelly in the Navy and Shaffer in the Air Force during World War II. In the last instance (12) it consisted of using available knowledge or hunches as to the backgrounds of successful and unsuccessful fliers to write multiple-choice biographical items, and of validating responses to these against a success-fail criterion. Thus men who had relatives who held private pilots' licenses proved more likely to succeed than did those without this kind of prior contact with flying. This finding led, in turn, to the hypothesis that prior favorable contact with flying makes for success, and other prior-contact experiences were canvassed in order to supply more experience items for the inventory. These items were in turn validated and retained only if they predicted success.

This method suggested modifications, developed simultaneously by Siegel and myself. In my case it was in the Career Pattern Study (32) and in studying success and failure in survival training in the Strategic Air Command (33). In Siegel's case it was in a doctoral dissertation (30). Siegel has followed through by publishing his inventory; I, by conducting further studies of the method and its applications with high school boys, with engineering applicants at the General Electric Co., and with telephone operators at the American Telephone and Telegraph Co.

Basically, the modification consists of pushing beyond low-order hypotheses concerning the relationship between past and future experiences to higher-order hypotheses that organize data on a greater range of experience by using constellations of experiences as a basis for inferring personality traits. Siegel's approach consisted of organizing presumably kindred experiences into clusters to constitute scales, and by internal consistency and correlational methods establishing the justifiability of his scales and of the trait names assigned to them. He has provided, in addition, some data on the predictive validity of these traits.

My approach was similar in my Strategic Air Command and

Career Pattern Study research, but in applying the method to telephone operators Martha Heyde and I have analyzed operator data obtained from application blanks and interviews in relation to turnover, in order to develop a hypothetical model of the stable and of the unstable telephone operator. From this model, described in terms of biographical and trait data, we derived a list of personality traits believed to be significant in turnover in that occupation. Actually and presumably related biographical and life-experience items were then written in multiple-choice form, from 15 to 30 items surviving the various editorial processes for each of the hypothesized personality traits.

We sought to measure the trait "independence-dependence" by answers to questions concerning the age at which the subject first started using make-up, choosing her own clothes, dating, taking overnight trips without her parents, etc. This inventory is now being given to operator applicants in major cities in several regions of the country, and turnover data are being collected on those hired. Three types of analyses of the results are planned. One is a factor analysis of the items to test our hypotheses concerning the trait or factor structure of our biographical data and experience variables. The second is a study of the relationship between these traits or factors and turnover. The third is a cross-validation study of the items against turnover criteria, to develop an empirical scoring key. Validated facts and empirical scoring keys will be compared.

Measures. Two types of measures are thus derivable from biographical inventories of the type with which some of us have been experimenting. One is the conventional empirical scale, of most interest to the classifier of students and job applicants and, although biographical inventories have not apparently been tried on them, of mental patients. The other is the trait or factor scale, of which Siegel developed ten for his general high school inventory and of which I have developed several for my custom-built inventories. It is the trait scales empirically validated against external criteria that are of most interest to us here, a potentially meaningful means of assessing personality.

Evaluation. How valid these biographical data measures are as indices of personality traits and how sound the procedure is for inferring personality traits from constellations of experience data is not fully demonstrated. I have devoted this much attention to this new approach to biographical data, because the results so far indicate that it may prove a valid and more objective method of assessing personality than the self-report methods that call for trait descriptions.

In closing this chapter, which has of necessity covered much ground briefly, I should like to relate the organization which I have used here to that used by Leary and Coffey (23) in their work on personality. They distinguish among public, private, and symbolic levels of personality measurement. The *public level* is that at which the individual appears to others, *performance* in my framework; the private level [conscious level in Leary's latest version (22)] is that at which he appears to himself, *self description* in my scheme; and the symbolic (private level in Leary's book) is that at which he reveals himself in projective materials, projection in my discussion. Leary's position is that each of these levels has its values and uses in personality assessment. I have already quoted Allport (1) to the same effect. While recognizing that at present we have data to justify the practical use of methods and information from only the public and private levels, from only the performance and self-descriptive approaches, it seems to me that we must agree with Leary and with Allport that all three levels or approaches should be used in the scientific study of personality if we are eventually to attain the understanding and the control that we desire.

References

1. Allport, G. W. The trend in motivational theory. *Amer. J. Ortho-psychiat.*, 1953, 23, 107-119.
2. Allport, G. W. and Vernon, P. E. *Studies in expressive movement.* New York, Macmillan, 1932.
3. American Psychological Association, Committee on Test Standards. Technical recommendations for psychological tests. *Psychol. Bull.*, 1954, 51, Supplement.
4. Bass, B. M. The leaderless group discussion. *Psychol. Bull.*, 1954, 51, 465-492.
5. Bordin, E. S. A theory of vocational interests as dynamic phenomena. *Educ. psychol. Measmt.*, 1943, 3, 49-66.
6. Cronbach, L. J. Assessment of individual differences. *Annual Review of Psychology, Vol. 7.* Palo Alto: Annual Reviews, 1956, 173-196.
7. Downey, J. E. *The will-temperament and its testing.* Yonkers, N. Y.: World Book, 1923.
8. Eriksen, C. W. Personality. *Annual Review of Psychology, Vol. 8,* Palo Alto: Annual Reviews, 1957, 185-210.
9. Eysenck, H. J. *The structure of human personality.* New York: Wiley, 1953.
10. Eysenck, H. J. La validité des techniques projectives. *Rev. de Psychologie Appliquée.*, 1955, 5, 231-234.
11. Flanagan, J. C., Fiske, D. W., Bass, B. M., Carter, L. F., Kelly, E. L., and Weislogel, R. L. Situational performance tests (a symposium). *Personn. Psychol.*, 1954, 7, 461-498.
12. Guilford, J. P. (ed.) Printed classification tests. *AAF Aviation Psychology Report No. 5.* Washington D. C.: Gov't. Printing Office, 1947.
13. Guthrie, E. R. Personality in terms of associative learning. In Hunt, J. McV., *Personality and the behavior disorders.* New York: Ronald, 1944, 170-213.

14. Heyns, R. W., and Lippitt, R. Systematic observational techniques. In Lindzey, G., (ed.) *Handbook of social psychology.* Cambridge: Addison-Wesley, 1954, pp. 370-404.
15. Hollander, E. P. The friendship factor in peer nominations. *Personn. Psychol.,* 1956, 9, 435-498.
16. Holtzman, W. H., and Sells, S. B. Prediction of flying success by clinical analyses of test protocols. *J. abnorm. soc. Psychol.,* 1954, 49, 485-490.
17. Jensen, A. R. Personality. *Annual Review of Psychology, Vol. 9,* Palo Alto: Annual Reviews, 1958, 295-322.
18. Kelly, E. L. Theory and techniques of assessment. *Annual Review of Psychology, Vol. 5,* Palo Alto: Annual Reviews, 1954, 281-311.
19. Kelly, G. A. *The psychology of personal constructs.* New York. Norton, 1955.
20. Kelly, G. A. Theory and techniques of assessment. *Annual Review of Psychology, Vol. 9,* Palo Alto: Annual Reviews, 1958, 295-322.
21. Landis, C., and Katz, S. E. The validity of certain questions which purport to measure neurotic tendencies. *J. appl. Psychol.,* 1934, 18, 343-356.
22. Leary, T. *Interpersonal diagnosis of personality.* New York: Ronald, 1957.
23. Leary, T. and Coffey, H. S. Interpersonal diagnosis: some problems of methodology and validation. *J. abnorm. soc. Psychol.,* 1955, 50, 110-124.
24. Lindzey, G., and Borgatta, E. F. Sociometric measurement. In Lindzey, G. (ed.) *Handbook of social psychology.* Cambridge: Addison-Wesley, 1954, pp. 405-448.
25. McClelland, D. C. Personality. *Annual Review of Psychology, Vol. 7,* Palo Alto: Annual Reviews, 1956, 39-62.
26. McQuitty, L. L. A statistical method for studying personality integration. In Mowrer, D. H. (ed.) *Psychotherapy: theory and research.* New York: Ronald, 1953, pp. 414-462.
27. Maller, J. B. Personality tests. In Hunt, J. McV. *Personality and the behavior disorders.* New York: Ronald, 1944, 170-213.
28. Meehl, P. E. *Clinical vs. statistical prediction.* Minneapolis: Univ. of Minn. Press, 1955.
29. Payne, R. W. L'utilité du test de Rorschach in psychologie clinique. *Rev. de Psychologie Appliquée,* 1955, 5, 255-264.
30. Siegel, L. A biographical inventory for students: I, II. *J. appl. Psychol.,* 1956, 40, 5-10, 122-126.
31. Stogdill, R. M., and Coons, A. E. (eds.) *Leader behavior: its description and measurement.* Columbus: Bureau of Business Research, Ohio State University, 1957.
32. Super, D. E., Crites, J. O., Hummel, R. C., Moser, Helen P., Overstreet, Phoebe L., and Warnath, C. F. *Vocational development: a*

framework for research. New York: Teachers College Bureau of Publications, 1957.

33. Super, D. E., and Luntz, L. Some uses of biographical inventories in describing adjustment and predicting success. Office for Social Science Programs, *Air Force Personnel and Training Research Center, Technical Memorandum 57-1.*

34. Sweet, L. Measurement of personal attitudes in younger boys. New York: National Council of YMCA's, *Occasional Studies No. 9*, 1929.

35. Wyatt, F. Some remarks on the place of cognition in ego psychology. *J. Proj. Techniques.*, 1953, 17, 144-151.

III

Foundations of Personality Measurement Theory in Multivariate Experiment

RAYMOND B. CATTELL
University of Illinois

P ERSONALITY ASSESSMENT has inspiration in many distinct fields, including such specialty areas as clinical, educational, counseling, and experimental psychology. No matter where objective testing arises, it is a pointless procedure to make measurements and scales that are unrelated to meaningful personality structures. Consequently personality assessment and basic theoretical research on personality become one and the same enterprise.

STRATEGY OF PERSONALITY RESEARCH

A brief digression on the strategy of personality research is essential here to justify my later inferences. Since we nowadays rightly emphasize explicitness of methodology and models, may I remind you that though the hunches on personality structure come from many fields of observation, the basic scientific methods in psychology by which such hypotheses are tested, revised, and re-created, are really of two kinds only, namely, the univariate, controlled experiment, as borrowed from classical physics, and the multivariate experiment, as illustrated in factor analysis, the multiple discriminant function, canonical correlations, etc. In the first approach, we try to hold constant everything but that which we are interested in manipulating and we then observe how one measure—the dependent variable—changes with the changes we produce in the independent variables. In the multivariate approach, on the other hand, we enter the experiment with a great number of variables, usually allowing them to vary as they vary in nature, without attempting to control them artificially in any way. We then tease out the relationships among them by the superior statistical potency of the methods which have been developed, principally in the life sciences, since the days of classical physics.

COMPARISON OF METHODS

There are advantages and disadvantages to both methods, though you would sometimes think from the pious expressions of brass instrument psychologists that all scientific purity lies with the classical univariate method. Actually, the multivariate method can claim three great scientific advantages. First, it can deal with patterns and wholistic concepts. A clinician in my presence once remarked to a psychologist that he proposed to do some experiments on the relation of the superego to school achievement. Whereupon the classical experimentalist, a man as direct as he was eminent, snorted, "What is a superego? I have never seen one."

The implications of this remark should really be "a plague to both their houses." So long as the older type of experimenter deals only with single variables he must remain blind to anything that requires demonstration as a complex pattern. But equally the clinician, although taking many variables into account, is unable objectively and scientifically to convince others, e.g., to show that the super ego is not a myth but a visible pattern, unless he commands the powers of mathematical analysis to determine and demonstrate a loading pattern. The multivariate statistical methods possess this power, and, as I shall hope to point out in my summary, it is possible to define the superego, various drives, and a number of complex temperament patterns to a useful degree of exactitude by factor analytic means. Furthermore, when these constructs are measured as factors, they can enter into exact experiment as readily as any single concrete variable.

The second advantage of the multivariate method is its sheer business efficiency. If you go to the labor of measuring, say, two hundred variables, in a hundred pairs of two, on a large population, you get by classical experiment evidence on 100 relationships. If, on the other hand, you do the same amount of experimental work and use a multivariate method of analysis, you throw light on the nature of approximately 2,000 relationships. That is to say, you possess the correlations in a matrix of 200 variables. Actually, this is something more than an enormous—twenty to one—gain in efficiency.

When the 100 relationships of the univariate experimental design are taken from many different samples, as commonly happens when an unfortunate reviewer of an area in the *Psychological Bulletin* is trying to make sense out of a hundred independent researches, the findings are essentially incomparable, statistically, because of coming from different samples, and they are of questionable comparability experimentally, because they are always attained by the idiosyncracies of the various investigators and their locations. The hypothesis-testing power, and especially the hypothesis-creating power of the multivariate experiment is here far greater, because we know that all the relations are comparable, having been made on the same group.

Additionally the factor analytic method has special revolving powers, in terms of discerning meaningful patterns among the correlations. We get what a philosopher might call "emergents" from the accumulated, criss-crossing relationships, such as can never come from reasoning about single relationships or from the blind game of partialling this influence out from that, one at a time. In personality research it means that we are enabled to detect the major *structures* operating across this whole field, whereas when one works with variables two or three at a time, trying to partial out this from that, one is apt to run around in the prison circle of one's own feeble vision of possibilities.

The third advantage of the multivariate method does not belong to its general use in psychology, but is specific to its application in the field of personality and clinical study. It resides in the fact that human beings decline to let you do controlled manipulative experiments on matters of vital emotional importance to them. If you wished to study the effect upon marital couples of a mother-in-law coming to stay in the home, you would not be well advised to go around issuing invitations to mothers-in-law, dropping in afterwards to see what this very independent variable has done to your dependent variables.

There are two objections to the manipulative experimental design in the field of personality. The first is that you ought not to do it, and the second is that, if you throw ethics aside and proceed, the artificial insult of the experiment may create a situation quite different from the naturally occurring one. When you chop pieces off a man's adrenal glands you do something more than reduce his adrenal functioning. The multivariate experimenter, like the clinician, allows life itself to make the experiments, in naturally functioning organic wholes, and then extracts the causal connections by superior statistical analytical procedures. If you stick to the controlled experiment in regard to emotional learning, etc., you are compelled like Mowrer, Miller and others to move increasingly away from human beings to animals. This leaves you with the impossible task of generalizing across from animal behavior to something vaguely analogous in human behavior. In fact, methodologically you have allowed the rat to lead you into a worse cul-de-sac than in any maze you ever constructed for him.

If now you look at the so-called clinical method with this broad dichotomy of method in mind you will notice that it has several close parallels to the multivariate method. Both deal with major emotional events in the lives of human beings, allowing life itself to provide the source of manipulation, and both work upon wholistic perceptions of patterns and relations, rather than upon single variables. Indeed, I think it can be seen that there is really *no such thing as a separate clinical method* (unless we are talking about a therapeutic method), for, when stripped down to its essential, formal procedures, the clinical method *is* the multivariate method. Unfortunately, though it is formally the multivariate method, it lacks scientific rigor, proceeding by intuition and fallible human memory, instead of being carried out on exact measurements by an electronic computer, using a far superior memory and a fully explicit statistical procedure. In terms of progress in the scientific study of personality, the clinician has his heart in the right place, but perhaps we may say that he remains a little fuzzy in the head. The salvation of the clinical method lies in filling out its cloudy procedures by structural statistics, decidedly more complex, incidentally, than those known to univariate methodology. Factor analysis is only one such statistical model, though it is the best we have achieved so far.

MEASUREMENT FOLLOWS STRUCTURE

But let us now return from this survey of foundations to my first assertion that measurement must follow structure. I am aware that this reiteration of "no testing without structure" makes me as popular among certain kinds of test constructors in educational and clinical psychology as a Baptist minister reminding people of the

Ten Commandments in an establishment for organized vice. But I would repeat that you may use the most impressive scaling procedures, refining Guttman, Coombs, and others to the nth power, and still be merely engaged in a sort of psychometric chess game, as far as any psychological understanding of psychological problems is concerned. If your scale is *not* guaranteed to deal with something psychologically meaningful and organic, it cannot help in psychological procedures. And, incidentally, it does not seem to be sufficiently realized that a Guttman scale, or any other scaling method *per se*, does not guarantee a factor pure scale. A correctly scaled scale may still be of any degree of factorial confusion.

When I mention a demonstrable functional unity in what follows, I refer technically not only to a pattern of covarying parts which can be demonstrated as a unique, replicable, determinate factor in terms of factor analysis, but also to a pattern which additionally could be shown to function as a whole by univariate, controlled experiment. That is to say, the pattern should show itself not only by a person who is higher in one element of it consistently being higher in the other elements, but also by the parts varying together from occasion to occasion when an experimental influence which changes this trait is brought to bear.

Within multivariate methods, this means that the factor pattern out of which the construct or concept arises, must be demonstrated not only by the classical R-technique, but also by the longitudinal P-technique. It may also be demonstrated by other factor analytic experimental designs, such as the condition-response design, in which one simultaneously factors in a single matrix both the various stimuli that might cause the pattern to change in level, and all the manifestations by which the pattern is recognized. In short, to ensure that a unitary trait is sound in wind and limb, it should be thumped in many different parts. Thus, in Scheier's work on the nature of anxiety, which has come out with certain clean cut results which I shall discuss in a moment, it was first demonstrated that some ten psychological and physiological variables repeatedly emerged as salients in a single factor in studies dealing with individual differences in anxiety level, i.e., by R-technique.

After this R-technique demonstration of the boundaries of anxiety as an individual difference trait, a longitudinal study was made in which the fluctuations (in these salient variables discovered on the R-technique factor) were measured from day to day under the various naturally occurring anxiety stimuli of daily life. A longitudinal factor analysis, by P-technique, then turned out much the same factor pattern as had been obtained by R-technique. There were some differences of emphasis, but it was clearly the same anxiety factor, marked by the same major variables.

A third phase of the research consisted in measuring a large number of people on this array of variables and then submitting them, in an analysis combining the factorial design of analysis of variance with factor analysis, to a number of what are commonly considered anxiety provoking stimuli, such as important examinations, a discussion of imaginary diseases, some probing of their economic condition, etc. Correlating in the stimulus differences with all the response differences, resulted in the reappearance of the same anxiety factor pattern. In this condition-response design, however, it was additionally loaded with the stimuli which are effective in *producing* the anxiety response pattern. Scheier's work on the measurement of anxiety thus illustrates the full present scope of multivariate method usage and shows how a practical measurement of high validity and determinateness can result.

This digression on complex issues of method may have been so brief as to evoke the comment that for those who knew them already, it was unnecessary and for those who did not, it was too short to carry the full implications. But we must move on with the statement that if this agreement is fully examined, it provides justification for believing factor analytic findings rather than clinical impressions. It also prevents our aligning ourselves, on the other hand, with that compulsively accurate psychometrics of scales which still narrowly persists in the old faculty psychology of supposing that where there is a single name there must be a single function.

A BRIEF REVIEW OF FACTOR ANALYTIC FINDINGS

Although factor analytic findings over the last fifteen years have been evaluated elsewhere (4), it will be helpful here to give a brief sketch of the substantive findings which are the necessary basis for the measurement theory I have to discuss. These results in 1958 are largely the outcome of certain aims and canons of research and method worked out in a first attempt to integrate the field, namely, my *Description and Measurement of Personality* (2) twelve years ago. In the first place, our laboratory has always aimed to gather data widely and simultaneously over the three chief possible media of personality observation—L-data or life records of behavior *in situ,* Q or questionnaire data, and T or objective test data. In the life record medium, personality is observed in the natural life situation, by time sampling, rating, or keeping of records on particular events, e.g., achievements, accidents, etc. This is, of course, the criterion medium, in the sense of being an external or cultural criterion for any testing. In the questionnaire medium the person responds by giving his impressions of himself, limited by his own self knowledge and willingness to disclose. In the objective [1] test medium, there is no question of introspective self-evaluation as in the questionnaire, but only of actual performance or response in a miniature situation, in which the subject does not know what aspects of his performance are being scored and interpreted.

At each age level at which investigations have been made we have always begun by operating in the first of these media, because it connects most readily with existing concepts in the field, permitting interpretations of the factors in popular, clinical, and general terms. An immediate integration of concepts is then possible because the measurements use the same words and situations of behavior as are covered by the clinicians, guidance psychologists, educators, and others. It also has the advantage that it permits use of a personality sphere concept, that is to say, the notion of a stratified sample of variables from the total realm of behavior. Incidentally, for those interested in perfecting the factor analytic approach, this ability to introduce a concept of *a population of variables* becomes very important.

Canons of Procedure

In adopting this simultaneous, three-fold observation of personality, it was our conviction that any important dimension of person-

---

[1] Some definition of "objective" is required, since there are commonly two degrees of objectivity in test construction: (1) objectivity of *scoring*, plus, (2) objectivity in the sense of *not involving self appraisal*. It is in the latter, complete, sense that "objective" is used here, and we would suggest the term *conspective* for a test that is only objective as to its scoring. This implies that it has a high conspect reliability; that is to say, complete agreement between two different psychometricists as to what the score would be. A test which is *not* conspective might be called a *rative test*, indicating that the score depends on the judgment of a single person and is made by rating rather than key scoring methods. The reader will notice that Edwards in his contribution has used the term objective in a way which allows both the true objective test as defined here and the conspective test to come under the same heading. However, psychologically and in terms of the history of test development, the difference between the conspective test and the true objective test is greater than that between the rative test and the conspective test, for it deals with the whole test character, whereas the latter deals only with the mode of scoring. For these adequate reasons, and to agree with the usage systematically adopted throughout 15 years of publication from our laboratory, we have used objective for the *non-self appraisal type* of test.

ality should break through all three, showing itself at once as a factor pattern in behavior rating data, in the questionnaire-response patterns, and in objective personality tests. This theory has been only partially vindicated, and some tantalizing exceptions persist. Throughout this discovery of structure as a basis for measurement it has been a canon of research procedure that factors shall be determined by simple structure principles, and other principles permitting a unique, objective factor solution quite independent of any psychological pre-conceptions which the observer may have about personality structure. Psychologists who have been using factor analysis by rotating for "psychological meaning" are merely having a pleasant game perpetuating their own superstitions or prejudices.

Some years ago I talked at Tubingen with the German psychologist, Kretschmer, who has done such striking clinical experimental work in bringing out the full nature of the schizothyme temperament pattern. Whenever I showed him an experimental pattern in factor analysis that agreed with his clinical impressions, he would say "factor analysis is a remarkably important scientific tool." But when I showed a pattern that corresponded to no known clinical pattern, his inclination was at once to assume it to be an artifact, and immediately to lose interest in it. This I cite only as a rather amusing and well developed instance of the attitude that, together with some defects of statistical education, has kept the clinical psychologist from understanding the importance of these factored measurement developments for his work.

Indeed, there is no need especially to pillory clinical psychologists, for psychologists in general seem rather prone, relative to physical scientists, to dependence on subjective conviction. Yet if we are dealing with a science rather than a religion, we should welcome objective methods which surprise us by turning up something that does not in the least fit what we knew before. Factor analysis has, in fact, produced surprises in the clinical field, for those who can see them, much as the microscope did in biology. Notably it has turned up at least a dozen clear cut patterns in the personality field, that contribute as much to the variance of behavior as any such familiar concepts as schizothymia, ego strength, dominance, etc., which have nevertheless never been visible to the naked eye of the clinician or named or discussed. These structures have not yet been accepted as the challenge to existing clinical theory and formulations that they really are, for they have power to yield predictions of criterion behavior impossible from the familiar concepts.

A third canon of our research has been that the factor patterns shall be *replicated,* in at least two independent researches, before we begin to give them serious theoretical consideration. To put this canon into effect requires considerable planning in research, to ensure that a sufficiency of identical variables to permit matching are carried over from one study to another. For in this day and age we can no longer go along with the idea that the identity of a factor in one study with that in another study can be established merely by the psychologist's impression of the psychological similarity of the two. There must be accurate carrying over of salients, and the use of a quantitative index, such as the salient variable similarity index, to ensure that the patterns really are alike.

A fourth principle has been that we should not be too hasty in interpreting the factors, but should be content to designate them by an index number in some agreed universal index among psychologists, such as that which I have proposed as an international index in the current issue of the Japanese *International Journal of Psychology.* A factor will commonly become a recognized part of the scenery, and a basis for measurement in a good unifactor scale, some years before its nature is fully understood. In the case of about half a dozen of the discovered factors, namely, ego strength, intelligence, anxiety, general neuroticism, schizothymia, and super ego strength, I think the pattern is sufficiently identical with anything that has ever been called by that name by a responsible psychologist, to justify using these customary names and interpretations—such as they are. In about another half dozen factors a pretty definite idea can be formed of the physiological, experiential, or dynamic influence responsible for the pattern. For example, surgency-desurgency level is essentially the level of general inhibition, and seems correlated with frequency of past punishment. The factor we have called Q3 seems to represent the degree of dynamic investment in the self sentiment, and so on. While these explanations are not as perfect and perhaps not as lurid as those that psychoanalysts are fed with their Freudian mother's milk, they have the advantage of dealing with demonstrable behavior patterns, and of permitting measurements of individual differences, with known validity and reliability, which can be made the basis of experimental investigation of theory. Surely it is high time that theory began to build itself around these measurable behavior patterns, frequently replicated in eight to a dozen researches, instead of the vaguely perceived and statistically unsubstantiated behavior patterns and sequences which many clinicians take as the basis for elaborate theories.

A last canon of design, in these experiments to put personality measurement on a functional basis, and functional concepts on a measurement basis, is that continuity should be established in the patterns over the whole developmental age range. That is to say, not only should the functional unity be established at one age level, by the above two handed use of R- and P-techniques, but the age range should be cut by such studies at three or four year intervals, to establish the mode of growth, as one might take slices across the stem of a plant. This is a big order, and it has not yet been filled, but sections have recently been taken at 12, 8, and 4 years of age and are in press.

LONGITUDINAL ANALYSES

The hypotheses of measurement here are that some patterns might be expected to persist over all age sections more persistently than others. For example, an ability like general intelligence, or a temperament trait associated firmly with some physiological or body-build component, would be expected to show itself, perhaps with some modifications, from the earliest testing period. On the other hand, an environmental mold pattern, such as the superego or a sentiment to a specific object, might be expected to appear only at a given age and to show more pronounced developmental change in the loading pattern. The work on personality factors was initially done, for good reasons, at the young adult level, but the researches of Coan, Peterson, Gruen, and others, maintaining the combinations of life record data, questionnaire data, and objective test data, show that all but three or four of the factors established in the adult level can be traced down through childhood and even into infancy. For example, in the factor analyses of time samplings of behavior, made at the four year old level, we can clearly see the cyclothyme-schizothyme factor, the dominance-submissiveness factor, the surgency-desurgency factor, the paranoid factor, the ego strength factor, and so on, operating in the nursery school world.

On the practical side, for the benefit of those who wish to do longitudinal research in personality over a sufficient interval, we are in process of constructing measures of these factors in the questionnaire medium. Thus, 14 of the 16 factors in the adult *16 Personality Factor Questionnaire* (3) can be demonstrated and set up in the range from 12 to 16 years of age, in a test called the *High School Personality Questionnaire* (5). Twelve of the factors can still be clearly recognized at the nine year level and are being put into the *Child Personality Questionnaire*. Peterson has made sets of questions, which must, of course, be given orally, which get at these personality factors at the nursery school level. There are many technical difficulties in getting a good series of personality factor questionnaires to operate meaningfully from the four year level right up through the adult level, but these difficulties must be overcome, because such longitudinal studies are essential both for understanding personality and for the success of applied psychology.

Indeed, there is both a great need and great opportunity at the moment for longitudinal studies in personality structure. Such studies will, first, establish more definitely the identity of the factors found at the earlier level with those at the later level, by repetitive measures on the same children at intervals; second, show which factors are most subject to environmental influences, and if so, to what environmental influences; third, show the general curve of change in these personality factors in the same sense as we have established the normal trend in the intelligence factor; and last, suggest in what way the pattern of behavior typically changes with age.

In regard to these changes in the test weights in the pattern to be measured, we may instance that the ego strength factor in four year old children loads freedom from temper tantrums, freedom from enuresis, infrequency of headaches and psychosomatic disorders, infrequency of manifestations of jealousy, etc. By eleven years of age, enuresis has dropped out of the loading pattern, the main emotional stability versus instability variables remain, and some new elements have come in. Similarly, in the dominance factor, disobedience, sulking and "talking back" are prominent in the time sampling variables at the early age, whereas by the adult level, these are no longer present. The disobedience has become unconventionality, but the talkativeness has disappeared and the dominant adult is, if anything, rather more silent than the average.

VALIDITY OF PERSONALITY MEASUREMENTS

In discussions on the validity of personality measurements, it is desirable constantly to distinguish between concept or construct validity, on the one hand, and external, or cultural, validity on the other. The former is defined by the correlation between a given objective test questionnaire or rating scale and the factor as derived from all known criterion variables. Thus we might validate a test against such factor constructs as anxiety, or against ego strength, or against surgency, or against schizothymia. The external or cultural validity is never validity singular but validity plural. That is to say, there are thousands of things against which a factor's predictive power could be tried and the correlations known in the interests of interpretation; but no one of them is *the* criterion. For instance, the use of the 16 PF test has yielded a great many significant personality factor correlations, for example, with success in school, prognostic rating in a clinic, automobile accident proneness, alcoholism, etc., and these have greatly enriched the original interpretations based on factor content alone.

One of the first inquiries to be made about the nature of a factor —indeed it should be *the* routine inquiry before making any more specific hypotheses—is to test whether it is largely hereditarily determined or substantially a product of learning and environment. Obviously, this is of basic importance both for theory and for the proper practical use of the measurement. Indeed, one of the chief claims of the factorally unitary measurement is that it permits something more than merely statistical prediction—namely, an estimate of criterion performance that takes into account whatever general psychological knowledge about the natural history of a trait permits us additionally to infer. Fortunately, some fairly extensive nature-nuture studies have already placed the principal factors in perspective, in relation to such older factors as Spearman's "g." For example, we know from multiple variance analysis studies that the cyclothyme-schizothyme factor is largely hereditarily determined, that a surgency-desurgency source trait is largely environmentally determined, that the level of dominance-submission is about 50-50 a product of constitution and familial-environmental influences, and so on.

Although the greater meaningfulness of personality measures based on factors arises from the possibility of building around each of these functional unities a rich natural history, the actual growth of such knowledge has barely begun, because of the extreme recency of satisfactory proof of the factors themselves. Meanwhile, the tests that can be and have been spawned with much greater ease have accumulated gargantuan standardizations, as well as the momentum of enormous numbers of past students whose gifts seem to be exclusively in the rituals of administering them. Like the first small mammals entering a world possessed by the dinosaurs, the lately arriving factored tests, have a validation largely in the future.

DYNAMIC CALCULATION

The most recent, and as yet scarcely noticed, development of factored measures lies in that area of dynamic calculation which is so vital to clinical psychology and to motivation theory. This rests on the discovery that the drive patterns in man can be established by the factoring of collections of objective motivational measures. Sex, self assertion, fear, and six other drive patterns have been replicated now in three successive studies by these means. Alongside these easily recognizable drive patterns, there occur patterns that closer scrutiny suggests can only be acquired dynamic sentiments, such as the self sentiment, the sentiment to religion, and the sentiment pattern of attitudes and interests acquired about one's profession.

In these studies an attitude is defined as a stimulus-response habit. By this model the strength of an interest, that is, the need to react, in regard to any course of action, can be expressed by a specification equation, weighting the tension levels of the various drives and sentiment systems of the strengths measured in the given individual. I must refer you to my recent book on *Personality and Motivation Structure and Measurement* for the postulates, and the chief equations, utilizable in the dynamic calculus which develops on this basis. The non-arbitrariness of the drive pattern—makes possible unambiguous measurements. For example, it is found that the achievement motive can be resolved into three distinctive components, a drive and two sentiment structures. On the basis of such unambiguous, functionally distinct and replicatable measurements, the experimental investigation of dynamic laws and motivational theories can go forward more exactly and more subtly than before.

FACTORING OF DRIVES

A development of crucial importance for clinical theories which these measurements have made possible, is the factoring of drives to determine, by P-technique, their quantitative contribution to the interests, attitudes, symptoms, and conflicts, conscious and unconscious, of the individual clinical case. Such a study is now being conducted by Williams, factoring each of 24 patients, to see the degree of agreement between the statement of each individual conflict based on the psychiatrist's experience with the case, and the description of the conflict quantitatively in terms of the dynamic calculus. If the agreement is reasonably good, I think we shall have demonstrated a very powerful new clinical tool. Parenthetically, I may add that to the extent that the agreement turns out to be imperfect, one may reasonably have doubts whether the psychiatrist or the dynamic calculus is wrong. In fact, our first step if the agreement is inadequate will be to bring in a second psychiatrist to see how far he agrees with the first!

NEW TYPES OF TESTS

The development of structured measurement in motivation has gone hand in hand with the invention of quite new types of objective tests, no longer requiring the actual scores on component interests and attitudes to rest on the verbal opinionnaire or the open-ended, projective type of test. These objective motivation measures include some devices using the so-called projective principles, together with physiological measures of motivation, learning measures, and many others. As far as theory is concerned, the interesting point of this analysis is that we seemed to get three distinct motivation strength factors, apparently corresponding to the id, ego, and superego contributions in any given interest.

PRACTICAL IMPLICATIONS

These theoretical implications will doubtless be much scrutinized and debated, but there are some immediately dependable conclusions for the practical man. First, the classical opinionnaire method of measuring attitude-interest strength by verbal self-evaluation has quite poor validity, accounting for only about a fifth to a tenth of the variance in the main motivation factors, however they are interpreted. Consequently, generalizations about attitudes and interests based only on this instrument could be highly fallacious as far as the total variance in interest strengths is concerned. Secondly, the projective tests, or misperception tests as we prefer to call them, are not clearly distinguished by any factors from the rest of the motivation measurement devices. Thus in the theoretical reconstruction suggested by this work, the classification of motivation measurements would fall principally into id, ego, and superego component measures, and the division into projective and non-projective, physiological and non-physiological, etc., signs of motivation strength become rather pointless.

MEASUREMENT OF STATES AND TRAITS

Any comprehensive view of progress in personality assessment must include the measurement of states as well as the measurement of traits. The work of Scheier (11) on the measurement of anxiety provides, as I have briefly mentioned, a very neat methodological demonstration of conceptual and statistical problems involved in separating states and traits. Scheier has now checked the anxiety state pattern in two independent factor analytic studies, and the anxiety trait pattern in no fewer than eight independent researches. There is enough similarity in the state and trait patterns to justify the popular habit of using the term anxiety for both. Both load a particular set of markers in the questionnaire realm, in objective personality tests, and in physiological response measures, though the emphases are interestingly somewhat different. For aught the early scale makers knew, there might have been four or five distinct and uncorrelated factors of anxiety rather than a single factor.

As it turns out there *does* seem to be a single factor of anxiety, but these premature scales mix this anxiety factor with the quite distinct neuroticism factor and a number of other irrelevant and contaminating factors. It is really not surprising that anyone surveying the literature of the past ten years is discouraged by almost every finding being matchable by an equal and opposite finding for even when investigators verbally defined anxiety in the same way, they frequently used a different test for it. It is rather early to see what the full impact of factor analytic work on anxiety measurement will be in giving a new momentum to insightful clinical research. The instrument *could* permit the emergence of a whole series of new laws and therapeutic certainties, replacing the present gropings toward scales of obscure meaning.

One of the certainties which emerged relatively early from this joint attack by Eysenck's laboratory and our own, was that anxiety and neuroticism are distinct factors. They have a slight obliquity, but, as I have shown with substantiating evidence, they can be measured with satisfactory reliability by objective tests, and, when so measured, it becomes evident that a person can stand at any position on one axis while occupying any position on the other. If the further, but far more tentative evidence by Eysenck's coworkers and ourselves, of a general psychoticism dimension is sound, then both anxiety and neuroticism are, additionally, independent of measured psychoticism.

These, however, are only local areas of illumination in the factor analytic picture, rendered clearer by our clinical familiarity with the phenomena. Outside these brightly lit spots, in the domains of the remaining dozen or more personality factors, definitely locatable but uninterpreted, there exists obscurities and some intriguing paradoxes, now engrossing the pure researcher. For example, for the last four years it has been known that two substantial second order factors can be found among the primary personality factors as represented in the 16 Personality Factor Questionnaire.

The first of these second order factors brings together the separate dimensions of ego weakness, high ergic tension, and the mysterious O factor, sometimes called guilt proneness, and which we have so far hung on to mainly by the symbol O. The second of these massive second-order factors reveals the existence of a common influence behind surgency, cyclothymia, dominance, and the factor which we have called parmia, which is short for high parasympathetic system dominance. These patterns were confirmed by the independent study of Karson, at the University of New Hampshire, and I think that we can now agree that the second of these two large factors gives substance to the Jungian concept of extraversion-introversion as a definite, invariant second order factor, rather than as the mere correlation cluster which it was once thought to be. That is to say, the general personality dimension of extraversion really expresses itself in five relatively independent primary factors: *surgency, dominance, parmia, cyclothymia,* and *lack of self-sufficiency.* The quality of an individual's extraversion therefore needs to be defined by his separate scores on these five components.

Although the second massive second order factor thus quickly fitted into a concept long popularly discussed, the first large pattern involving ego weakness, ergic tension, etc., as I have described, could not be immediately interpreted. However, when Scheier began his work with objective anxiety measurements, he included the 16 Personality Factor Questionnaire in his study and when he determined the loading of his objective test anxiety factor on these questionnaire measurements, the pattern of loadings turned out to be exactly the same as that found in the factorization of the questionnaire itself. In other words, the second order factor among the questionnaires is identical with the first order factor among the objective test measurements. On looking at the psychological picture this begins to make good sense for it tells us that high anxiety is contributed to by ego weakness, by high ergic tension, that is to say, frustration of drive expression, and by the temperamental guilt proneness component.

Without time for expanding these comments, I would point out that we now have three instances where a second order factor in the questionnaire realm has become recognized and confirmed as a first order factor in objective, instrumental tests. The perplexing lack of relationship between the questionnaire and behavior rating factors on the one hand, which mutually agree well, and the objective test factors on the other, which have previously defied alignment, therefore begins to resolve itself. The objective test factors are second order factors to the primaries found in the other media of observation. This is only one illustration of the increasing interconnection and illumination of structure which is now beginning to take place in the factor analytic realm. However, I want to add a technical word of warning. I think this fitting together of the jigsaw puzzle can continue only insofar as we all give far more attention to good technical precision in our first order factor analyses than has been typical of work in the last ten years. In particular, far greater diligence is necessary in getting accurate rotation, to a plateau of maximum percentage of variables in the hyperplane, whenever simple structure is alleged to be obtained.

AVOIDANCE OF GENERAL THEORY

If I have referred insufficiently to general theories, it is because I believe that psychology particularly needs to guard itself at this stage of development from getting into cloudy regions of grandiose theory, instead of seeking well established laws and concepts, susceptible to accurate measurement. In a healthy science, wider theories arise from well determined regularities, which we call laws. If you give yourselves a few seconds thought on this, I think you will realize that the unquestionable, dependable laws in psychology can probably be counted on your fingers, not in the hundreds with which they can be counted in the physical sciences. This is both a cause and a consequence of the psychologist's readiness to escape, at the drop of a hat, into philosophy. The despair which motivates this escapism is a justifiable reactive depression to the very small amount of progress made in psychology relative to the enormous amount of labor that has gone into research over the past thirty years, especially in the clinical and personality area.

Of course, if we get too dissatisfied with ourselves, in relation to the chemists and physicists' accomplishments, we can always look across at the still more chaotic and barren backyard of our neighbors, the sociologists. We are not quite at the head of the list in terms of getting nowhere in a great hurry. Several shrewd observers have pointed out one feature that constantly seems to distinguish research in the social sciences from research in the physical sciences: the physical sciences typically show an architectonic growth, in terms of one research building constructively upon another, whereas in the social sciences there are an enormous number of unrepeated researches, in which particular variables are used by a particular investigator and never touched again by anyone. The resulting scenery is a shanty town of one story hovels instead of the skyscrapers which the physical sciences build.

I think there are three major, and doubtless many minor, reasons for this. First, we have tried to ape the physical sciences by concentrating on the univariate controlled experimental method, instead of the multivariate experimental method which is alone truly adapted to the far more numerous variables and complex determination with which we deal. Second, our work needs far more mathematical discipline than our students have been willing to acquire. Third, there has been insufficient social organization of research. By this last I mean that we have been inclined to ascribe our failures wholly to defective technical methods when frequently they are due to defective coordination of research. Better social organization can come either from the organization of teams and institutions or through more sensitive conscience and vision in the individual research worker. One of the immature features of our science seems to be a bizarre teenager sense of honor, which dictates that no individual with claims to creativity could possibly use the same variables as any other individual and certainly not stop to replicate any extensive experiments previously done. There is also what I would call magpie research in which the investigator seems attracted for purely emotional reasons by the glitter of a particular variable or piece of apparatus, e.g., the psychogalvanometer, social prejudice, colored inkblots, sociometric count, or what have you, and centers his research on a mere variable without any broader theoretical or conceptual framework.

Solution: Organization and Division of Labor

I believe a great deal of progress could be made by a very simple practice indeed, namely, that of putting other peoples' variables into one's correlation matrix. People can continue to hold quite different theories about what is happening behind these variables, but at least if we linked hands on some marker variables we could with comparative certainty begin to relate and debate the theories through the intercorrelation matrices. We do this as a routine procedure in our own factor analyses, taking a minimum of two marker variables for each well known factor, for example, from the work of Eysenck, Guilford, and other previous researches, when we start new investigation on the next factor of theoretical interest. Factor analyses carried out *without* such markers from the known *terra firma* are strictly uninterpretable. They inhabit a solipsistic universe of their own, with no past and very little future, and might as well be carried out upon the moon. On the other hand, an overlap of variables, must sooner or later, mean an overlap of integration of ideas. If people want to be productive, they should get their variables together.

This brings me to consider an important respect in which the development of our own personality assessment researches may be considered to lack integration. The charge must be admitted that factor analysts are so engrossed in establishing the form and nature of factors, with statistical elegance, in laboratory measures, that they have made quite inadequate effort to show the clinician, the educator, the industrial psychologist, and others what these factors mean in more popular terms, and particularly to interpret them in terms with which the general psychological theorist is familiar. But let us not mistake the principle of division of labor, which is necessary in a highly specialized world, for any lack of integration, which is not. It happens that a rather unusual assemblage of skills, apparatus, and organized facilities is necessary for the effective advance of knowledge through applying factor analysis to establishing functional unities in behavior.

One needs, first, research time, resources and subjects enough to permit lengthy measurement of a large range of variables; second, a research team with talents in the direction of proceeding from general theoretical concepts about personality to actual miniature-situational objective test designs; third, a sure touch in the finer statistical issues in the area of multivariate analysis; and last, an electronic computer, well furnished with programs for the principal factor extraction and rotation procedures. The combination of mathematical competence and clinical insight in psychologists, as now trained, is far from common, and the other conditions are positively rare; so it is not surprising that there are fewer than half a dozen laboratories in the English-speaking world, and none that I know of outside it, where this basic research is being intensively pursued.

However, although such research centers cannot easily be expanded to the requisite number, there is no need for them to be so few as they are. Any large university psychology department should be able to organize an effective laboratory in this area. Viewed in broader terms of national effort there are unmistakable similarities to our backwardness in the area of intercontinental ballistic missiles. Both have the pattern of insufficient planning of funds and facilities for the scale of work required, and the lack of ability to bring representatives of different departments together. In our case the coordination failure has shown itself especially, until recently, in obtaining strong teams combining clinicians and multivariate statistical experimenters.

The second necessary objective in the organization of research is the expediting of external cultural validation of these functional unities, once they are established and have had good tests set up for them in the laboratory. I believe it cannot be too much stressed that this is a task which cannot effectively be done by the same team or organization as had been designed for the basic internal validation just described. Instead this is the proper field for the vaster group of professional, applied psychologists in clinical, educational, and industrial research. There is always a lag between the conclusion of laboratory research and its use in the field, and one wonders if this lag could not, with a little better cooperation, be cut down from ten to five years. We all know the theory that if a man in the backwoods invents a better mousetrap the world will, in a few days, make a beaten track to his door, but in an age of advertising and vested interests he is more likely to be paid to bury the invention.

Through the momentum of custom alone, and the ego involvements of personal prowess with ink blots or Binet, the majority of clinical and educational psychologists are inclined to continue with the instruments they were taught to use at college, though instruments of twice as high a validity may be open to evaluation in research reports. For example, many clinicians are only just beginning to realize that the factored questionnaire of today is something quite different from the ad hoc questionnaires of former years, and there is quite a good probability that it would give them better clinical diagnoses and prognoses than are obtainable from their current tools. Others, failing to realize the modern demands for research specialization which I have just stressed, seem to expect that the factor analysts will not only investigate structure but also supply them with the clinical validities of such tests, and they sit back and wait, ignoring their own vital role in test development. But the test construction itself is today a full time and highly specialized task. The amount of planning, skill, and labor involved in factorizing literally hundreds of variables, checking by replication the factor structure in independent studies, and constructing unifactor scales from such variables is enormously greater than that involved in the older style questionnaires and tests, which most of us could make up almost overnight. It is, however, true that the factor analyst has usually been content to dump his finished product before the clinician in the journals and to return to his computer and his laboratory.

Unfortunately, even the applied psychologist who realizes his role in the teamwork of science, has been inclined to look at this abstract contrivance with about as much enthusiasm and insight as a Bikini native looking at an atom bomb. He rightly fears that it is something which will involve radical changes in his mode of practice and thinking. Often he is inclined to defend himself from having to think in objective structural concepts by saying that a factor is an artificial mathematical monstrosity which will have no potency in his human clinical world. The result is that though a number of well factored tests highly relevant to clinical practice have become available over about the last five years, the activity which should have led to their external validation has been utterly inadequate. The important point, however, is that on the few occasions when their external validity has been crucially tried, it has turned out to be very good.

Turning from practice to basic theory, one notes that these external validities are vital to the full interpretation of personality factors and structural relations for factors cannot be interpreted in the laboratory alone. In the case of the 16 P.F. Test external validation has come in rapidly and freely, leading to great strides in the interpretation of these factors which only five years ago had little attached to them except the letters of the alphabet—just like the nutritional vitamins before chemical analysis and synthesis. Thus, although factor C might be tentatively interpreted from its descriptive ratings and questionnaire responses as ego strength versus ego weakness, this hypothesis only received the degree of confirmation it really required with the ensuing demonstration that it is significantly and positively correlated with leadership in face to face groups, that it is higher in successful than unsuccessful psychiatric technicians, that it correlates with school achievement among students of the same intelligence level, that it is negatively correlated with accident proneness, that it is substantially negatively correlated with anxiety proneness, and so on.

Similarly, the finding that high F factor or surgency-vs-desurgency, is substantially positively correlated with being chosen and voted a group leader, that it has one of the principal loadings in the second order extraversion factor, that it increases with alcohol, that it declines steadily with age from adolescence to middle age, that its level is largely a product of environment rather than heredity, that it increases significantly under frontal lobotomy and under psychotherapy, provided valuable extension of the original factor hypothesis that desurgency is a form of generalized inhibition, associated with frontal lobe action and with frequency of punishing, repressive past experience. This degree of insight into its nature could never have been achieved from the direct content of the factor, either in ratings or in the questionnaire responses.

Accordingly, the great need in the social organization of research at the present moment is a concerted plan for taking all factor analytically well established personality source traits and having their social validities, their changes with age, their relevance to clinical prognoses, their educational predictive value, etc., systematically examined. No one clinical, counseling, or other applied psychological center can hope to do this alone or for all the factors. But a planned division of labor, in which certain laboratories or clinical centers make systematic studies of the life history of one factor and others of another could lead to an enormous increase in the practical effectiveness of personality measurement in applied psychology in the next five or ten years.

In conclusion, I hope I have given some convincing reasons why the construction of personality measurement scales should be wedded to concepts of personality structure, and some evidence that the objective structuring of personality has come of age sufficiently to make this possible. How soon this marriage will be fruitful, in terms of major gains in the power and insightfulness of applied psychology, depends on how soon teachers of applied psychology cease thinking in terms of catalogues of tests and set out to teach tests and measurements as an epilogue to courses in personality. The psychology of structure and growth comes first: the tests are merely an appendix to such an exposition. If after all this discussion, you were to ask me why I personally prefer factor scales to other scales, e.g., simple homogeneous scales, I think I should have to say because the former are psychologically interesting and the latter are dull. When you are through with a complicated scaling ritual you have perhaps at best eased a neurotic compulsion; but with factor scales you can have a lot of fun finding how people tick.

References

1. Burt, C. L. Scale analysis and factor analysis. *Brit. J. Psychol.*, 1953, 6, 5-23.
2. Cattell, R. B. *Description and measurement of personality.* New York: World Book Co., 1946.
3. Cattell, R. B. *The objective-analytic personality factor battery.* I.P.A.T., 1604 Coronado Drive, Champaign, Ill., 1956.
4. Cattell, R. B. Personality and motivation structure and measurement. New York: World Book Co., 1957.
5. Cattell, R. B. and Beloff, H. The High School Personality Questionnaire. I.P.A.T., 1604 Coronado Drive, Champaign, Ill., 1954.
6. Cattell, R. B., Blewett, D. B., and Beloff, H. The inheritance of personality: a multiple variance analytic determination of approximate nature-nuture ratios for primary personality factors in Q-data. *Amer. J. Hum. Genet.*, 1955, 7, 122-146.
7. Coombs, C. H. A theory of psychological scaling. *Engin. Res. Bull.*, No. 34, Ann Arbor, Univ. of Michigan, 1952.
8. Edwards, A. L. Chapter 6. This Book.
9. Guttman, L. A basis for scaling qualitative data. *Amer. soc. Rev.*, 1944, 9, 139-150.
10. Peterson, D. R. and Cattell, R. B. Personality structure in nursery school children as revealed by teacher ratings. *J. clin. Psychol.*, (In press).
11. Scheier, I. H. and Cattell, R. B. Confirmation of objective test factors and assessment of their relation to questionnaire factors: A factor analysis of 113 ratings, questionnaire and objective test measurements of personality (In press).
12. Williams, R. J. An attempt at definition and measurement of "conflict." Unpublished Ph. D. Thesis, Univ. of Illinois Library, Urbana, Ill., 1958.

IV

Differential Validity in Some Pattern Analytic Methods

Louis L. McQuitty
Michigan State University

A THEORY of personality structure is a starting point for the development of numerical methods for the objective assessment of personality. This chapter starts with a simple-minded theory concerning the way in which personality is structured. It outlines the theory and traces the development of a series of pattern analytic methods that have derived logically from the theory. The methods can be used to investigate the fruitfulness of the theory.

Most clinical theories accept the concept of syndromes of symptoms. A syndrome of symptoms is a combination of characteristics that implies a disease of some kind. If a person is mentally ill, then the manifestation of this condition can presumably be described as a syndrome of behavioral symptoms. For every disease entity there is a unique syndrome of symptoms. There is presumed to be a one-to-one correspondence between disease entities on the one hand and syndromes of symptoms on the other. The process of diagnosis is to discover the syndrome of symptoms portrayed by a patient and then assign to him the disease corresponding to that syndrome.

An examination of syndromes of symptoms reveals that many symptoms are common to more than one syndrome. There is not a one-to-one correspondence between symptoms and syndromes. In other words, there is not one symptom that is unique to each syndrome, such that if a given symptom is present then a corresponding syndrome is known to be present. Nearly every symptom can and does occur in more than one syndrome. Analogously, most every symptom can and does occur as a manifestation of more than one disease; there is not a one-to-one correspondence between symptoms and diseases.

In the field of mental health, symptoms are characteristic responses, and syndromes of them are patterns of characteristic responses. Following this translation still further, mental diseases are personality types. This approach gives a particular definition to the concept of a personality type. The personality type is the internal property that causes a person to portray a particular pattern of responses. It is a hypothetical contruct; it is assumed in order to explain why an individual gives a particular pattern of responses, just as a disease is interpreted to be the cause of a particular syndrome of symptoms even when nothing more than the syndrome has been observed in the patient.

There is presumed to be a one-to-one correspondence between personality types and patterns of responses, such that if a given pattern of responses is characteristic of a person, it means that the individual possesses a particular personality type. There is not, however, presumed to be a one-to-one correspondence between individual responses and personality types. Rather, most individual responses are presumed to be characteristic of more than one type; different types can cause the same response. As a consequence, a given response sometimes means one personality type and sometimes another type, just as a given symptom sometimes means one disease and at other times a quite different disease.

Carrying the analogy of personality types to disease entities still further, it is helpful to realize that a person can have more than one disease at a time. Analogously, it is assumed that a person can be characterized by more than one personality type. In fact, it is assumed that he can be characterized by many personality types. The number of types desirable to attribute to a person will depend on the level of abstraction that we wish to achieve in classifying people.

The Classification Problem

One problem with which we are concerned is the development of numerical methods that can start with the symptoms characteristic of patients and that can be used to classify the patients objectively into meaningful disease categories. An analogous problem is to start with responses to the individual items of a test, using these to classify the subjects into meaningful personality types.

The classification problem is complicated by the lack of a one-to-one correspondence betwen responses and personality types. In one person, the response to a given test item may be determined by one personality type but in another person the same response to the item may result from a different personality type. For example, a medical type of person may respond correctly to a question about chemistry because he has learned it in the advanced study of medicine. A chemical engineering type of person, on the other hand, may respond correctly to the same item because he learned it in the advanced study of engineering, but the two types of persons would possess this identical knowledge in different patterns of other information about physiology and mathematics.

The fact that the correct answer to an item is caused by two different personality types means that it has differential validity. In the one case, it indicates a medical type, and in the other it indicates an engineering type. In order to know which of these two types is indicated by a correct answer to the chemical item, we must know the answers to other items. If the correct answer to the chemical item occurs in a pattern of correct answers about physiology and incorrect ones about mathematics we then know that the correct chemical answer indicates a medical rather than an engineering type.

DIFFERENTIATION VERSUS DISCOVERY OF TYPES

Because the chemical answer has high validity for indicating both engineering and medical types, it necessarily has low discrimination for differentiating between the two types; it would be discarded as an item in a test designed to differentiate between the two types. Instead we would use the mathematical and physiological items in differentiating between engineers and doctors. But we are concerned here with a more difficult problem in objective classification. In the example, we assumed that the engineering and medical types are given; we know who are doctors and who are engineers. Instead of starting with known categories of subjects, we wish to start with characteristic responses to selected items and classify subjects into categories which are determined in some objective fashion by the responses to the test items.

For our purpose we require valid items; the items we seek must be indicative of types; but we cannot insist on items that are invariantly valid in the sense that they measure the same thing or things for all persons. This latter kind of item, with invariant validity, is the kind desired in most test construction methods, as illustrated especially well in factor analysis. In factor analysis, an item is assumed to measure the same thing for all people. This is not to say that it measures only one factor; it may in fact assess several factors, as indicated by loadings on several factors. The point is that whatever an item measures it is assumed to do this with near equal efficiency for all people of the universe under study. In this sense, its degree of validity is invariant; it measures nearly equally well the same stuff for all people.

Items of invariant validity are not the ones with which to start in an effort to isolate types, when the types are to be determined by the responses to test items themselves. The reason for this is that we have assumed there is not a one-to-one relationship between types and responses. There is no response which is known to mean one type and only one type.

Not being able to use items of high invariant validity, we seek then the next best thing, viz., items of high differential validity. Responses to these items manifest types but they manifest different types in different people; this is the sense in which they have differential validity. Even though the items by themselves have differential validity, patterns of responses to them are presumed to have invariant validity; each pattern of responses to these items is presumed to mean one and only one personality type, thus manifesting a one-to-one correspondence between types and patterns.

Our purpose is to isolate response patterns which have invariant validity with respect to types. In order to do this we first attempt to define a type. In this effort, there are alternative ways of proceeding. We could, for example, attempt to define types in such a manner that we could recognize their manifestations observationally in people. We could then observe people and select representative types. We could study them and attempt to write items to which the types would give differential patterns of answers. However, the observational isolation of types has not proved particularly fruitful, historically.

We have used a different initial approach in our efforts to study types. Eventually we will wish to combine the two approaches, using them in mutually assistant fashions. Our approach is to give a statistical-like definition to both patterns of responses and personality types. We use the statistical definition to enable us to develop the techniques of analysis for isolating patterns and types. Then we propose to study both the response patterns and representatives of the types in order to learn more about the characteristics of the types. Our first patterns will doubtlessly be incomplete and overlapping but nevertheless subject to refinement, elaboration, and improvement through repeated application of the methods used.

We first assume that we have a test that contains items with differential validity. Considerable time should be given to the selection of such items in terms typological theories. We have not yet addressed ourselves to this problem, being concerned initially with the statistical definition of types and the methods of numerical analysis for isolating both patterns and types.

SOME PATTERN-ANALYTIC METHODS

Since several pattern-analytic methods have already been developed, it will be helpful to review two of them in relation to our set of assumptions before outlining our statistical definitions of types and the methods of analysis which flow from them.

Two major kinds of pattern-analytic methods are appropriate to two different classes of data, ordered and unordered. The responses to the individual items of a test are an illustration of unordered data, at least until the responses have been allocated to a scale according to some operational definition. After allocation to a scale, responses to the items then illustrate ordered data.

Profile Analysis

One general pattern-analytic approach is profile analysis; the items are first ordered to a scale and responses to them are used to allocate people to the scale. This operation is performed with respect to several scales so that every subject has a profile of standing on the scales. A further step in the method is to classify the subjects into categories according to some index of similarity among profiles, as illustrated in a method by Cronbach and Gleser (1). In this approach, the meaning of a standing on any one scale is assumed to be a function of the standing of the subject on the other scales. This point can be illustrated with reference to two categories of profiles, labelled A and B. The profiles for category A are all very much alike as are also those for category B, but those of A are different from those of B, except for Scale 3 on which the subjects of both A and B all have the same standing as shown in Figure 1.

If we assume that the profiles of categories A and B are manifestations of Types I and II respectively, the common standing on Scale 3 has two different meanings. In profile A, it means Type I, but in profile B, it means Type II. This result shows that the standing has differential validity. The items of a scale, however, are usually chosen to minimize differential validity. In building a scale, we

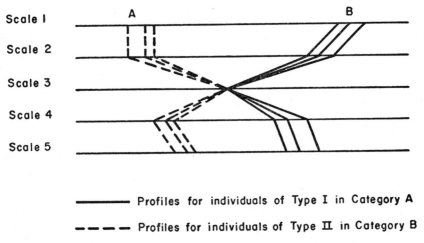

——————— Profiles for individuals of Type I in Category A

— — — — Profiles for individuals of Type II in Category B

FIGURE 1. Hypothetical Profiles Illustrating Differential Validity for the Common Standing on Scale 3.

usually attempt to define a unitary trait that is common to all people, and then we attempt to select items that measure this trait in all of our subjects; we attempt thereby to select items with high invariant validity, but items must have relatively low differential validity to the extent that they have high invariant validity; if an item measures one thing well for all subjects, as required by invariant validity, it can not then measure more than one thing as required by differential validity. Efforts to select items with invariant validity in building scales necessarily limits the potentiality of differential validity. If differential validity is nevertheless found with such scales, the result suggests the worthwhileness of searching for items with high differential validity and analyzing them in a manner particularly designed to discover the manifestation of types.

Lubin's Approach

Not all pattern-analytic methods which have been applied to unordered data, *viz.*, the responses to the individual items of a test, have been applied in a manner that selects items with high differential validity. Some pattern-analytic approaches have been applied instead in ways which maximize invariant validity and thereby tend to minimize differential validity. An example is a study by Lubin (2) in which he used what I have called an accumulative method of pattern analysis (4).

Lubin's approach involved selecting items in relation to an external criterion for a pattern-analytic method of scoring. He first selected from a group of many items the one item *x* that was most highly related to the external criterion. Next he treated this item successively in a pair with every other item until he found the one pair of items *x* and *y* that had the highest pattern score with the criterion. Proceeding in an analogous fashion, he retained items *x* and *y* and tried them successively with every other item until he found the triplet *x, y,* and *z* that had the highest pattern score with the external criterion. Thus he selected his items accumulatively one item at a time. By selecting the one item with the highest relationship to the criterion, however, he selected an item with high invariant validity. This action not only limited the differential validity of the item selected but also the interaction variance it can have with other items and consequently the differential validity of the next item selected.

In the Lubin approach, the first pair of items must not only include the first item (with high invariant validity), but the pair itself must have high invariant validity with the criterion, thereby limiting the interaction variance that later items can have with those already selected. This whole process continues to limit interaction variance. Since interaction variance is the essence of differential validity, differential validity is continually limited throughout the selection process.

This outline of influence on validity of the Lubin method of selecting items for pattern-analytic scoring is not to argue that the Lubin study should never have been performed. On the contrary, it becomes an example of an effective use of the extreme case. If pattern-analytic scoring of items of this kind had proved more successful than the usual methods of selection and scoring, it would have been a strong endorsement of all items for pattern-analytic scoring. Lubin, however, did not find his approach to be superior to the usual methods. We only have evidence that items with relatively high invariant validity do not yield unusually promising pattern-analytic scores, leaving the possibility that items may still be found with differential validity and promising pattern-analytic scoring.

METHODS FOR SELECTING ITEMS WITH DIFFERENTIAL VALIDITY

In our own approaches the methods are appropriate to the selection of items with high differential validity, where differential validity is defined to mean that an item response is determined by different internal constructs in different people. The occurrence of the same item response in two different patterns of responses to other items is assumed to be tentative evidence that an item response is determined by two different constructs. Thus, if two subjects both answer a difficult chemical question correctly but the first subject also answers many physiological questions correctly while failing mathematical items, and the other subject answers the mathematical questions correctly while failing the physiological items, we might say that the first subject answered the chemical questions correctly because he was a medical type, and the second subject answered correctly because he was an engineering type. We would thus be treating the concept of "type" as a postulated, internal construct, attributing to it the power of determining patterns of answers to items.

By seeking item responses with different validity as evidenced by their occurrence in different response patterns, we are in fact seeking items with high interaction variance. We want item responses which have various meanings depending on the combination of other item responses with which they occur.

In developing our approaches, we have assumed that typological theories are relatively inadequate; we suspect that they do not now describe the types that will ultimately prove most fruitful in objective, numerical analyses. Not knowing the nature of types to hypothesize, we have tried to develop methods that would depend maximally on the concatenation in the data and minimally on assumptions implicit in the method of analysis.

We have not known the level of abstraction to apply in the isolation of types. Consequently, we have developed methods for a hierarchical classification of response patterns. At the lowest level of classification, there is very little abstraction; the subjects are classified into many categories, and every category contains few subjects, all of whom have relatively many common responses. As the classification proceeds to successively higher and higher levels of classification, there is more abstracting; there are fewer categories of subjects and every category contains more subjects who have fewer common responses. In other words, at the lower levels of classifications, relatively unique characteristics are instrumental in determining the many types. As the classification proceeds, these relatively unique characteristics are disregarded in favor of more general ones which are descriptive of larger categories of people. Thus in the course of the analyses we proceed from the unique individual to relatively unique types; then to more and more generalized types, until at the top level of classification we may have in the extreme case only one type of person and all members with only a few common responses. This approach makes it possible to compare the types of the successive levels in terms of such considerations as meaningfulness, statistical significance, reliability, validity, and the prediction of criteria, thereby providing insight into which types might most fruitfully be regarded as in some sense "real."

DEFINITIONS OF TYPES

By the approach just described, we have attempted to give maximal influence to the data in determining what is to constitute "real" types. Nevertheless, in developing objective numerical procedures for the isolation of types, we must give sufficient meaning to the concept of type so that statistical operations will flow logically from the definition.

Binary Types

Our first statistical definition was to define a type as a pair of persons so chosen that each member of the pair is more like the other member than he is like any other person. Types of this kind were arbitrarily called species to emphasize by analogy with the Linnean botanical classification system that the types are at the lowest level of classification, as shown in Figure 2.

Similarly, a genus was defined as a pair of species so chosen that each member of the pair is more like the other member than it is like any other species. In an analogous fashion, families, orders, classes, etc., were defined. In this approach, every species contained two persons, every genera four persons, every family eight persons and analogously in a geometric progression so that the types of each successive level are twice as large in number of persons as those of the next lower level. The method which derives from these definitions of types is called binary agreement analysis (6).

The emphasis on a classification by twos in the definition of types was not based on a typological theory; it was done, instead, in order to simplify the statistical operations and thus facilitate the development of numerical method for classifying people, realizing that an approximate method might enhance the development of a more sophisticated solution.

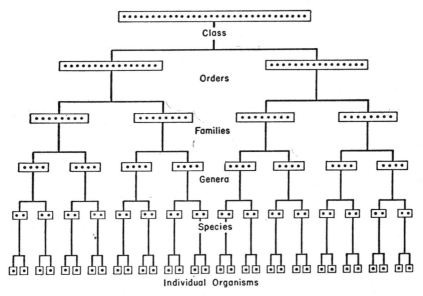

FIGURE 2. A Simplified and Incomplete Linnaean Chart.

In developing and applying binary agreement analysis a particular problem stood out as a result of features within all sets of data analyzed; some highest agreement scores were reciprocal. Consider, for example, the matrix of Table 1.

In this matrix subject A has his highest agreement with subject B, and B, in turn, has his highest score with A; this is a reciprocal agreement score in the sense that A is not only highest with B but B is also highest with A. Some highest agreement scores are non-reciprocal, as illustrated in the one mediating between individuals I and J; I is highest with J, but J is highest with K.

The definition of types as used in binary agreement analysis was entirely satisfactory so long as highest agreement scores were reciprocal, but when they were non-reciprocal, a problem arose. In the above example, if I were classified with J because it is highest with J, then J could not be classified with K with which it is highest, i.e., so long as we continued to classify in pairs exclusively. In binary agreement analysis, we solved this problem arbitrarily. We classified J with K rather than J with I if and only if the score for J-K were larger than the one for I-J. Individual I was then classified in terms of its second highest agreement score, at the species level, i.e., with L in the matrix of Table 1. In cases such as this, species J-K and I-L usually come together at the genus level to solve the problem in a more meaningful manner at the second level of classification.

Generalized Agreement Analysis

The joint occurrence of reciprocal and non-reciprocal scores led naturally to the concept of multiple reciprocity where I, J, K, and L, for example, might all be highest, each with respect to every other one; the scores would all be tied and they would be larger than any score which any one of the individuals would have with any other individual. However, empirical data do not generally reveal this condition, yet theories of types argue for it. We assumed that the failure of empirical data to reveal the conditions is due to chance error in raw data; we therefore developed a method that includes a technique for correcting agreement scores for chance errors, called generalized agreement analysis (3).

Once we had introduced the concept of corrected agreement

TABLE 1

AGREEMENT SCORES BETWEEN INDIVIDUALS HYPOTHETICAL DATA

	A	B	C	D	E	F	G	H	I	J	K	L
A		115	110	105	100	109	104	88	44	40	35	30
B	115		109	104	99	110	105	89	43	39	34	29
C	110	109		103	98	102	102	85	42	38	33	28
D	105	104	103		99	101	103	84	40	37	34	29
E	100	99	98	99		100	101	84	40	38	32	30
F	104	110	102	101	100		103	83	41	36	33	28
G	104	105	102	103	101	103		99	38	37	31	29
H	88	89	84	84	85	83	99		57	58	54	53
I	44	43	42	40	40	41	38	57		108	106	107
J	40	39	38	37	38	36	37	58	108		110	106
K	35	34	33	34	32	33	31	54	106	110		108
L	30	29	28	29	30	28	29	53	107	106	108	

scores we were able to use a more realistic definition of types in the development of statistical methods for isolating them. We defined a species as a category of subjects of such a nature that everyone in a category is more like what is common to members of the category than he is like any one in any other category. In this approach, a species of two often has a larger *corrected* agreement score when it grows into one of three, because of the greater dependability of agreements by three individuals over those in two. This fact enables individual I of Table 1 to have a higher corrected score with J-K than it does with L; thus requiring that I be classified initially in a category with J-K with which it has its highest corrected agreement score.

Elementary Linkage Analysis

A criticism of generalized agreement analysis is that it is laborious. However, the fact that it works enables us to propose a simple definition of types which can be applied to a matrix of scores to yield a rapid, numerical method for isolating types.

The method is called elementary linkage analysis (5). A type is defined as a category of people of such a nature that everyone in a category is more like someone else in the category than he is like anyone in any other category. This definition is applied easily in classifying people into categories once one has a matrix of agree-

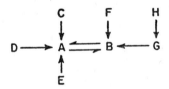

FIGURE 3. Type I.

ment score (or some other index of likeness) between people. Consider the matrix of Table 1 again. The first step is to underline the highest entry in each column, as has already been done in the table. We then select the highest entry in the entire matrix. In the present example it is 115 and mediates between individuals A and B. These two individuals are shown in Figure 3 with a double arrow mediating between them to indicate that they are a reciprocal pair.

The highest entry in a matrix is always reciprocal. The next step is to find all individuals who have either A or B most like them. This is done by reading across the rows of individuals A and B in

Table 1, and thus finding that C, D, and E have A most like them; they are classified in Figure 3 with A. F, and G having B most like them are classified with B. These new additions to the type, individuals C through G are called first cousins because they join directly to a member of the reciprocal pair. We then examine the rows of the first cousins to see if anyone has these individuals most like them; we find that H has G most like it. No other individual has a first cousin most like it, and consequently no other first cousin brings another individual into the type. Row H of Table 1 is examined and it is found that there is no individual who has second cousin H most like it. Consequently, we have exhausted the first type; no other individuals classify into this type. Individuals A through H have now all been withdrawn from the matrix of Table 1 to constitute the first type. The method is then repeated with the reduced matrix to isolate the next type, etc., until all individuals are classified. The one reciprocal pair in the reduced matrix mediates between individuals J-K which are joined by first cousins I and L to complete the second type as shown in Figure 4 and exhaust the matrix. In this approach everyone is classified into a category so that he is more like some person in the category than he is like anyone in any other category.

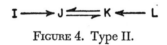

FIGURE 4. Type II.

When everyone has been classified into a category, the types may be called species, arbitrarily. One can then take an index of association between the species and repeat the process to classify the species into genera and analogously for higher levels of classification.

Successive Agreement Analysis

A defect in elementary linkage analysis is the fact that the initial classification for every individual depends on indices of association between pairs of people; these are subject to error, and mistakes made in classification at the first level might be reflected at later levels.

After having developed elementary linkage analysis, our purpose was to develop a rapid method which could use large sets of data and classify in depth with maximal validity. An electronic computer method was developed for this purpose. A type is here defined as a category of people of such a nature that everyone in a category is more like what is common to the members of his category than he is like what is common to the members of any other category of the same size. It is called successive agreement analysis to indicate that an individual is first classified with the one person with whom he has most in common, then with the two persons with whom he has most in common, then with the three persons he has most in common, etc.

Successive agreement analysis as practiced is not as comprehensive as the definition just given would seem to imply. Not everyone is necessarily classified with the one person with whom he has most in common; it is done, instead, only for those who have the highest agreement scores; these are the most dependable classifications. Likewise, not everyone is necessarily classified with the pair of persons with whom he has the most in common; only those that have the highest agreement scores with the most dependable pairs are thus classified. A similar failure to classify everyone at the quadrad and even the quintad level may occur, but eventually everyone is usually best classified at some rather early level and then usually at all subsequent levels.

Successive agreement analysis starts with a matrix of agreement scores such as shown in Table 1. Then the N highest agreement scores are selected out, where N is some arbitrary number, usually maximal for computer capacity, and often equal to the number of subjects represented in the matrix. In some cases, every individual will be represented in at least one of the N highest agreement scores, but in other cases some one or more subjects will be omitted while others are represented several times. Nevertheless, these N highest diadic scores are the ones with which individuals are apt to have their highest agreement at the triadic level. The next step is to compute the agreement score between every individual and every pair to produce a matrix of triadic scores as shown in Table 2. The N highest triadic scores are then selected out.

Usually these will include the classification of some individuals who were omitted in the classification at the diadic level. The process proceeds in an analogous fashion at successive higher and higher levels representing classification in depth and allowing an investigator to make comparative studies of the successive levels in terms of such considerations as predictive abilities, reproducibility and psychological meaningfulness.

It is essential to emphasize one characteristic of successive agreement analysis, for it depends on an assumption which can lead to errors if it does not hold for the data under analysis. Reference to Table 2 will help explain the assumption. In this table, individual L is not included in the highest N pairs listed in the left hand column. It is assumed first that N will eventually join a category which contains one of these N pairs. Suppose that this occurs at the quadradic level. It is assumed that individual L will have a higher score in this quadrad than he would have in any other quadrad if we had started with any other N pairs. A similar assumption is made for all individuals. In general, the assumption says that the N highest pairs are sufficient in order to realize the best classifications later on.

Some Findings

Some of these methods have been tried sufficiently to suggest hypotheses for further study. A first suggestion is that there are items whose responses have differential validity, measure different things in different people. When the value of these items is assessed in terms of invariant validity, they are found to have rather low validity. It is possible that nearly all items may have at least some differential validity. We may have in general underestimated the validity of all items by attempting to do this in terms of invariant validity exclusively.

TABLE 2

Agreement Scores Between Individuals and Pairs of Individuals
Hypothetical Data

	A	B	C	D	E	F	G	H	I	J	K	L
A C	x	—	x	—	—	—	—	—	—	—	—	—
A E	x	—	—	—	x	—	—	—	—	—	—	—
A G	x	—	—	—	—	—	x	—	—	—	—	—
A I	x	—	—	—	—	—	—	—	x	—	—	—
A K	x	—	—	—	—	—	—	—	—	—	x	—
B D	—	x	—	x	—	—	—	—	—	—	—	—
B F	—	x	—	—	—	x	—	—	—	—	—	—
B H	—	x	—	—	—	—	—	x	—	—	—	—
B J	—	x	—	—	—	—	—	—	—	x	—	—
C E	—	—	x	—	x	—	—	—	—	—	—	—
E G	—	—	—	—	x	—	x	—	—	—	—	—
G I	—	—	—	—	—	—	x	—	x	—	—	—

The x's exist where the score would mediate between an individual and a pair containing that individual; the table is restricted to scores for groups of three different individuals.

When we have compared our types with external criteria, we have found those at the lower levels such as species and genera to be more predictive than the higher level ones, where the categories might be expected to be more reliably determined. This outcome suggests that there are many relatively unique types and that large samples of subjects are essential in order to isolate them in a dependable fashion. We thus need pattern-analytic methods which can classify several hundred subjects. Electronic computers with high storage capacity make this goal possible of realization.

References

1. Cronbach, L. J., and Gleser, Goldine C. Assessing similarities between profiles. *Psychol. Bull.*, 1953, *50*, 456-473.
2. Lubin, A. H. Methodological study of configural scoring. Personnel Res. Branch, Tech. Note 42, B-8-251-36, The Adjutant General's Office, Washington, D. C.
3. McQuitty, L. L. Agreement analysis: classifying persons by predominant patterns of responses. *Brit. J. Statist. Psychol.*, 1956, *9*, 5-16.
4. McQuitty, L. L. Isolating prediction patterns associated with major criterion patterns. *Educ. Psychol. Measmt.*, 1957, *17*, 3-42.
5. McQuitty, L. L. Elementary linkage analysis for isolating orthogonal and oblique types and typal relevancies. *Educ. Psychol. Measmt.*, 1957, *17*, 207-229.
6. McQuitty, L. L. A pattern analysis of descriptions of "best" and "poorest" mechanics compared with factor-analytic results. *Psychol. Monogr.*, 1957, 71, No. 17 (whole No. 446).

V

The Unimportance of Test Item Content

Irwin A. Berg
Louisiana State University

T he content of objective personality and interest test items customarily has been selected with face validity in mind. Personality inventories typically use items which inquire concerning how one feels about being in crowds or whether one often has nightmares. Similarly, interest tests use content which centers on one's enjoyment of mechanical puzzles, building birdhouses, listening to music, etc. Rarely does one find an item dealing with frequency of nightmares on a vocational interest test nor, by contrast, a birdhouse item on a personality test. In general, psychological tests in these areas use items that are reasonably tidy from the standpoint of possessing obviously appropriate content. However low the correlations might be between such test scores and suitable behavioral criteria, the face of validity shines in every item.

Content and Early Personality Tests

This has been particularly true of the earlier personality tests. The content of these older tests sampled a wide range of what was regarded as significant behavior and accordingly had a heavy interlarding of items that dealt with symptoms of maladjustment. Then, it was usually assumed that the subject would give honest answers when taking the test. The notion of a direct relationship between item content and what was being measured was probably a heritage from achievement testing procedures. After all, achievement tests in subject matter fields such as geography, arithmetic, history, etc., have been used for centuries while psychological tests, as we know them, have been in existence for but a few decades. If one wishes to measure achievement in geography, for example, one uses a test that asks questions about geography. That is only common sense and admits no debate. Thus it was natural to apply the same technique to personality and interest measurement by using items which unmistakably mirrored the area being measured. If personality adjustment were being assessed, the items were straightforward in asking whether the subject "worried more than most people" or whether he "often had bad dreams at night." This approach worked in its fashion. It did not produce very good measures of personality, but it produced better measures than we had before. It was obviously a good start in the right direction.

There were a number of straws in the wind which indicated that the *a priori* face value of item content might not be worth much in some behavioral areas. At first glance, it seems reasonable to postulate a close relationship between accident frequency and reaction time on the assumption that the slowpoke would be prone to mishaps. As early as 1929, however, Farmer and Chambers (30) reported that correlations between reaction time and number of accidents for several occupational groups hovered around zero. Curiously, in motor vehicle driver testing, reaction time measures are often included even now in "dummy" car testing apparatus, apparently on the invalid assumption that those who can get their feet off the gas pedal and on the brake will have fewer accidents. It is only fair to observe that this particular response measure may be included less for its predictive efficiency than for its sales value in influencing business executives who hire the testing.

Concern for Face Validity

While psychologists would not be misled by face validity in such situations when they were in the iron grip of a string of zero criterion correlations, they sometimes appear to cling to other unsupported beliefs concerning objective personality tests. Indeed, they sometimes express such beliefs in print. In 1945, for example, Meehl (47) found it necessary to take Hutt (38) to task for asserting that "structured" personality tests were based on the assumption that the items would have the same meaning for all subjects who took the test. This is probably still a fairly prevalent misconception; however, as Meehl emphatically points out, neither the *Minnesota Multiphasic Personality Inventory* (MMPI) nor Strong's *Vocational Interest Blank* (VIB) make this assumption.

A tremendous number of articles concerning these two tests have been published (over 800 on the MMPI alone) and it should be quite clear that from the MMPI or VIB standpoint, it is not important whether the meaning is the same or different for all subjects, nor does it matter whether the subject is being truthful or even a good judge of his own behavior. If a subject responded "true" to an item such as "I like to mingle in crowds," it is not important whether he *really* liked crowds or not. The important thing is what behavioral correlates can be empirically identified with such a response. If most people like crowds and most paranoids significantly do not, we have a good item for measuring paranoia. Furthermore, with similar levels of statistical significance, any content could be used for such an item whether it dealt with crowds, horses, or Socrates. These last few sentences may be unnecessarily sounding the alarm long after the guard is roused and on the alert; yet the point is of such import that excessive zeal may be tolerated.

Thus far it has been noted that personality and interest test items do not need to have *a priori* meaningfulness. The MMPI and VIB have fully demonstrated this, and they are very good tests indeed. Rather paradoxically, however, while in practice adhering to empirical test rather than *a priori* item content, Hathaway and McKinley (36) in the MMPI and Strong (57) in the VIB paid a good deal of attention to the content of their test items. The MMPI used 26 carefully described categories of items which ranged from general health to psychotic symptoms, and the VIB employed lists of occupations, amusements, etc. There was an obvious concern for face validity in content. Just why this was so is hard to say; however, it may have been a sardonic deference to what users of the tests might expect to find. Be that as it may, the VIB used only items which had some clear-cut relationship to vocations and the work-a-day work. The MMPI has mostly items with content of reasonable face validity for personality measurement; however, it also has a sizeable number of items which are admittedly enigmatic when scrutinized in this way.

It appears, therefore, that while objective personality and interest tests pay rather careful attention to item content, at least two of the best and most widely used tests of this type do not depend for scoring purposes upon an appropriate or fitting response being made to the test content. As an elaboration, Meehl's (47, p. 300) remark has pertinence, "Thus it puzzles us but does not disconcert us when this relation cannot be elucidated, the science of behavior being in the stage that it is. That 'I sometimes tease animals' (answered False) should occur in a scale measuring symptomatic depression is theoretically mysterious, just as the tendency of certain schizophrenic patients to accept 'position' as a determinant in responding to the Rorschach may be theoretically mysterious."

The present paper is an attempt to offer an explanation which seeks to dispel a portion of the theoretical mystery to which Meehl refers and to gather evidence from various sources in an attempt to demonstrate that particular content of objective personality and interest tests is unimportant. This is not to say that no content whatsoever is essential for personality and interest tests. Some sort of stimulus pattern is required, of course; however, virtually any content of any sense modality should be suitable and under some conditions the content may be so insignificant as hardly to deserve the name. I believe the available evidence indicates that items dealing with jobs, social activities, attitudes, adjustment, etc. are quite unnecessary for objective personality, interest, and similar tests. One can use such content if he so desires; but one can equally well use abstract designs, sounds, lists of foods, lights, imaginary questions, spiral after-effect, and content of an equally wide range. In this sense, then, item content is unimportant.

THE DEVIATION HYPOTHESIS

Before reviewing the evidence for the unimportance of particular item content, it seems appropriate to offer some theoretical explanation of why content is not important. At present this can be stated only as a hypothesis, though one which has been supported at a number of points by empirical test. This is the Deviation Hypothesis which has been set forth in several previous publications (12, 13). An outline of the hypothesis will serve as a framework for the remainder of the present paper. There are literally hundreds of studies dealing with isolated empirical demonstrations of the prediction, with varying degrees of success, of certain facets of behavior from other, ostensibly unrelated facets of behavior. The commonest examples of this are the variety of clinical measurement devices, although there are many others. The question at hand is how we can account for the predictive usefulness described in so many of these researches. What, in other words, is the common thread running through such myriad studies which deal with bits and pieces of behavior? It is to these questions that the Deviation Hypothesis is directed.

The Deviation Hypothesis is based upon biased responses. The emphasis, however, is not placed upon the bias itself but rather upon the *departures from an established pattern of bias*. This latter is the important factor; indeed, it is the key to the problem before us. In a "true-false," "head-tails," "agree-disagree" response situation, for example, the responses rarely follow a normal probability distribution where the stimulus pattern is relatively unstructured. Instead of a 50-50 percentage distribution of responses, one often finds 80-20 or some equally skewed pattern indicating bias. Cronbach (26, 27) has described a large number of such response sets, as he called them, in psychological testing; and other writers (17, 24, 33, 43, 52) have also provided evidence for the existence of bias. The Deviation Hypothesis is not directly concerned with the responses which contribute to the pile-up, in the 80 per cent who call "heads" when a coin is flipped, for example. Rather the interest is centered in the 20 per cent who go counter to the "heads" response and say "tails" or possibly something else or even say nothing at all.

The persons who deviate from the established pattern of bias in such insignificant responses as responding "tails," "dislike," "disagree," and so on are not merely different in such minor or noncritical aspects of behavior. They are also different in critical or significant aspects of behavior—or so the Deviation Hypothesis would have it. The noncritical aspect of behavior is a reflection of a critical aspect; the two go hand in hand. The critical aspect is a personality manifestation. It may be aberrant adjustment such as schizophrenia or chronic anxiety or it may be some other aberrant condition such as genius, mental retardation, accident proneness, creativeness, chronic heart disease, or any other condition which may be objectively defined on some behavioral dimension. Thus we would include physicians as well as kleptomaniacs, engineers as well as scholastic under-achievers as being capable of suitable objective, operational definition.

Accordingly, the Deviation Hypothesis has been stated (13, p. 159), "Deviant response patterns tend to be general; hence those deviant behavior patterns which are significant for abnormality (atypicalness) and thus regarded as symptoms (earmarks or signs) are associated with other deviant response patterns which are in noncritical areas of behavior and which are not regarded as symptoms of personality aberration (nor as indicators, signs, earmarks)." It should be emphasized that abnormality is to be taken in the literal meaning of "away from normal." In this sense psychotics or lawyers, for example, show certain responses which distinguish them from each other and also from the rest of the general public. Everyone makes many responses which are quite like those made by the majority of people. Everyone also makes certain other responses which are peculiarly his own or peculiarly shared by a special group. These certain other responses are, of course, not shared by a majority of people; hence they are the responses designated as *deviant* and may be precisely defined statistically in terms of the level of significance by which they depart from the common response. Insofar as can be ascertained, these deviant responses are the product, singly or in combination, of past learning, inherited structure, and organic or physiological state. Thus it may be said that the deviant responses which differentiate engineers from physicians, for example, are chiefly the product of past learning whereas organic factors (possibly at times associated with inherited defect) are presumed to be the basis for any deviant responses exhibited by patients with chronic heart disease.

Very likely, learning pervades to some degree all aspects of deviant responses, including those responses which are rooted in hereditary or physiological aberration. Habits of living to take a case in point, may produce stress which culminates in cardiac disorder in the manner described by Selye (51). In other cases, presumably, a weakness of heart structure would require new learning, that is habits which would avoid taxing the weak heart. According to the Deviation Hypothesis, both conditions should produce deviant response patterns, though not necessarily the same pattern. It should be emphasized that these are but illustrations, not evidence, of how learning might be involved in what appears to be essentially an organic condition.

Particular Stimulus Content is Unimportant

Thus, what has been said is that no particular content is needed for interest and personality tests, nor, for that matter, in a wide variety of other behavioral measures. What is needed are stimuli that will elicit deviant responses or, more accurately, stimuli which will produce "response sets" or biases from which deviant response patterns may be statistically identified. Such stimuli should be relatively unstructured since lack of structure facilitates the appearance of bias. Accordingly, the hypothesis with respect to item content has been stated (13, p. 160), "Stimulus patterns of any sense modality may be used to elicit deviant response patterns; thus particular stimulus content is unimportant for measuring behaviors in terms of the Deviation Hypothesis." Attention is called to the fact that this statement makes no assertion that any item is just as good as every other for discriminative purposes. Such a claim would be patently absurd.

What is meant is that if an item concerned with nightmares, for example, distinguishes schizophrenics from normal persons at the five per cent level of confidence, one can locate equally valid items which are utterly different in content, items with content such as interlaced triangles, musical sounds, autokinetic phenomena, etc. But if interlaced triangles are found to be equivalent to nightmares as an item, it certainly does not follow that a drawing of interlaced circles would be just as good as either, or that some musical sound must perforce be as valid as all three. While such might be the case, empirical demonstration is absolutely necessary to make the necessary determination of possible item equivalence. In other words, the same procedure that was used to ascertain the value of the nightmare item must also be applied to the interlaced triangle item—or any other item.

From what has been said, it should be possible to use a series of abstract designs for test items and do about as good a job of measuring personality as can be done with traditional verbal items of the "I am troubled with insomnia" variety. Content other than abstract designs could, of course, be used; but this example will do for a beginning. The *Perceptual Reaction Test* (PRT) (16) has been used for this purpose since it was developed to elicit "set." It is composed of 60 abstract designs drawn with ruler and compass, and the subject checks either *Like Much, Like Slightly, Dislike Slightly,* or *Dislike Much* for each design. Only seven minutes, on the average, are required by normal subjects to take the test. It would really be a much more effective comparison if the PRT had several hundred designs since most of the personality tests in wide use have hundreds of items. Be that as it may, a number of studies have been completed which indicate that even a mere 60 designs of no particular meaning can do a good job of reflecting certain facets of personality.

VARIETY OF USABLE STIMULI

Berg and Collier (15) found that groups of high anxiety subjects operationally identified by the Taylor Anxiety Scale and the Sway Suggestibility Test made significantly more extreme choices (*like much* or *dislike much*) on the PRT when compared to low anxiety subjects. Lewis and Taylor (41) obtained quite comparable results with the same test; however, their findings demonstrated that the extreme choices were not preferences for extreme position, as Berg and Collier thought, but were actually preferences for extreme option content in the PRT. A much more detailed study of the diagnostic possibilities of the PRT was published by Barnes (7). Using 1,700 normal persons (1,000 males, and 700 females) as controls, Barnes administered the PRT to 546 (360 males, 186 females) clinic and mental hospital patients. By identifying the deviant responses, Barnes was able to construct clinical scales as follows: *Delta,* for general NP disturbance; *Psi,* for psychotic condition; *Sigma,* for schizophrenia; *Chi,* for character disorder; *Psi-Chi,* for separating diagnostically psychotic and character disorder states. In Barnes' (7, p. 290) words, "It is concluded that response set on the PRT is related to personality factors, that it has a degree of reliability which compares well with other tests of personality factors, and that it can be used to assess personality disorder."

The PRT was also used by Hesterly and Berg (37) to measure maturity in relation to schizophrenia. The PRT responses of groups of normal children aged 8, 10, and 12, were compared with normal adults; and the younger age groups were found to have response patterns most different from adults with the difference decreasing for the older age group. Since immaturity is commonly associated with schizophrenia, it was postulated that no significant difference would be found for the deviant response patterns of adult schizophrenics and normal young children. This was found to be the case. The youngest groups of normal children were different in deviant response patterns from normal adults but not different from adult schizophrenics.

Thus it appears that with a simple test composed of only 60 meaningless designs, we can measure certain aspects of personality by means of the Deviation Hypothesis in the same way that the usual objective personality inventories do when using traditional verbal content. By the same token, it would not be surprising to find a relationship between behavior disorders and responses to other nontraditional personality test content such as a list of foods. Wallen

(61) and Gough (34), for example, showed that neurotic males indicated that they disliked significantly more foods than normal males.

In another study, Wallen (62) found a similar, significantly greater number of food aversions in various clinical diagnostic categories such as intra-cranial injury, anxiety neurosis, hysteria, epilepsy, etc. when compared to normal males. In a comparison of number of food aversions and scores on a test of adjustment, Altus (4) found a correlation of .497 between the two measures for data obtained from Army illiterates. Smith, Powell, and Ross (55) found that high-anxiety individuals, as identified by the Taylor Manifest Anxiety Scale, showed significantly more food aversions than low-anxiety subjects. These studies were not done as investigations of the Deviation Hypothesis since they antedate publications of this concept. However, they illustrate an aspect of the unimportance of particular item content; and like many other studies concerned with critical and noncritical responses, they can be fitted comfortably into the deviant response concept.

Stimuli for conditioned response, autokinetic and spiral after-effect perceptions involve noncritical areas of behavior in the sense that the responses are not regarded in themselves as symptoms or earmarks. However, several studies have indicated that deviant patterns in noncritical facets of such behavior are reflections of deviations in critical areas. Taylor (58) and Spence and Taylor (56) found that anxious subjects, as identified by her Manifest Anxiety Scale, were consistently and significantly superior in all measures of eyeblink conditioning and extinction compared to nonanxious subjects. Voth (60) tested 845 mental hospital patients and 423 normal subjects with the autokinetic phenomenon. He found that distinctive patterns of deviant responses were characteristic of certain patient groups. Schizophrenics, epileptic, and anxiety patients among others, revealed more pronounced apparent movement when compared to normal groups. Manic-depressive and involutional patients either experienced no apparent movement or the movement was much less extensive than normal. Price and Deabler (49) and Freeman and Josey (31) used the Archimedes spiral after-effect as a means of differentiating patients with organic brain damage and patients with memory impairment from normal subjects. Aaronson (1) used a similar technique with an epileptic population.

VARIATIONS IN RESPONSE MEASURES

Perhaps because of its essential role in ordinary communications, deviant language behavior has for centuries been recognized as related to psychological states. The staccato speech of manic patients, the painfully labored utterances characteristic of certain depressions, or the neologisms of schizophrenia are cases in point. More recently, subtler aspects of language have been examined with respect to their value as indicators of disturbed emotional states. These studies may be mentioned as additional examples of bits of research which lend support to the assertion that particular item content is unimportant for personality assessment. These studies can also be fitted into the broad framework of the Deviation Hypothesis, although they were not intended as tests of that hypothesis.

None of the studies has scaled the responses in the usual objective personality test fashion; however, it seems feasible that this could be done should it be deemed advantageous to do so. Chodorkoff and Mussen (21), for example, found that schizophrenics chose inferior definitions on a special vocabulary test when compared to normal subjects. Lorenz and Cobb (44, 45) reported that psychoneurotic patients used more verbs and pronouns but fewer adjectives and prepositions as compared to a normal control group. As client adjustment improved during a series of therapeutic interviews, Berg (14) found a decrease in the ego words, "I," "me," "my," and an increase in the empathic words "you," "we," "us." Other studies, such as those by Fairbanks (29), Mann (46), and Roshal (50) among others, indicate that vocabulary variability relates to personal adjustment. Thus what one says and how one says it are apparently capable of manifesting deviant response patterns. On this basis, then, language behavior could serve for personality assessment purposes. Although any such test might prove to be unwieldly and inconvenient, a test could be prepared from such responses judging from the available evidence.

The list of studies which employ various forms of content to reflect various facets of personality would run into the thousands. Figure drawings, to mention but one class, have been used in numerous studies to investigate such matters as obesity (40), facial disfigurement (2), and homosexuality (6), on the hypothesis that the responses were related to personality. A few studies indicate that auditory content may also be validly utilized as measures of personality variables. A long-play record of musical sounds has been developed by Cattell and Anderson (19) which is probably the first use of musical excerpts for diagnosing mental illness. Simon and others (53) have reported differences in the recognition of mood in music for patient populations and for normal subjects. The "tautophone" (35), a device which emits sounds which resemble spoken words but which are actually meaningless, has been employed as a personality test.

No studies have been found in which sense modalities such as taste, smell, tactile sensitivity and the like have been used in connection with personality measurement. One study by Singer and Young (54), however, indicates that response bias exists in responses to olfactory stimuli; hence it may be possible to use this sense for personality assessment. Theoretically, of course, all senses should provide content which may be used in this way. In practice, sense modalities other than vision are relatively cumbersome to use for personality testing purposes. This may account for the vast preponderance of personality measures which involve reading or looking at something. It should, however, be obvious that a wide range of content can be used and has been used in appraising personality.

What is essentially a deviant response technique has been employed in studies of physical diseases, some of which have psychosomatic components. Various stimuli patterns have been used, such as those found in the Rorschach, TAT, Blacky Test, MMPI, etc. A sampling of such studies includes disorders such as uterine dysfunction (25), peptic ulcer (18), rheumatoid arthritis (22), dermatosis (48), leprosy (42), constipation (5), and others. To what extent personality variables influenced or determined the course of these diseases or to what extent the diseases produced certain personality changes is unknown. The significant point is that, even in such cases, a variety of stimulus content can be used to differentiate them from normal subjects on the basis of deviant responses.

Some scales which have emphasized content with direct face validity, such as the authoritarian personality F scale (3), have been shown actually to measure a considerable amount of simple acquiescence and not only fascist proclivities. This has been shown by studies such as those of Bass (10), Cohn (23), Chapman and Campbell (20). By its use of a wide range of content and its use of atypical responses, the MMPI moved in the direction of de-emphasizing item content. This is particularly borne out in the use MMPI makes of subtle items, that is, items which are quite unrelated in terms of face validity to the personality dimensions they measure.

If it is *only* the deviant responses that are important, no matter how elicited, and not the test item content, one should be able to obtain a fairly definite relationship between valid clinical scales and a simple count of the number of deviant responses. Barnes (8) did this with the MMPI, by just counting the total number of atypical responses (X's on the MMPI record form) and correlating the number of atypical responses with the clinical scales. The atypical responses, of course, were drawn from all of the MMPI scales and no attention whatsoever was given to the content. Barnes found the simple atypical response total correlated .93 with the Sc scale and .87 with the Pt scale, which is about as high as the reliability of these scales. Ordinarily, one would expect to find a less impressive relationship; however, the great attention paid by the MMPI to clean criterion groups and the use of a wide variety of item content probably permitted a more effective expression of deviant responses. In another study, Barnes (9) showed that atypical "true" answers on the MMPI without regard to item content represented the psychotic factor of Wheeler, Little and Lehner (64); atypical "false" answers had a heavy loading for the neurotic factor.

IMPORTANCE OF DEVIANT RESPONSE PATTERNS

Thus the important variable is not content *per se* but rather a pattern of deviant responses. Such responses can be elicited by a wide range of stimuli as the evidence presented here illustrates. Occasionally, the question comes up of whether some deviant behavior pattern in a noncritical area is necessarily symptomatic of a critical personality deviation. Some persons wear strange clothing or indulge in weird hair styles; thus they exhibit responses which are deviant. But, as has been pointed out, they may not necessarily be deviant in a critical area of behavior. This is true; however, it must be emphasized that a burnoose on Fifth Avenue or hair parted crosswise from ear-to-ear each represent but one deviant response. A pattern or series of deviant responses would be another matter. Every normal person exhibits some deviant responses in noncritical areas to a variety of stimulus content and he is still considered to be normal. The crucial point is that people who are deviant in a critical area of behavior exhibit a significantly larger number of deviant responses in noncritical areas. The pattern of deviant responses is also distinctive with respect to the critical behavior deviation.

A single deviant response is practically never sufficient to measure or otherwise identify personality characteristics. The same, of course, is true of a single item on a personality test of conventional content. A male transvestite who dons female wearing apparel might ostensibly be regarded as offering an example of a single deviant response which is indicative of critical behavior aberration. Yet actually such preference for women's clothes is probably, not one, but rather a large number of deviant responses. That is, the transvestite would probably use lipstick and perfume, rouge his cheeks, enamel his nails, walk with mincing gait, separately put on a number of articles of female clothing, etc. Each of these should be appropriately regarded as separate deviant responses, adding up to a respectable total.

Since everyone exhibits some deviant responses, it seems unlikely that a single response will suffice for identifying significant aspects of personality. Attempts to use a few simple deviant response measures, such as the handedness studies of Wile (65), Goddard (32), and Doll (28), met with very limited success in their investigations of the relationship of left hand-preference to feeblemindedness and neurotic reactions. Yet these studies did indicate that hand preference could probably be used as one deviant response item. A large number of such items might conceivably be scaled into a respectable personality test. Be that as it may, there is good reason to believe that a wide variety of content can be used for personality test items; however, as has been the case in the past, a lengthy series of items will be necessary, whatever content may be used.

The evidence reviewed here is believed to indicate that there is nothing of special value in particular item content for objective personality and similar tests. Verbal content of the traditional kind used in personality tests is not essential; for a wide variety of content may be employed with equal effectiveness. Indeed, any content which produces deviant response patterns will serve, judging from the available evidence. The important thing is not particular content, but rather a series of deviant responses and operationally clean criterion groups. These are the absolute essentials for using deviant responses to measure personality. Thus it is possible to use items of traditional content to assess personality; however, conditioned responses, spiral after-effect, abstract designs, autokinetic phenomena, musical sounds, language behavior, drawings and other content may also be used. Some test items, of course, will be better for certain purposes than others, just as some items of conventional content are better than others for certain testing purposes. But whatever the content, valid discriminations of a number of facets of personality can be made. Accordingly, for personality and similar tests, a particular item content is unimportant.

References

1. Aaronson, B. S. Age, intelligence, aphasia, and the spiral after-effect in an epileptic population. *J. clin. Psychol.*, 1958, 14, 18-21.
2. Abel, T. M. Figure drawing and facial disfigurement. *Amer. J. Orthopsychiat.*, 1953, 23, 253-264.
3. Adorno, T. W. et al. *The authoritarian personality*, New York: Harper, 1950.
4. Altus, W. D. Adjustment and food aversions among army illiterates. *J. consult. Psychol.*, 1949, 13, 429-432.
5. Altus, W. D. Constipation and adjustment among illiterate males. *J. consult. Psychol.*, 1950, 14, 25-31.
6. Barker, A. J., Mathis, G. K., and Powers, C. A. Drawing characteristics of male homosexuals. *J. clin. Psychol.*, 1953, 9, 185-188.
7. Barnes, E. H. The relationship of biased test responses to psychopathology. *J. abnorm. soc. Psychol.*, 1955, 51, 286-290.
8. Barnes, E. H. Factors, response bias, and the MMPI. *J. consult. Psychol.*, 1956, 20, 419-421.
9. Barnes, E. H. Response bias and the MMPI. *J. consult. Psychol.*, 1956, 20, 371-374.
10. Bass, B. M. Authoritarianism or acquiescence: *J. abnorm. soc. Psychol.*, 1955, 51, 616-623.
11. Berg, I. A. The reliability of extreme position response sets in two tests. *J. Psychol.*, 1953, 36, 3-9.
12. Berg, I. A. Response bias and personality: the Deviation Hypothesis. *J. Psychol.*, 1955, 40, 60-71.
13. Berg, I. A. Deviant responses and deviant people: the formulation of the Deviation Hypothesis. *J. counsel. Psychol.*, 1957, 4, 154-161.
14. Berg, I. A. Word choice in the interview and personal adjustment. *J. counsel. Psychol.*, 1958, 5, 130-135.
15. Berg, I. A. and Collier, J. S. Personality and group differences in extreme response sets. *Educ. psychol. Measmt.*, 1953, 13, 164-169.
16. Berg, I. A. and Hunt, W. A. and Barnes, E. H. *The perceptual reaction test.* Evanston, Ill.: 1949.

17. Berg, I. A. and Rapaport, G. M. Response bias in an unstructured questionnaire. *J. Psychol.*, 1954, 38, 475-481.
18. Blum, G. S. and Kaufman, J. B. Two patterns of personality dynamics in male peptic ulcer patients are suggested by responses to the Blacky Pictures. *J. clin. Psychol.*, 1952, 8, 273-278.
19. Cattell, R. B. and Anderson, J. C. The measurement of personality and behavior disorders by the IPAT Music Preference Test. *J. appl. Psychol.*, 1953, 37, 446-454.
20. Chapman, L. J. and Campbell, D. T. Response set in the F scale. *J. abnorm. soc. Psychol.*, 1957, 54, 129-132.
21. Chodorkoff, B. and Mussen, P. H. Qualitative aspects of the vocabulary responses of normals and schizophrenics. *J. consult. Psychol.*, 1952, 16, 43-48.
22. Cleveland, S. E., and Fisher, S. Behavior and unconscious fantasies of patients with rheumatoid arthritis. *Psychosom. Med.*, 1954, 16, 327-333.
23. Cohn, T. S. Is the F scale indirect? *J. abnorm. soc. Psychol.*, 1952, 47, 185-192.
24. Cottle, W. C. and Powell, J. O. The effect of random answers on the MMPI. *Educ. psychol. Measmt.*, 1951, 11, 224-227.
25. Crammond, W. A. Psychological aspects of uterine dysfunction. *Lancet*, 1954, 267, 1241-1245.
26. Cronbach, L. J. Response sets and test validity. *Educ. psychol. Measmt.*, 1946, 6, 475-494.
27. Cronbach, L. J. Further evidence on response sets and test designs. *Educ. psychol. Measmt.*, 1950, 10, 3-31.
28. Doll, E. A. Anthropometry as an aid to mental diagnosis. *Pub. New Jersey Trng. Scho.*, 1916, 8, 1-7.
29. Fairbanks, H. The quantitative differentiation of samples of spoken language. *Psychol. Monogr.*, 1944, 56, 19-38.
30. Farmer, E. and Chambers, E. G. A study of personal qualities in accident proneness and proficiency. Industrial Health Research Board of Great Britain, 1929, Report No. 55.
31. Freeman, E. and Josey, W. E. Quantitative visual index to memory impairment. *Arch. Neurol. Psychiat.*, 1949, 62, 794-796.
32. Goddard, H. H. The height and weight of feebleminded children in American institutions. *J. nerv. ment. Dis.*, 1902, 39, 217-235.
33. Goodfellow, L. D. The human element in probability. *J. gen. Psychol.*, 1940, 33, 201-205.
34. Gough, H. G. An additional study of food aversions. *J. abnorm. soc. Psychol.*, 1946, 41, 86-88.
35. Grings, W. W. The verbal summator technique and abnormal mental states. *J. abnorm. soc. Psychol.*, 1942, 37, 529-545.
36. Hathaway, S. R. and McKinley, J. C. The Minnesota Multiphasic Personality Inventory (Manual). New York: Psychol. Corp., 1943.

37. Hesterly, S. O. and Berg, I. A. Deviant responses as indicators of immaturity and schizophrenia. *J. consult. Psychol.*, 1958, 22, 389-393.
38. Hutt, M. L. The use of projective methods of personality measurement in army medical installations. *J. clin. Psychol.*, 1, 134-140.
39. Jackson, D. N. Content and style in personality assessment. Princeton, N. J. Educational Testing Service, RM-57-11, 1957.
40. Kotkov, B. and Goodman, M. The Draw-a-Person Tests of obese women. *J. clin. Psychol.*, 1953, 9, 363-364.
41. Lewis, N. A. and Taylor, J. A. Anxiety and extreme response preferences. *Educ. psychol. Measmt.*, 1955, 15, 111-116.
42. Lord, E. Group Rorschach responses of thirty-five leprosarium patients. *J. Proj. Tech.*, 1954, 18, 202-207.
43. Lorge, I. Gen-like: halo or reality? *Psychol. Bull.*, 1937, 34, 545-546.
44. Lorenz, M. and Cobb, S. Language behavior in manic patients. *Arch. Neurol. Psychiat.*, 1952, 67, 763-770.
45. Lorenz, M. and Cobb, S. Language behavior in psychoneurotic patients. *Arch. Neurol. Psychiat.*, 1953, 69, 684-694.
46. Mann, M. B. The quanitative differentiation of samples of written language. *Psychol. Monogr.*, 1944, 56, 41-74.
47. Meehl, P. E. The dynamics of "structured" personality tests. *J. clin. Psychol.*, 1945, 1, 296-303.
48. Narciso, J. C., Jr. Some psychological aspects of dermatosis. *J. consult. Psychol.*, 1952, 16, 199-201.
49. Price, A. C., and Deabler, H. L. Diagnosis of organicity by means of spiral aftereffect. *J. consult. Psychol.*, 1955, 19, 299-302.
50. Roshal, J. J. G. The type-token ratio as a measure of changes in behavior variability during psychotherapy. In Snyder, W. U. *Group report of a program of research in psychotherapy.* State University, Pa.: Pa. State Univ. Press, 1953, 94-104.
51. Selye, H. *The stress of life.* New York: McGraw-Hill, 1956.
52. Shelley, H. P. Response set and the California Attitude Scale. *Educ. Psychol. Measmt.*, 1955, 16, 63-67.
53. Simon, B., Holzberg, J. D., Alessi, S. L., and Garrity, D. A. The recognition and acceptance of mood in music by psychotic patients. *J. nerv. ment. Dis.*, 1951, 144, 66-78.
54. Singer, W. B. and Young, P. T. Studies in affective reaction: III. The specificity of affective reactions. *J. genet. Psychol.*, 1941, 24, 327-341.
55. Smith, W., Powell, E. K. and Ross, S. Manifest anxiety and food aversions. *J. abnorm. soc. Psychol.*, 1955, 50, 101-104.
56. Spence, K. W. and Taylor, J. A. The relation of conditioned response strength to anxiety in normal, neurotic, and psychotic subjects. *J. exp. Psychol.*, 1953, 45, 265-272.
57. Strong, E. K., Jr. *Manual for Vocational Interest Blank for Men.* Stanford: Stanford University Press, 1935.

58. Taylor, J. A. The relationship of anxiety to the conditioned eyelid response. *J. exp. Psychol.*, 1951, 41, 81-92.
59. Vinson, D. B. Response to electroshock therapy as evaluated by mirror drawing. *J. clin. exp. Psychopathol.*, 1952, 13, 201-210.
60. Voth, A. C. An experimental study of mental patients through the autokinetic phenomenon. *Am. J. Psychiat.*, 1947, 103, 793-805.
61. Wallen, R. W. Food aversions of normal and neurotic males. *J. abnorm. soc. Psychol.*, 1945, 40, 77-81.
62. Wallen, R. W. Food aversions and behavior disorders. *J. consult. Psychol.*, 1948, 12, 310-312.
63. Welsh, G. S. and Dahlstrom, W. G. *Basic readings on the MMPI in psychology and medicine.* Minneapolis: University of Minnesota Press, 1956.
64. Wheeler, W. M., Little, K. B. and Lehner, G. F. The internal structure of the MMPI. *J. consult. Psychol.*, 1951, 15, 134-141.
65. Wile, I. S. The relation of left-handedness to behavior disorders. *Am. J. Orthopsychiat.*, 1932, 2, 44-57.

VI

Social Desirability and Personality Test Construction

ALLEN L. EDWARDS
The University of Washington

By an ojbective test, I shall mean any test for which the method of scoring responses to the test materials is rigorously defined. This use of the term objective implies nothing about the nature of the test materials designed to elicit responses. It refers only to the method of scoring responses. With an objective test, the method of scoring can be succinctly described by means of a scoring key. The scoring key tells us what to do with each of the responses made by the subject. For example, in a True-False objective test, the scoring key may tell us that True responses to certain items in the test are to be weighted 1 and False responses are to be weighted 0. For other items, the True responses are to be weighted 0 and False responses weighted 1. The subject's score on this test becomes the sum of the weights assigned to the responses he has made.

Although the definition I have given for an objective test implies nothing with respect to the nature of the test materials, my discussion of objective personality tests will be restricted to those tests for which the test materials are verbal statements or items. The task set for the subject by the testing situation is one of self-description in terms of the statements or items contained in the test. Objective tests of this kind are commonly known as personality inventories, schedules, or questionnaires.

In the typical personality inventory, the number of possible responses available to the subject is fixed by the nature of the test so that the subject must choose one of the several alternatives presented to him. I shall refer to these various alternatives as response categories. An objective personality inventory may have any number of response categories. However, we seldom find inventories with more than five response categories and, in most cases, the inventories in current use have only two or three response categories. These are usually of the form: True-False, Yes-No, Agree-Disagree, Like-Dislike, and so forth. When three response categories are provided, the third category is typically an Undecided category.

Although it is not a necessary condition for an objective personality inventory, we generally find that only one of the response categories is keyed. By a keyed response, I shall mean the response that is assigned a non-zero scoring weight. With a True-False test, designed to measure a personality variable, the keyed response is the one that we believe is more likely to be given by those who have a greater degree of the variable than by those who have a lesser degree. For example, in an inventory designed to measure introversion, the following item might appear: I keep in the background on social occasions. If we believe, for one reason or another, that those who have a high degree of introversion are more likely to answer True to this item than those who have a lesser degree of introversion, the keyed response would be True.

It will be convenient to confine the present discussion to those objective personality inventories in which a limited number of response categories are available to the subject and in which only one of the possible responses is keyed. The points I wish to make, however, have general implications and would, I believe, apply also to those inventories in which differential weights are assigned to multiple categories.

METHODS USED IN DEVELOPING INVENTORIES

In constructing objective personality inventories, three somewhat different procedures have been followed. Cattell (4) and Guilford (16, 17), for example, have used factor analysis techniques in developing their personality inventories. The *Minnesota Multiphasic Personality Inventory* and the *Vocational Interest Blank*, on the other hand, were constructed by Hathaway and McKinley (20) and Strong (26), respectively, using a procedure which I shall call the method of criterion groups. Still a third approach is the one used by Allport, Vernon, and Lindzey (1) in constructing the *Study of Values,* and which I have also used in developing the *Personal Preference Schedule* (9). This latter approach, I shall refer to as the construct approach.

If the factor analytic approach is followed, one starts initially with a large pool of items. Subjects are asked to respond to each item and the responses to all possible pairs of items are correlated. The resulting intercorrelation matrix is factor analyzed in anticipation of obtaining a smaller number of factors than items. By rotation of the factor matrix, simple structure may be found. Then, those items with high loadings on a given factor and low loadings on all other factors are placed together. By examining the content of the items with high loadings on a single factor, an attempt is made to see what they have in common. These items, for the factor analyst, will constitute a scale for measuring a single personality variable. Thus Cattell (3, p. 81) has found a factor on which a high score indicates: that the subject prefers an art gallery to a game of cards on a fine afternoon; that he does not generally succeed in keeping his emotions under control; that he does not dislike being waited on in personal matters; and that he does not believe that racial characters have more real influence in shaping the individual and the nation than most people believe. Yet, at the same time, he does admit to fits of dread or anxiety for no apparent reason; he does try to bluff his way past a guard or doorman; and he has been known to be a sleepwalker and to talk a great deal in his sleep. Cattell has tentatively labelled this personality variable as "Bohemian Unconcernedness."

It is not that a factor analyst would necessarily start out with the notion of developing a scale designed to measure "Bohemian Unconcernedness." As a matter of fact, it is characteristic of the factor analytic procedure that not one but several scales result from the application of factor methodology—one for each of the factors obtained. It is also characteristic of the factor analyst that he has no necessary prior notion of what these factors may be, if found, nor what they may relate to. The name assigned a factor or scale is based upon an examination of the content of those items with high loadings on the factor and what these items will be is not necessarily known in advance. Furthermore, the number of factors obtained is limited only by the number of items initially used. And the initial number of items, in turn, is limited only by the capacity of the modern electronic computer.

The criterion group approach demands that we have two contrasting groups of subjects available. For example, one of these groups may consist of individuals labelled as schizophrenic by psychiatrists and the other of individuals not so labelled. These two groups are given a set of items and differences in the responses of the two groups to each item are examined. Tests of significance may be applied as a basis for selecting those items for which there is a statistically significant difference in response between the two criterion groups. Thus, it may be found that a significantly larger number of schizophrenics than normals answer True to the item: I frequently have pains in my feet. This item will then be selected for inclusion in a scale—along with any other additional items that differentiate between the two groups. Item selection is rigorously empirical, and the person who uses the criterion group approach is, in general, not at all concerned with item content. He asks only that the items included in the scale be those that have been found to differentiate between the two groups of interest. The name assigned to the variable supposedly measured by the scale is based on the nature of the criterion groups used in their selection. Thus, MMPI scales have been constructed to measure schizophrenia, delinquency, depression, hysteria, low back pain, and so forth. The number of scales which can be constructed following the criterion group approach is limited only by the number of contrasting groups that can be found.

If the goal of the criterion group approach is to develop a scale useful in the prediction of membership or lack of membership in groups comparable to the original criterion groups, the procedures followed seem highly appropriate. But if scores on the scale so developed are treated, as they so often are, as measuring variation along a single continuum or dimension of personality, that is another matter. No matter how rigorously the criterion groups are defined, it does not seem at all possible that they can ever be made comparable in all respects but one. It may be possible, of course, to equate them for such variables as age, sex, socioeconomic status, and so forth, but it is well known that as the number of variables on which two groups are matched is increased, there is a corresponding decrease in the number of cases that meet the requirements for membership in the criterion groups. If we retain substantial N's in both groups, then we may have groups differing with respect to the criterion, but this criterion will of necessity be complex—a multiplicity of many things.

Perhaps the reason so many scales have been developed to measure clinical rather than normal personality variables is because criterion groups for clinical variables are available in hospitals and institutions. We should keep in mind, however, that a scale developed in this manner can never be better than the criterion group which provided the basis for item selection. Thus, if a criterion group is established by psychiatric judgment and if psychiatric judgment is fallible, as it surely is, this may mean that if we use the judgments of other psychiatrists to establish the criterion group, it will not be the same as the original criterion group. This, in turn, may result in a different set of items being selected for inclusion in the scale than those selected on the basis of responses of the original group. Two scales so developed, although supposedly predicting the same criterion, may bear little relation to one another.

In using the construct approach to the development of a personality scale, the psychologist starts with at least a vague notion of a personality variable that is of interest to him. He may have noted, for example, that some people seem to desire to be the center of attention. They like to entertain others, to tell amusing stories, to make themselves conspicuous by wearing unusual clothing, and, in various ways, to draw attention to themselves. These isolated bits of behavior may be subsumed under a construct which is tentatively labelled exhibition. The objective of the construct approach is to develop a scale which, it is hoped, will measure the construct of interest. When this approach is used in the development of an inventory, one does not start with a heterogeneous collection of items. Rather the attempt in the initial stage of item formulation is to "map the construct." The kinds of items we seek are those which are believed to be relevant to the construct.

When a sufficient pool of items is available, the responses of an unselected group of subjects to the items are then analyzed. Correlational and factor analytic techniques may be used in the attempt to select homogeneous items for inclusion in the scale. Or total scores for the subjects may be obtained on the complete set of items and the individual items analyzed in terms of total scores. This, of course, is, in a sense, a criterion group approach, but with one important difference. The criterion groups, in this instance, are established on the basis of their behavior with respect to the items, rather than in terms of an external criterion.

A major limitation of the construct approach is that the items included in the scale are dependent upon the manner in which the investigator has mapped the construct initially. For example, one investigator's construct of exhibition may not be the same as another's. Thus, although they may use the same labels, the mapping of the construct may be quite different with the result that the items in the two scales may also be different. Further research with the scales, along the lines suggested by Peak (25) and by Cronbach and Meehl (7), with respect to construct validity may prove of value in clarifying the difference between the two constructs represented by the two scales.

ITEM ENDORSEMENT AND SOCIAL DESIRABILITY SCALE VALUE

Regardless of the approach used in the development of a personality scale, there are certain common problems relating to the finished product. One of these relates to what I have come to call the social desirability variable and it is this problem that I now wish to discuss.

You are all familiar with the methods devised by Thurstone for scaling attitude statements. A number of statements relevant to some issue or institution are collected and these are submitted to a judging group. The judging group is not asked to respond in terms of whether they agree or disagree with each statement, but only to judge the degree of favorableness of each statement on, say, a 9-point scale. On the basis of the distribution of judgments for each statement, scale values are obtained by either the method of equal-appearing intervals or the method of successive intervals.[1] The scale value of a given statement is taken as an indication of its location on a psychological continuum such that high values indicate very favorable statements and low values very unfavorable statements.

I have applied these methods in scaling statements of the kind that we ordinarily find in personality inventories. The instructions given to the judging group are such that they are not asked to respond in terms of whether they agree or disagree with each statement, or in terms of whether they think it does or does not describe them, but rather they are asked to judge the degree of social desirability or undesirability of each statement. In other words, I ask them to rate how desirable or undesirable they would consider the behavior or characteristic in other individuals. On the basis of the distribution of judgments, a scale value is obtained for each statement by one of the psychological scaling methods. The scale value of a statement is taken as an indication of the location of the statement on a psychological continuum ranging from highly so-

---

[1] These and other methods of psychological scaling are described by Edwards (12) and Guilford (18).

cially undesirable to highly socially desirable. High scale values indicate statements that are socially desirable and low scale values statements that are socially undesirable.

Suppose that we have obtained social desirability scale values for a large number of statements. The statements are then printed in the form of a personality inventory. A new group of subjects is given the inventory and they are asked to respond to each statement in the usual manner of obtaining self-descriptions. For each statement we find the proportion of those responding Yes or True and we then plot these proportions against the corresponding, but independently obtained, social desirability scale values. The first time that I did this I found a linear relationship between the two variables. The product moment correlation between the proportion endorsing an item and the social desirability scale value of the item was .87 (8).

Calvin Wright (28) repeated this study with a minor variation. He gave 140 items to 127 college students and asked them to rate the degree to which each statement characterized them on a 9-point scale. The mean rating assigned to the statements in self-description was then correlated with the social desirability scale values of the statements. The product-moment correlation between these two variables for this sample was .88.

Using a Q-sort to obtain self-descriptions with the same statements and with still another sample, I found correlations of .87 between mean Q-sort rating and social desirability scale value for 50 females and .84 for the same variables for a group of 50 males (10).

I have also scaled the items in the *Interpersonal Check List* for social desirability. The ICL was then given to another group of subjects who were asked to describe themselves without signing their names to their test booklets. The product-moment correlation between probability of endorsement and social disirability scale values for the 128 items in the ICL was .83 (11).

These findings have subsequently been confirmed by various investigators with still other samples of items. Kenny (21), for example, scaled 25 personality items, originally used in an investigation by Zimmer (29), for social desirability. The rank order correlation between the social desirability scale value and the proportion endorsing an item was .82 for these 25 statements. Hanley (19), working with items from the MMPI, reports correlations of .89 and .92 between probability of endorsement and social desirability scale values for 32 items randomly selected from the Sc or Schizophrenia scale, and correlation of .82 and .86 between probability of endorsement and social desirability scale value for 25 items selected at random from the D or Depression scale.

I believe it is possible to generalize, on the basis of the studies described, and to state that, whenever we have a personality inventory in which the items in the inventory vary with respect to their social desirability scale values, we may expect to find a substantial positive correlation between probability of endorsement of an item and social desirability scale value of the item. Consider one possible implication of this finding. Although Hanley (19) established the relationship between probability of endorsement and items in the Sc scale of the MMPI using only 32 of the 79 items in this scale, his selection of items, he states, was random. Let us assume, therefore, that the relationship would hold for the complete set of 79 items. Now, recall how the Sc scale was developed. To be included in the Sc scale, an item had to differentiate significantly between a group of diagnosed schizophrenic patients and a group of normal controls. This means that either a significantly larger proportion or a significantly smaller proportion in the schizophrenic group had to endorse an item compared with the corresponding proportion in the normal-control group. But, on the basis of Hanley's findings, we have evidence that the relationship between the proportion in the normal group endorsing an item and social desirability scale value is linear with a product-moment correlation of .92 expressing the degree of the relationship. In essence, then, if an item was to be included in the Sc scale, the proportion in the schizophrenic group endorsing the item would be likely to deviate significantly from the linear regression line relating probability of endorsement to social desirability scale value for the normal group.

Does this mean that the relationship between probability of endorsement and social desirability scale value is not linear for the schizophrenic group? That is one possibility. Another is that the relationship is linear for the schizophrenic group, but that for this group the regression line is parallel to that obtained for the normal group, differing from it only in terms of the Y intercept. Still another possibility is that both the Y intercepts and the slopes of the regression lines differ for the two groups. Or, perhaps the social desirability scale values of the items established by the judgments of the schizophrenic group would differ from those established by judgments of the normal group. I do not know the answers to these questions, but they could easily be obtained through research. We do have some evidence, from a study by Klett (22), indicating that social desirability scale values based upon the judgments of diagnosed psychotic patients, are related to the social desirability scale values of the same items obtained from judgments of a non-psychotic group. Klett, for example, reports a correlation of .88 between the social desirability scale values based upon the judgments of psychotic patients and scale values based upon the judgments of college students.

THE SOCIAL DESIRABILITY HYPOTHESIS

Some years ago, Cronbach (5, 6) called attention to the importance of response sets as factors influencing scores on psychological tests. It was his observation that individuals may show very stable response tendencies to items in tests such that these tendencies are relatively independent of item content. The number of True responses that a person gives to a set of items may possibly be a measure of a general tendency to agree, or, as Cronbach called it, acquiescence. Similarly, the number of False responses that a person gives to a set of items may be a measure of a general tendency to disagree or dissent, that is, to be negative. If an Undecided category is provided, the number of such responses may be a measure of a general tendency to avoid committing oneself or to be evasive.

If the majority of the items in an inventory are keyed True, then a high score on the inventory may measure not only the variable of interest but also the tendency of the subject to acquiesce. Similarly, a low score may not necessarily indicate a lack of the variable, but only the tendency of the subject to respond negatively. Comparable complexities may enter into the interpretation of a score when the majority of the items are keyed False.

I do not, however, consider the tendency to respond True or the tendency to respond False as of primary importance in personality inventories. My reason for this belief is that both of these response set hypotheses, at least in personality inventories, have been shown to lead to predictions which are contrary to fact, whereas an alternative hypothesis leads to predictions that are in accord with fact. This alternative hypothesis, I have called the social desirability or SD hypothesis (13).

The SD hypothesis proposes that, just as individual differences have been found in the tendencies of subjects to respond True, Undecided, or False, regardless of item content, so also are there individual differences in the tendencies of subjects to give socially desirable responses to items in personality inventories, regardless of whether the socially desirable response is True or False. I have devised various scales to measure this tendency and these scales are referred to as Social Desirability scales or SD scales (9, 13).

An SD scale is relatively easy to develop. Suppose we take any heterogeneous set of personality statements and scale them for social desirability. We desire items heterogeneous with respect to content simply because we do not wish subjects who are to be given the developed SD scale to believe we are measuring some particular personality variable, such as, for example, dominance. On the basis of the evidence cited previously, we expect to find a linear relationship between probability of endorsement of these items and their social desirability scale values. To develop an SD scale we take those items with socially desirable scale values and key the True response. For those items with socially undesirable scale values, we key the False response. A person's score on the scale is simply the number of times he has given the keyed response in self-description, that is, the number of socially desirable responses he has given. As I have said earlier, I have developed a number of such SD scales, but most of the research that has been done to date is based upon a scale consisting of 39 items from the MMPI (13).

Now, let us suppose we take any existing personality inventory of interest and examine the scoring key for the items contained in the inventory. If the trait being measured by the inventory is itself a socially desirable trait, then we would expect to find a majority of the keyed responses to be socially desirable also. The scoring key for the trait, in essence, would be much the same as the scoring key we would obtain if we keyed the responses as we would in developing an SD scale. If the inventory were scored by each key, we would expect to find a high and positive correlation between the scores resulting from each key. This should, in general, be true for all personality inventories designed to measure traits which are themselves considered socially desirable. Similarly, if a high score on a given personality inventory indicates a trait that is itself considered socially undesirable, then the scoring key for this inventory should be just the reverse of the scoring key we would obtain if we keyed the same items as in an SD scale. Scoring the inventory by each key, we would expect to find a high negative correlation between the scores resulting from each key, that is, the trait key and the SD key.

In the cases described, it could be argued that the resulting correlations were artifacts of the scoring keys applied to the same items. By having available a separate and independently constructed SD scale, based upon a different set of items, and by correlating scores on this SD scale with those of a given personality inventory, we are no longer correlating two sets of scores necessarily dependent by virtue of scoring the same set of items by two keys which are not themselves independent.

CORRELATIONS BETWEEN THE SD SCALE AND OTHER SCALES

A person with a high score on the SD scale can be described as one who has given a large number of socially desirable responses in self-description, whereas a person with a low score can be described as one who has given relatively few socially desirable responses in self-description. If this is a stable and consistent personality characteristic, we should find it evidenced in performance on a variety of other personality inventories, regardless of the particular traits supposedly being measured by these inventories. For example, suppose we have an inventory on which a high score indicates a socially desirable trait. Then individuals who are likely to give socially desirable responses in self-description are also likely to obtain high scores on this inventory. We should expect, therefore, that individuals who score high on the SD scale will also score high on the trait, whereas individuals with low scores on the SD scale will score low on the trait. As a result, we should find a positive correlation between scores on the SD scale and on the trait inventory.

Consider, for example, the Guilford-Martin (15) scales designed to measure Cooperativeness, Agreeableness, and Objectivity. High scores on these three scales indicate traits which, I believe, would be considered favorable or socially desirable. The product-moment correlations between scores on these three scales and scores on the original 79-item SD scale for a sample of 106 college males and females are .63, .53, and .71, respectively (9). There are three MMPI scales on which high scores would be considered as indications of socially desirable traits: The Dominance, Responsibility, and Status scales. The tetrachoric correlations between scores on these scales and scores on the 39-item SD scale, as reported by Merrill and Heathers (24) for a sample of 155 males, are: .49, .52, and .61, respectively.

If we consider inventories on which high scores would be taken as indications of socially undesirable traits, then, following the same line of reasoning as we did earlier, we should expect to find negative correlations between scores on these inventories and scores on

the SD scale.[2] Within the MMPI we can find a wide variety of
scales for which high scores indicate socially undesirable traits.
Tetrachoric correlations were obtained by Merrill and Heathers (24)
between scores on these scales and scores on the 39-item SD scale
for a sample of 155 males. The tetrachoric correlations are as follows:

MMPI Scales	Correlation with the 39-Item SD Scale
Neuroticism	−.50
Dependency	−.73
Hostility	−.75
Manifest Anxiety	−.84
Social Introversion	−.90

For the various clinical scales of the MMPI, Merrill and Heathers
(24) report the following tetrachoric correlations with the 39-item
SD scale for the same sample:

MMPI Scales	Correlation with the 39-Item SD Scale
Hs Hypochondriasis	−.52
Pt Psychasthenia	−.85
Sc Schizophrenia	−.77
D Depression	−.61
Pd Psychopathic Deviate	−.50
Hy Hysteria	.08
Pa Paranoia	−.09
Ma Hypomania	−.13

The three lowest correlations with SD are those of .08, −.09,
and −.13 with Hysteria, Paranoia, and Hypomania, respectively.
As a result of my work with the SD scale, I have become so ac-
customed to finding substantial correlations between SD and scores
on other inventories that, when low correlations are obtained, I
seek for an explanation in terms of the relationship between the
social desirability scale values of the items and the manner in which
the item responses are keyed.

[2] According to Berg's (2) deviant set hypothesis, if a subject tends to make responses
avoided by the majority of a group of subjects, this tendency may be related to other
forms of deviancy from normative standards. On the SD scale, deviant responses would
result in low scores. On the SD scale, then, deviancy would be more or less synony-
mous with "social undesirability" which, in turn, has been shown to be related to
"abnormality," as measured by the clinical scales of the MMPI.

FACTORS INFLUENCING CORRELATIONS WITH SD

In general, a low correlation between scores on the SD scale and scores on another personality inventory could result from at least two conditions. We know, for example, that, if the trait being measured by an inventory is itself socially undesirable, then, in general, most of the keyed responses will, in turn, be socially undesirable. To obtain a high score on the inventory, the subject must, in fact, attribute to himself socially undesirable characteristics. Suppose, however, that it is possible to obtain at least some items such that the keyed response is a socially desirable response, yet the variable itself is socially undesirable. For example, it might happen that, using the method of criterion groups, some of the items included in the clinical scales of the MMPI are such that the keyed response is a socially desirable response. Then to these items, a socially desirable response would be keyed as indicating a socially undesirable variable. If a scale contains a number of such items, then this would tend to lower the correlation between scores on the scale and scores on the SD scale.

Some evidence on this point is available. A study by Hanley (19) indicates that approximately 75 per cent of the items in the Sc scale have socially undesirable scale values, with 25 per cent falling in the neutral and socially desirable categories. For the D scale, on the other hand, only approximately 52 per cent of the items have socially undesirable scale values, whereas 48 per cent have scale values falling in the neutral and socially desirable categories. Hanley classified the items in these two scales according to whether the True response was keyed or not keyed in determining scores on the scales. With the dichotomy, keyed and not keyed, point biserial correlations were obtained with the social desirability scale values of the items as the continuous variable. For the Sc items, the point biserial correlation was .84 and for the D items it was .58. These findings indicate that the keying of items in the D scale is somewhat less related to the social desirability scale values of the items than in the case of the Sc scale. We should, therefore, expect to find, as we have consistently found, that scores on the D scale correlate lower with scores on the SD scale than do those on the Sc scale.

There is another possible way in which we might obtain a low correlation between scores on the SD scale and scores on another personality inventory. We might, for example, have an inventory in which a substantial number of the items have social desirability scale values in the central section of the psychological continuum.

That is, these items may be relatively neutral with respect to their social desirability scale values. If we have a number of items with neutral scale values, a subject whose responses are primarily influenced by social desirability considerations will be in a quandary as to how he should respond. If the scale value of an item is truly neutral, then there is no socially desirable or undesirable response that can be made by a subject in answering it. In this situation, we might argue, his responses are more likely to be influenced by the content of the item. The correlation between SD and scores on the inventory should thus decrease as the number of neutral items in the inventory is increased.

SUBTLE ITEMS

Some years ago, Wiener (27) attempted to classify the items in the various MMPI scales into two groups, one of which he called subtle and the other obvious. For five of the MMPI scales he was able to find two such groups of items. The three scales, Hysteria, Paranoia, and Hypomania, for which low correlations with SD are reported by Merrill and Heathers (24), are among the five. The two additional scales are the D and Pd scales. Hanley (19) has suggested that subtle items are those with neutral social desirability scale values. I have expressed the opinion that not only may a neutral item be a subtle item, but that any item for which a socially desirable response is keyed as a sign of socially undesirable trait would be a subtle item (13). In the case of socially desirable traits, a subtle item would be one for which the socially undesirable response is keyed. Recall that I define socially desirable and undesirable responses on the basis of an item's social desirability scale value.

Let us accept this hypothesis concerning subtle items, for the moment, and see if we can predict what we should find when we correlate scores on the SD scale with those on the subtle and obvious scales of the SD scale with those on the subtle and obvious scales of the MMPI. For the obvious scales, we should have more items for which the keyed response is a socially undesirable response than in the case of the subtle scales. The subtle scales, on the other hand, should contain more neutral items and/or more items for which the keyed response is a socially desirable response than in the case of the obvious scales. If this argument is sound, then we should find a substantial negative correlation between the SD scale and the obvious scales. For the subtle scales, the correlations with SD should definitely be lower, with the magnitude and sign of the correlation depending solely upon how many neutral items the scale contains and upon the number of items for which the socially desirable response is keyed. If we have many items for which the socially desirable response is keyed, the correlation with SD should be positive in sign.

At my suggestion, Fordyce and Rozynko (14) drew a sample of 50 MMPI records from the files of a VA hospital and obtained product-moment correlations between scores on the 39-item SD scale and total scores on the D, Pd, Pa, Ma, and Hy scales. They then calculated the correlations between the SD scale and the separate subtle and obvious scales. The results are as shown below:

MMPI Scale	Correlations with the 39-Item SD Scale		
	Total	Obvious	Subtle
D	−.69	−.78	.33
Pd	−.67	−.85	.27
Pa	−.52	−.72	.06
Ma	−.08	−.53	.40
Hy	−.28	−.71	.54

Note that in every instance the negative correlation of SD with the obvious scale is greater than it is with the total scale consisting of both subtle and obvious items. This is as it should be. The correlations between SD and the subtle scales, on the other hand, are all positive in sign. These findings support the contention that the subtle scales contain neutral items and/or items for which a socially desirable response is keyed to a greater extent than do the obvious scales. The fact that the positive correlations between SD and the subtle scales are not of the same magnitude as the negative correlations between SD and the obvious scales indicates that the subtle scales contain fewer keyed socially desirable responses than the obvious scales contain keyed socially undesirable responses.

I have spent considerable time with the MMPI and social desirability. This is not because I believe the MMPI to be the only personality inventory in which the social desirability variable operates. It is rather because the MMPI is such a widely used personality inventory that the data in which I was interested were readily available. The points I have made would apply, I believe, equally well to any other inventory of the True-False kind.

Minimizing Social Desirability

If we do not desire scores on objective personality inventories to be influenced by the social desirability variable, what can we do about it? One suggestion is that we can attempt to correct for social desirability by means of such scales as the SD scale. For example, if we know the correlation between the SD scale and scores on another personality inventory, then we can predict the score that a person would receive on the inventory by means of a linear regression function of these scores on the SD score. If we then subtract the predicted score from the actual score, it can readily be shown that these deviation scores will be uncorrelated with the SD scores. Unfortunately, however, the correlations between SD and scores on various personality inventories are of such magnitude that the residuals or deviation scores may represent little more than error variance. It is well known that the reliability of difference scores is, in general, considerably lower than the separate measures involved in the difference scores.

Another possibility would be to search for items that are relatively neutral with respect to their social desirability scale values. I do not know whether this is a hopeless search or not. I can only say that, on the basis of my experience in scaling personality items, the number of items with relatively neutral scale values is much smaller than the number I find with socially desirable or socially undesirable scale values.

Along the same lines, we might seek items such that the socially desirable response is the keyed response in scales designed to measure socially undesirable variables. For scales designed to measure socially desirable variables, we would, of course, attempt to find items for which the socially undesirable response is keyed. The five subtle scales of the MMPI are perhaps the closest approximations we have, at the present time, to scales of this kind. Additional research directed toward the development of subtle scales designed to measure normal personality variables is needed.

A third approach to the minimization of social desirability in personality inventories is the one I have used in developing the Personal Preference Schedule. In this inventory, an attempt is made to minimize the operation of the social desirability variable by pairing statements representing different personality variables on the basis of their social desirability scale values in such a way that the social desirability scale values of the two statements are comparable. The subject is then asked to choose between the two statements.

In this way, we hope to minimize the probability of the choice being determined by social desirability considerations alone. I shall not take time to cite the considerable evidence available which bears upon the extent to which this forced-choice type of inventory does minimize the social desirability variable. It is cited in detail in my book on the social desirability variable in personality assessment (13).

Status of the Personality Inventory

And now—what of the future of the objective personality inventory? Let us first go back to the past. In 1945, Kornhauser (23) published the results of a survey in which he queried specialists about their satisfaction with various psychological tests. One of the questions in the survey had to do with their satisfaction with existing personality inventories and also with the Rorschach. The results were more or less a tie, with 51 per cent expressing some degree of satisfaction with personality inventories and 49 per cent with the Rorschach.

I do not have the results of a comparable survey for the year 1958 rather than 1945. I do not think I would be overstating the case, however, if I said that probably all of us who have attempted to develop objective personality inventories are not overly satisfied with the results of our efforts. There is much that remains to be done in the way of research before we will have personality inventories that are judged as satisfactory as, let us say, achievement tests.

References

1. Allport, G. W., Vernon, P. E., and Lindzey, G. *Study of values.* (Rev. ed.) Boston: Houghton Mifflin, 1951.
2. Berg, I. A. Response bias and personality: the deviation hypothesis. *J. Psychol.,* 1955, 40, 61-72.
3. Cattell, R. B. *Personality.* New York: McGraw-Hill, 1950.
4. Cattell, R. B. *The Sixteen Personality Factor Questionnaire.* Champaign, Ill.: Institute for Personality and Ability Testing, 1950.
5. Cronbach, L. J. Response sets and test validity. *Educ. psychol. Measmt.,* 1946, 6, 475-494.
6. Cronbach, L. J. Further evidence on response sets and test design. *Educ. psychol. Measmt.,* 1950, 10, 3-31.
7. Cronbach, L. J., and Meehl, P. E. Construct validity in psychological tests. *Psychol. Bull.,* 1955, 52, 281-302.
8. Edwards, A. L. The relationship between the judged desirability of a trait and the probability that the trait will be endorsed. *J. appl. Psychol.,* 1953, 37, 90-93.
9. Edwards, A. L. *Manual for the Personal Preference Schedule.* New York: Psychol. Corp., 1953.
10. Edwards, A. L. Social desirability and Q sorts. *J. consult. Psychol.* 1955, 19, 462.
11. Edwards, A. L. Social desirability and probability of endorsement of items in the Interpersonal Check List. *J. abnorm. soc. Psychol.,* 1957, 55, 394-396.
12. Edwards, A. L. *Techniques of attitude scale construction.* New York: Appleton-Century, 1957.
13. Edwards, A. L. *The social desirability variable in personality assessment and research.* New York: Dryden, 1957.
14. Fordyce, W. E., and Rozynko, V. The correlations between the SD scale and the subtle and obvious scales of the MMPI. Unpublished study. Cited by A. L. Edwards, *The social desirability variable in personality assessment and research.* New York: Dryden, 1957, p. 47.

15. Guilford, J. P. *The Guilford-Martin Personnel Inventory.* Beverly Hills, Calif.: Sheridan Supply Co., 1943.

16. Guilford, J. P. *An Inventory of Factors* STDCR. Beverly Hills, Calif.: Sheridan Supply Co., 1940.

17. Guilford, J. P., and Martin, H. G. *The Guilford-Martin Inventory of Factors* GAMIN, Abridged Edition. Beverly Hills, Calif.: Sheridan Supply Co., 1943.

18. Guilford, J. P. *Psychometric methods.* (2nd ed.) New York: Mc-Graw-Hill, 1954.

19. Hanley, C. Social desirability and responses to items from three MMPI scales: *D. Sc. and K. J. appl. Psychol.,* 1956, 40, 324-328.

20. Hathaway, S. R., and McKinley, J. C. Manual for the Minnesota Multiphasic Personality Inventory. (Rev. ed.) New York: Psychol. Corp., 1951.

21. Kenny, D. T. The influence of social desirability on discrepancy measures between real self and ideal self. *J. consult. Psychol.,* 1956, 20, 315-318.

22. Klett, C. J. The social desirability stereotype in a hospital population. *J. consult. Psychol.,* 1957, 21, 419-421.

23. Kornhauser, A. Replies of psychologists to a short questionnaire on mental test developments, personality inventories, and the Rorschach test. *Educ. psychol. Measmt.,* 1945, 5, 3-16.

24. Merrill, R. M., and Heathers, Louise B. The relation of the MMPI to the Edwards Personal Preference Schedule on a college counseling center sample. *J. consult. Psychol.,* 1956, 20, 310-314.

25. Peak, Helen. Problems of objective observation. In L. Festinger and D. Katz (Eds.), *Research methods in the behavioral sciences.* New York: Dryden, 1953, pp. 243-299.

26. Strong, E. K., Jr. *Vocational Interest Blank for Men.* Stanford Univer., Calif.: Stanford Univer. Press, 1938.

27. Wiener, D. R. Subtle and obvious keys for the Minnesota Multiphasic Personality Inventory. *J. consult. Psychol.,* 1948, 12, 164-170.

28. Wright, C. E. Relations between normative and ipsative measures of personality. Unpublished doctor's dissertation. Univer. of Washington, 1957.

29. Zimmer, H. Self-acceptance and its relation to conflict. *J. consult. Psychol.,* 1954, 18, 447-449.

VII

Objective Scoring of Projective Tests

Wayne H. Holtzman
The University of Texas

Ever since L. K. Frank's first use of the term "projective method" in 1939 (15), there has been a rapid mushrooming of techniques for encouraging an individual to reveal aspects of his personality by the way in which he perceives, organizes, or relates to potentially affect-laden, ambiguous stimuli. Stemming largely from psychoanalytic theory, such projective techniques range all the way from free association in relatively unstructured situations to rather highly structured, formalized devices such as the Thematic Apperception Test. Before considering the problems of quantification and objective scoring, it might be instructive to examine closely the assumptions implicit in the projective method as contrasted to those underlying psychometric tests and measurement theory.

Projective Compared with Psychometric Methods

Unlike the standardized aptitude test, the projective approach deals with the idiomatic expression of the individual as revealed in the context of his needs, fears, strivings, and ego-defensive behavior. As Frank has so aptly stated, "The essential feature of a projective technique is that it evokes from the subject what is, in various ways, expressive of his private world and personality process." (16, p. 47).

Given any projective technique where the subject is offered a wide latitude in which to reveal himself, the particular sample of responses obtained is assumed to reflect significant aspects of the subject's personality organization, if only the examiner can find the key to its interpretation.

Macfarlane and Tuddenham have pointed out that such an isomorphic assumption concerning the subject's test protocol and his personality leads to three corollaries that are rarely explicit: (a) belief that a protocol is a sufficiently extensive sampling of the subject's personality to warrant formulating judgments about it; (b) belief that the psychological determinants of each and every response are basic and general; and (c) belief that projective tests tap the durable essence of personality equally in different individuals (27, p. 34). Many of the more wary, sophisticated projectivists would argue that none of these three assumptions *necessarily* follows from the basic assumption underlying the projective method—that even the best of projective test protocols is but a tiny fragment of the total personality, fraught with innumerable possibilities for misinterpretation. Nevertheless, in actual practice it is difficult to avoid falling into the dogmatic position of over-interpretation in an attempt to weave together a consistent picture of the personality dynamics presumably reflected by the clinical techniques employed. It can be argued that elaborate, clinical interpretations of personality from projective protocols often reveal more about the personality of the clinician than that of the subject.

In contrast to a projective technique, a psychometric test is based upon the fundamental assumption that an obtained score on the test reflects a hypothetical "true" score which is characteristic of the attribute in question for a given individual under specified testing conditions and at a given moment in time. Any deviation of the obtained score from the true score represents error of measurement which can be assessed provided one is willing to make certain assumptions about the nature of such errors. By defining the true score so that it includes all constant errors of measurement, the discrepancy between obtained and true score becomes a random error component. Since a random event by definition is uncorrelated with any other event, a general theory of measurement can be developed out of which components of error variance can be estimated, both with regard to the concept of reliability and the concept of validity (18).

Contrary to the opinion of some writers (37), such psychometric theory is not necessarily limited to a nomothetic universe where one is interested in group or inter-individual differences. As Cattell (6) has been quick to point out, one can legitimately utilize psychometric theory for idiographic purposes by considering k different measures on m different occasions for a single person. Nor need psychometric theory be restricted to consideration of one response variable at a time—the oft heard criticism that a psychometric, statistical, or quantitative approach is too atomistic to provide more than a ridiculous caricature of the individual personality. While it is true that most contemporary uses of test scores deal with isolated traits, or at best with linear combinations of several traits, the advent of configural scoring methods (30), the possibilities of profile analysis (19), and other complex, multivariate procedures open new vistas for effective utilization of psychometric theory in the study of the individual personality.

Use of psychometric theory as a basis for assessment of personality commits one to a trait theory of personality. Postulating some sort of "true" score as a hypothetical construct to be inferred from observed scores is tantamount to saying that John Doe has X amount of the trait in question. It is not necessary, however, to think of John's possession of the trait as a "fixed" quantity. An individual's true score remains invariant only so long as the specific testing conditions remain constant and there is no real change in the individual with respect to the trait in question. A primary purpose of test standardization is to minimize constant sources of error that are ordinarily confounded with the inferred true score. Only errors of measurement that are random in nature can be adequately assessed and taken into account by the usual concepts of reliability and validity within contemporary psychometric theory.

Rosenzweig (37) has observed that assessment procedures can be ordered on a continuum depending upon the degree of structuring and control introduced by the assessor. At one extreme are the completely qualitative, unstructured methods of psychoanalysis, free association by a patient in the presence of an analyst. At the other extreme are highly structured paper-and-pencil tests which meet all the standards of psychometric theory. Projective techniques are seen as falling somewhere in between the particular position on the continuum depending upon the degree of standardization and control. In most instances, the projectivist has tried to preserve the qualitative, idiographic essence of the projective method while also searching for ways in which to categorize, quantify, and standardize the response variables underlying test behavior. He would like to have a technique for assessing personality which covers a wide band of the above continuum with a high degree of power throughout the range. Very few psychologists indeed have completely and consistently refrained from some form of abstraction later leading to quantification.

As soon as an individual decides to classify and enumerate any characteristics of a subject's responses to a projective technique, however crude and elementary the system, he has shifted from a purely projective point of view to a psychometric frame of reference. Such measurement may be quite nominal and only faintly resemble full-blown quantification. Nevertheless he has made the first and most significant step by classification of responses. For example, to classify a given response to an inkblot as a W assigns meaning to the response that transcends the idiosyncratic, private world of the subject. Unless one considers such symbols as W, D, and d, mere short-hand devices that have no real meaning beyond calling one's attention to certain aspects of the protocol, the symbols take on nominal characteristics of measurement. Those subjects who use the whole inkblot are seen as one class of individuals (W-tendency type), while those who use only a small part of the inkblot for their response are seen as another class (d-tendency type).

Such symbols of classification can be considered "signs" depicting specified characteristics abstracted from the raw protocol. More or less elaborate patterns of signs can be derived, either rationally or empirically, which point toward a syndrome or personality attribute to be inferred from the protocol. The pattern of signs may be complex and highly conditional so that predictive statements of the "if A and B but not C, then X" type can be formulated. Or the set of admissible signs may all contribute to some sort of "global" measure like the adjustment score derived from the Rorschach by Munroe's Inspection Technique (32). Such clusters of signs may have some pragmatic value in predicting a criterion, but they have a disjunctive quality or arbitrariness which makes any theoretical interpretation exceedingly difficult. In most instances when a series of responses is classified, some types of response will appear more than once. Counting of such response frequencies is the first step in the construction of a quantitative scoring system. A Rorschach protocol with 10 movement responses would be thought of as indicating a greater tendency to see movement than a record with only two movement responses. Such a statement implies a crude kind of ordinal scale by which people can be ordered according to their degrees of M-tendency, provided the total number of responses is controlled.

As one becomes engrossed with the counting of symbols it is very easy to forget the nature of the projective material being classified. In his eagerness to make a given technique meet the demands of both psychometric and projective theory, the psychologist often compromises the two sets of conflicting standards to the point where the technique fails to accomplish either aim. There are some projective devices that should always be treated by qualitative methods of analysis since almost any attempt to abstract quantitative scores will fail to have any meaning. Other projective techniques may be altered sufficiently to yield scores meeting acceptable psychometric standards while at the same time preserving the projective nature of the task. It is too much to expect a technique designed originally as a purely projective method to lend itself to a meaningful kind of quantification without some revision, and in many projective techniques no amount of revision will produce adequate scores in the true psychometric sense.

Frank (16) has divided the projective techniques into five general kinds: constructive, interpretive, constitutive, cathartic, and refractive. The constructive methods consist of those techniques which require the subject to arrange materials into larger configurations or to produce drawings as in the Draw-A-Person Test. The interpretive methods are primarily verbal-associational techniques such as the Thematic Apperception Test. The best known example of a constitutive method is the Rorschach in which the subject must organize relatively amorphous, unstructured inkblots into meaningful concepts. While most projective techniques may stimulate cathartic reactions, some, such as play therapy with dolls, are designed specifically for this purpose. The last of Frank's classes, the refractive method, is based upon the fact that any conventionalized mode of communication—handwriting, gestures, and other forms of expressive movement—may be used as an approach to the individuality of a person.

The above classification serves as a convenient basis for a more detailed discussion of scoring problems and quantifications in the analysis of projective techniques. Since cathartic methods cut across the other procedures, and since the analysis of expressive movement and individual style of communication can be considered as a special topic apart from more conventional projective methods, only the first three of Frank's classes will be discussed. Considerably more attention will be given to the Rorschach and related techniques than to the constructive or interpretive methods, partly because the

Rorschach has been studied longer and more exhaustively than any other projective test and partly because it provides an unusually good illustration of various problems of quantification encountered throughout the projective-psychometric continuum.

CONSTRUCTIVE METHODS

The way in which a child or adult arranges miniature life toys, draws a figure of a man or woman, or builds mosaics from colored pieces can reveal a great deal about his personality. Generally speaking, however, such creative productions are very difficult to analyze in any objective, quantitative fashion. Most clinicians only use qualitative procedures when dealing with constructive methods. Occasionally the characteristics of a construction may be classified to formalize its description, but inferences regarding personality, whether based upon symbolic interpretations or more direct expressions by the subject, remain at the clinical intuitive level. Of course, rating scales for recording clinical judgment can be employed with such materials, as with any other individual response or style of expression. But it is not difficult to see why quantification in the psychometric sense has failed to prove useful in the analyses of drawings or other creative products, even though the situation may be rather highly structured as in the Bender-Gestalt Test. Usually the construction has to be viewed as a whole or as only a very small number of separate units analogous to test items. The configuration, color, shading, and other characteristics of a drawing are complex, defying quantification in the usual sense. Nevertheless, in some special cases, fairly successful attempts have been made to score objectively certain limited aspects of such productions. Several of these will be briefly discussed.

Drawing a human figure has been employed rather extensively as a projective technique in recent years, largely due to the persistent studies of Karen Machover (28). Working primarily from a psychoanalytic point of view in which the drawing is assumed to reflect the body image of self, Machover and others have developed systems of graphic analysis utilizing a sign approach to the scoring of drawings. For full use of the system, the subject must draw both a man and a woman so that comparisons of self-sex and opposite-sex figures can be made. A good example of this graphic sign method is the scale of figure drawing items which is presumed to measure field-dependency (50). Sets of 40 items for men and 45 for women were constructed by Machover on the basis of a preliminary analysis. Criterion groups for the initial selection of items consisted of college students with high and low field dependence as measured by a battery of perceptual tests. A total score is obtained by summing the number of signs checked during the detailed analysis of the two figure drawings. Some of the signs are completely objective such as transparency, lack of ears, or hair shaded. Others, like consistency rating and rigidity rating, are subjective and require a clinical judge. For the most part, however, the list of signs is sufficiently objective to merit further study.

Graphic signs have been used with similar success by Pascal and Suttell in the objective scoring of drawings in the Bender-Gestalt Test (34). The test consists of nine geometric forms that are copied by the subject. The number of scorable signs on each design varies from 10 to 13, with seven additional signs dealing with the total configuration of all nine drawings. Each sign is given a numerical weight varying from one to eight. The size of the weight was empirically determined in earlier studies differentiating normals from such groups as psychotics and organics.

A single score is obtained by summing the weights of positive signs, the higher the score the more pathological the record. Although much valuable information may have been sacrificed at the expense of obtaining a single quantitative index, the resulting score has sufficiently high reliability and validity in a variety of situations to prove highly useful as a screening procedure.

A third variation of semi-structured drawing which represents an attempt at objective quantification is the Drawing-Completion Test described by Kinget (23). Eight squares are presented to the subject, each containing small, but suggestive, stimuli such as a dot, a wavy line, or a black square, around which the subject draws whatever he wishes. Kinget has attempted to develop a graphic system with a series of crudely quantitative variables, some based on content analysis and others dealing with style and expressive features of the drawings. A personality profile is constructed by recording signs and then adding them together in more abstract categories, somewhat like the first attempts to quantify the Rorschach. While the rationale behind the scoring system is highly speculative and smacks of arm-chair analysis without adequate empirical support, the method itself is interesting and sufficiently novel to deserve careful study.

Working with spontaneous finger paintings, a construction which has proved very difficult to quantify, Dorken (10) has developed a series of objectively defined rating scales for energy output, affective range, contact with reality, and clarity. Pictorial norms were used as points of reference to anchor the scales. The variable, Affective Range, illustrates the technique. "Spontaneous" colors, red and yellow, were each assigned scale values of three, blue and green were given values of two each, and the "somber" colors, black and brown, were each scored one. Combination colors were scored in relation to this primary scale. Test-retest reliability ranged from .13 to .84, depending upon the sample and time interval between administrations. By using a series of finger paintings, reasonably adequate summary scores on the four variables defined by Dorken should be possible.

It is significant to note that in each of the above examples of attempts to achieve objective scoring of projective techniques, the degree of quantification is pretty much limited to the complex sign approach in which numerous signs are scored, weighted, and summed to yield some sort of "global" but quantitative, measure which is purported to reflect important dimensions of personality. Ideally, the sign approach should begin with sufficient theoretical rationale to construct a coherent system. After careful operational definition of each sign, the objectivity of scoring should be determined by having at least two trained individuals independently score a large number of protocols. In some instances where several signs have similar rationales in their definition, their consistency should be examined empirically in a study to validate the construct which they theoretically represent (7). In most cases, however, a straight empirical analysis without regard for the construct in question will be undertaken with the practical view in mind of establishing a weighting system that has maximum efficiency for predicting some criterion. In any case, the burden of proof concerning the reliability and objectivity of any proposed scoring system rests with the individual who proposes it.

INTERPRETIVE METHODS

Assessing personality from the way in which an individual reveals his fantasy life in telling a story or interpreting a scene goes back through centuries of mankind. However, the first notable attempt to develop a projective test for uncovering a person's needs, wishes, and related fantasies by having him tell stories was made by Morgan and Murray in 1935 (31). In the past 20 years, Murray's Thematic Apperception Test (TAT) has become a standard projective technique, second only to the Rorschach in its widespread use both in the clinic and laboratory. Numerous other interpretive methods —Rosenzweig's Picture-Frustration Study (36), Bellak's Children's Apperception Test (22), and Shneidman's Made-A-Picture-Story Test (43), to mention but a few—stem more or less directly from Murray's pioneering work and attest to the fruitfulness of the basic method.

Interpretive methods range all the way from one end of the projective-psychometric continuum to the other. Representative of the purely projective approach is the standard TAT analyzed entirely in a qualitative manner, focusing upon the content of stories and stylistic aspects of the story telling as illustrated by Stein (44), such analysis draws heavily upon careful deduction and clinical intuition. Only one step removed from this intuitive approach is the more formal kind of qualitative analysis in which various characteristics of each story are classified according to theme expressed, kinds of affect, need categories, and the like. Such qualitative systems tend to vary considerably according to the predilection of the analyst. Representative of the diverse approaches to analysis of TAT protocols is Shneidman's (43) compilation of systems used by 15 different authorities working with the same TAT record.

Several investigators have developed sets of rating scales to be used with the TAT. One of the most extensive systems is Hartman's (21) consisting of five-point scales for 65 categories covering thematic elements, feeling qualities, topics of reference, and more formal characteristics, each of which can be scored for a given story. Total scores are obtained by summing ratings across stories. While such scales utilize the clinical skill of the interpreter, serious difficulties often arise when one is concerned with the objectivity of the scoring. When categories deal with the manifest aspects of a story, independent raters can generally agree at a satisfactory level to insure fair objectivity. But as soon as attention is focused upon covert aspects of the response or upon the personality of the story-teller rather than his production, agreement falls off sharply (46).

The reason for this greater subjectivity when dealing with the personality of the subject is apparent when one examines closely the nature of the factors influencing response to a TAT picture. Holt (22) discusses nine different determinants of the manifest response, ranging from situational context to personal style of the story-teller. The interpreter is faced with the very complex task of weighing the probable influence of each factor before he can arrive at an interpretation of the subject's personality. It is somewhat like having an equation with nine variables, several of which can be partially discounted while most remain unknown quantities. Several judges will weigh the unknowns quite differently, resulting in widely varying ratings.

This difference between *test-oriented systems* dealing with formal characteristics of the response and *personality-oriented systems* in which the interpreter makes direct inferences concerning the personality of the story-teller is fundamental. The more superficial or concrete the system, the more objective the scoring and the less relevant the derived variables to the personality of the subject. Young (51) developed a set of 23 well-defined traits, such as Anxiety, Dominance, and Need to be Loved, which could be used in rating the personality of the interpreter as well as the subject. Fifteen trained interpreters independently rated 12 TAT stories from seven different individuals, a total of 84 responses, on each of the 23 traits. Ratings on the same 23 traits were obtained for each of the 15 interpreters by a sociometric method. Even though the average agreement among interpreters was fairly high for such personality-oriented variables, differences in the interpreters' ratings proved significantly related to their own personalities, demonstrating the intrinsic subjectivity of such methods of analysis.

Several fairly objective variables dealing with story content seem sufficiently relevant to important aspects of the story-teller's personality to merit special attention. McClelland and his colleagues (26) have carefully developed the personality construct, Achievement Motive, and have demonstrated how it can be reliably scored in TAT stories. The scoring involves simple classifications of response elements by objective criteria that are then summed to yield an overall index of the individual's Need-Achievement score. A number of experimental studies are also cited indicating the validity of the personality construct.

A similar careful derivation of two test-oriented variables of relevance to the story-teller's personality was undertaken by Eron (12). Using well-anchored rating scales, Eron and co-workers developed fairly objective measures of emotional tone and outcome that could be applied to single responses and summed to get an overall score. Both variables have satisfactory inter-scorer reliabilities, .86 for emotional tone and .75 for outcome. Eron is chiefly concerned with the development of norms for TAT themes that can be used to define the general characteristics of each card in terms of the ease with which certain themes are evoked. Such data for the TAT can be roughly thought of as analogous to difficulty level or other item-parameters in aptitude tests. A recent application of Eron's approach demonstrates how Guttman's scaling method can be employed using normative TAT data to construct a uni-dimensional scale for need-Sex (1).

A final example of an objective approach to the scoring of the TAT is one devised recently by Dana (9). Three fundamental aspects of test behavior—approach to the situation, normality of response, and rarity of response—were used by Dana to define three variables amenable to objective scoring, Perceptual Organization, Perceptual Range, and Perceptual Personalization. Inter-scorer reliability in terms of percentage agreement between independent judges ranged from 76 to 94 for the three scoring categories in a study of 150 TAT stories. The unique aspect of Dana's approach is the fact that these three variables are sufficiently pertinent to a large variety of projective techniques to permit inter-test comparisons for sharpening the validity of the personality constructs involved.

Variations of the sentence completion method provide much more suitable data for psychometric development than the TAT. The technique consists of providing the subject with a list of incomplete sentences to which he responds with whatever completions come to mind. By wise selection of sentence stems, content fairly similar to the thematic apperception methods can be obtained. Of course the response is much more highly structured and discrete from one item to the next than is the case with the TAT. Herein lies the chief virtue of the method with respect to quantification.

Rotter and Willerman (38) developed one of the first sentence completion tests with high objectivity. Designed for large-scale screening purposes in the Army Air Force, their 40-item version yielded a single adjustment score having inter-scorer reliability of .89 and split-half reliability of .85. A refined version of this test designed for college students, the Rotter Incomplete Sentences Blank (39) has an objective scoring manual with reported interscorer reliability of .96 and split-half reliability of .84, unusually high for a projective technique.

Trites and his colleagues (47) developed a military version of the sentence completion method to a high degree of objectivity while at the same time dealing with a number of response-categories rather than just one. A scoring manual was written on the basis of 1038 test protocols which yielded interscorer agreement ranging from .80 to .96 for eight major variables, Conformity, Ego Esteem, Gregariousness, Sexuality Attitudes, Air Force-oriented Motivation, Hostility, Insecurity, and Unscorable Response. Although there is little direct evidence to support the validity of these variables with respect to the personality constructs implied, in a later factor analysis of inter-item correlations where the items had been scored dichotomously as indicating either a positive or negative attitude with reference to adjustment to flying, Trites (48) obtained four factors which were meaningfully linked to several of the original major variables.

It is instructive to note the characteristics of the sentence completion method which are responsible for achievement of satisfactory psychometric standards. Unlike the TAT, the number of discrete items can be very large, making possible an atomistic treatment of test elements without undue distortion of the technique. Where the TAT has at most 20 pictures, each with an infinite variety of complex responses possible, the sentence completion method has highly structured items for which the variety and extent of responses are relatively limited. The more circumscribed nature of the technique makes possible the development of an objective scoring manual for any variables that may be present in the response. That such psychometric treatment does not necessarily reduce the usefulness of a projective method is demonstrated by the repeatedly high validity obtained for the Rotter Incomplete Sentences Blank in assessing level of personal adjustment (39).

Constitutive Methods

The Rorschach test stands alone among projective techniques in the amount of attention, both clinical and experimental, which it has received during the past twenty years and illustrates problems encountered in scoring responses to constitutive methods. Quantitative analysis of responses to inkblots has ranged all the way from one extreme of the projective-psychometric continuum to the other. Some writers (25, 41) have pointed out how the Rorschach can be dealt with in a purely qualitative manner, emphasizing the dynamic and symbolic nature of the content and leaning heavily upon psychoanalytic theory and the intuitive skills of a clinician. Associations to inkblots are seen as only one step removed from completely free association in the psychoanalytic session. Others (20, 33) have shown how highly structured and completely objective multiple-choice methods can be applied to the study of individual differences in the perception of inkblots. And curiously enough, the same 10 inkblots are used throughout!

To what extent are these various degrees of structuring and quantification based upon sound principles of measurement theory? Does the Rorschach really span the entire projective-psychometric continuum with the high degree of power claimed by some of its proponents?

The most rudimentary form of quantification in the Rorschach is the assigning of symbols to certain kinds of responses which are then looked upon as signs pointing to various personality attributes or nosological classes. An excellent example of such a classification of qualitative signs is the analysis of verbalization described by Rapaport (35), who presents a very careful rationale for the scoring of such pathognomic verbalizations as confabulations, contaminations, confusion, absurd responses, and ideas of reference. Such signs are not additive except in the very crude sense that a number of positive signs in a single record tend to pile up in confirming the diagnosis.

The widely used "formal" scoring methods for the Rorschach represent attempts to measure the perceptual variables implicit in the response. The complex nature of the stimulus permits a wide latitude of location, of determinants, and conceptual content. Once decisions have been made as to what constitutes a discrete response, the number of such responses to a given inkblot or to all 10 Rorschach plates can be determined. Although there are some minor problems encountered in deciding when a verbalization is truly a response for purposes of scoring, one can safely assume that interscorer agreement as to number of responses (R) is quite high regardless of the judge's theoretical position. Similarly, the scoring of location, at least in its gross elements of whole, usual large detail, or small and unusual detail, does not pose serious problems in the attaining of reasonable objectivity. Aside from specialized uses of content such as Elizur's anxiety score (11), the categorizing of concepts into human, animal, and other generic classes is quite straightforward also. The greatest difficulties in achieving scoring objectivity arise in the realm of response-determinants.

Trying to determine those stimulus attributes which are responsible for eliciting a given response amounts to a kind of global psychophysics for which the general laws have yet to be worked out. Although logical in their conception, most scoring systems for determinants involve a number of highly arbitrary decisions, the wisdom of which is highly debatable. The subjectivity of the method, the influence of factors extraneous to the blots such as the examiner-subject interaction (40) and variation in style of inquiry (17) raise troublesome questions concerning the meaning of scores once achieved.

Presumably the inquiry phase of the Rorschach is designed to discover the characteristics of the inkblot which prompted the subject to give a response. The subject is asked by rather vague and indirect questions to introspect, to analyze the perceptual process and report to the examiner what about the blot suggests, for example, "a bloody finger," or "a pretty flower." A helpful subject who senses what the examiner is after may reply by saying, "It's shaped like a man's thumb and is colored red, suggesting blood." More than likely, however, the subject will say, "It just looks like it to me," leaving the examiner about where he started. And even if the subject does mention the color as playing a part in the concept, do we have any way of knowing whether the subject would have reported blood in the absence of color? How do we know it wasn't the combination of form and shading that suggested a bloody thumb? The unfortunate fact is that we simply don't know, although recent studies by Baughman (2) provide a better basis for guessing.

Zubin (52) has recognized this problem and has tried to overcome it by introducing a much more exhaustive inquiry than the usual brief, indirect questioning. In addition to asking many more questions per response, he has experimented with inquiry immediately following the response rather than waiting until all 10 inkblots have been administered. Sixty scales were constructed that could be applied in scoring a single response, provided the inquiry was sufficiently exhaustive. Five scales deal with location, six with the objective attributes of the stimulus, six with determinants or the relative importance of stimulus attributes in the formation of the percept, 14 with interpretation categories such as surface texture or strength of movement, three with organization activity, 15 with content, and 11 with other aspects of the single response such as reaction time and popularity. In addition, there are six scales dealing with variables present in the protocol as a whole. When one stops to think that Rorschach records frequently contain upward of 50 responses, the amount of energy invested in scoring 60 scales on each response is tremendous.

If a sufficient amount of information were available about the objective stimulus attributes and the correlates between these attributes and characteristics of the response, the amount of work required to utilize Zubin's system might be justified. However, the very nature of the complex stimulus confronting the subject in the form of an inkblot defies all but the crudest, global type of description as far as the specific stimulus attributes are concerned. With respect to the determinants or global psychophysics of the reported percept, even a highly trained introspectionist would be hard put to verbalize accurately the relative importance of various inkblots characteristics in forming the percept. Since the greatest value for the Rorschach is claimed to be the study of psychopathology where the subject's ability to introspect accurately may be seriously impaired, there appears to be little real hope of obtaining the kind of information necessary to use many of the scales Zubin has proposed. Although Zubin's system may not really increase the objectivity of scoring for the Rorschach, since it is comprised largely of five-point scales for recording clinical impression, his exhaustive approach immediately points out the fundamental weaknesses inherent in the standard methods of scoring.

In addition to the fact that objective scoring for most inkblot variables cannot be achieved without the use of arbitrary rules, the standard Rorschach is inherently poor as a psychometric device in some other important respects. Providing the subject with only ten inkblots and then permitting him to give as many or as few responses to each card as he wishes characteristically results in a set of unreliable scores with sharply skewed distributions, the majority of which fail to possess the properties of even rank-order measurements. One record with an R of 20 may be comprised of single responses to the first nine cards and 11 responses to Card X, while another may consist of two responses per card. Any of the usual scores with the possible exception of form level will have quite different meanings in the two contrasting protocols even though the total number of responses is constant. Add to this the difficulties arising when R varies from less than 10 to over 100, and it is easy to see why most quantitative studies involving the standard Rorschach yield confusing or negative results.

In a general review of statistical methods applied to Rorschach scores, Cronbach (8) has considered several ways in which the confounding effect of R upon most other variables can be reduced. (a) Computing percentage ratios of each variable over R; (b) removing the linear effect of R by partial regression techniques; (c) reducing the effect of R by plotting the variable against R and drawing a freehand line fitting the medians of the columns (a crude form of curvilinear partial regression); or (d) dividing the total sample into a number of subgroups that are homogeneous with respect to R before proceeding with any quantitative analysis of other variables. The usual procedure of computing percentage ratios is highly unsatisfactory because of the crude metric qualities of most Rorschach variables and the lack of a linear relationship between R and other variables. In a study of 790 cases, Fiske and Baughman (14) demonstrated that the relationships between R and other scoring categories are usually complex and nonlinear. Consequently the usual linear regression methods for removing the confounding effect of R will generally fail. Given a standard free-response Rorschach, the only procedure which has any real promise for controlling R is to form subgroups according to R and analyze each one independently. But even this very inefficient procedure leaves unanswered the serious criticism that two records with identical number of responses may be quite different in meaning due to different patterning of responses across the 10 cards.

Recognizing the serious problems in the interpretation of scores when R is a variable, most clinicians make allowance for R in a crude intuitive way. Buhler (5) goes one step further by trying to structure the test administration so that three to five responses will be given to each blot. Blake and Wilson (4) avoid the problem in part by considering only the first response to each card. However, having only 10 responses from which to obtain scores, many of which occur rather rarely, creates a whole host of new problems in attempting to achieve satisfactory standards of measurement.

Standardization of testing conditions and development of procedures for administering the Rorschach to large groups at a time represents another attempt to achieve more objectivity. Munroe (32), Harrower (20), Sells (42), and others have demonstrated the feasibility of group procedures provided one is willing to sacrifice certain aspects of the more unstructured, personalized individual Rorschach. The usual procedure is to project each inkblot on a large screen for three minutes while the subject writes down his responses in a standard booklet. The number of responses is uncontrolled, the subject is usually given a very simple, direct inquiry concerning the role of shape, color, movement, and texture, and location is indicated by drawing the outline of his percept on a miniature replica of the blot.

Most of the scoring difficulties inherent in the standard Rorschach are aggravated still further by use of such group methods. Where one at least has the opportunity for such things as the recording of verbalizations and individualized inquiry to help clear up scoring problems in the standard Rorschach, the group method deprives the examiner of all but the most superficial cues for scoring determinants, increasing further the arbitrary nature of the system.

If one uses standard paper-and-pencil aptitude tests as a model to be emulated, the most highly structured, psychometrically sound form of the Rorschach would appear to be a multiple-choice test with sufficiently standard instructions to permit its use with large groups of subjects. Under pressure of screening demands during wartime, Harrower and others (20) developed a multiple-choice version in which the subject chooses from a list of thirty concepts those three which look best to him for the particular blot in question. Fifteen of the 30 available concepts presumably indicate psychopathology while the remainder reflect normality. Harrower's own system of scoring is unusual and unnecessarily complicated. Normal answers are arbitrarily weighted "1" for any concept involving human movement, "2" for any that represent a popular response, "3" and "4" for those which involve color-form integration, and "5" for space responses. The set of abnormal answers is assigned weights varying from "6" to "9" in a similar arbitrary fashion. The total score obtained by summing the weights for the concepts chosen is confused in its meaning because of the arbitrary weighting system.

More recently, O'Reilly developed a simpler multiple-choice form with 12 choices per blot, four from psychotic records, four from neurotic records, and four from normals. The subject is asked to select the two concepts which best describe the inkblot. Answers are weighted on a three-point system with "1" for normal and "3" for psychotic. Almost complete separation of normals from psychotics was achieved in a cross-validation, although the neurotics had only slightly higher total scores than did the normals.

Another interesting, objective approach utilizing the multiple-choice format is the concept evaluation technique developed by McReynolds (29). Using Beck's list of good and poor responses according to form level (3), McReynolds selected 25 good and 25 poor concepts spread throughout the 10 Rorschach plates. The subject is shown the location of the concept and asked to indicate whether or not the inkblot looks like the concept. Generally given after a standard Rorschach as part of the testing-the-limits phase, McReynolds' concept test yields an objective, scorable, reliable, and well-defined measure of the degree to which the subject can discriminate good from poor concepts. One of the main advantages of McReynolds' test is the fact that the number of discrete stimuli (intact areas of inkblots) has been increased from 10 to 50 by breaking up the standard 10 Rorschach plates into smaller components. This point is a highly significant departure from the usual ipsative method of allowing repeated response to the same stimulus and probably accounts for the satisfactory internal consistency (split-half reliability of .82) that McReynolds obtained.

As Harrower (20) has pointed out, the highly structured multiple-choice versions of the Rorschach are no longer equivalent to the standard individual Rorschach except for the inkblots themselves. One could go a step further and question whether or not tests that have completely fixed response alternatives can even be considered projective techniques. In all respects they appear to be objective tests of perception which may have implications for the measurement of important personality traits. The course of development from an unstructured projective technique to a completely structured objective test is complete.

A New Solution

The fundamental question of how to develop psychometrically sound scoring procedures for responses to inkblots while also preserving the rich qualitative projective material of the Rorschach has been approached from a new point of view at The University of Texas.[1] The major modifications undertaken consist of greatly increasing the number of inkblots while limiting the number of responses per card to one, and extending the variety of stimulus colors, pattern, and shadings used in the original Rorschach materials. From an exploratory study it was concluded that a test containing 45 inkblots, to each of which only one response is given, would be feasible to construct and would probably tap essentially the same variables as the classical Rorschach method. Special efforts might have to be made, however, to develop materials which have high "pulling power" for responses using small details, space, and color and shading attributes to compensate for the tendency to give form-determined wholes as the first response to an inkblot.

Such a test would have several advantages over the standard Rorschach: (a) The number of responses per individual would be relatively constant. (b) Each response would be given to an independent stimulus, avoiding the weaknesses inherent in the Rorschach where all responses are lumped together regardless of whether they are given to the same or different inkblots. (c) Making a fresh start in the production of stimulus materials, especially in

[1] Initial impetus for this research was given the writer by a Faculty Research Fellowship from the Social Science Research Council, Inc., of New York. More recently the research program has been supported by a grant-in-aid from the Hogg Foundation for Mental Health, The University of Texas.

view of recent experimental studies of color, movement, shading, and other factors in inkblot perception, would yield a richer variety of stimuli capable of eliciting much more information than the original 10 Rorschach plates, And finally, (d) A parallel form of the test could easily be constructed from item-analysis data in the experimental phases of test development, and adequate estimates of reliability could be obtained independently for each major variable.

The research to date has borne out all original expectations. Two matched alternate forms, A and B, of the Holtzman Inkblot Test have been developed, each containing 45 inkblots. Two additional blots are common to both forms of the test and appear as practice blots before the others. Instructions to the subject are similar to those used in the standard Rorschach with the exception that the subject is asked to give just the primary response to each card, and a brief, simple inquiry is made after each response where necessary to clarify the location or determinants. Administration of the test is easier than the Rorschach, and the subject generally finds giving only one response per card is a fairly simple task.

Six major variables are scored for each response, while a number of minor variables or qualitative signs are scored when deemed appropriate. The major variables were selected and defined according to the following criteria: (a) The variable had to be one which could be scored for any legitimate response. Variables which only rarely occurred were set aside for the moment. (b) The variable had to be sufficiently objective to permit high scoring agreement among trained individuals. (c) The variable had to show some *a priori* promise of being pertinent to the study of personality through perception. And (d) each variable must be logically independent of the others. Location, Form Appropriateness, Form Definiteness, Color, Shading, and Movement Energy Level were selected for intensive study and provided the basis for item-analyses in the final selection and matching of inkblots for Forms A and B.

Location as a variable was defined strictly in terms of the amount of blot used and the extent to which the natural gestalt of the blot was broken up by the response. A three-point weighting system was adopted with "0" for wholes, "1" for large details, and "2" for small areas, making possible a theoretical range of scores from 0 to 90.

The scoring of color was based entirely upon the apparent primacy or importance of color, including black, gray, and white, as a response-determinant. When the subject named the color in his response, scoring was relatively simple. On rare occasions, when it was apparent that the response would have been highly improbable without the presence of color, credit for color was given even though never mentioned by the subject. A four-point system similar to the Rorschach was adopted with "0" for completely ignoring color and "3" for use of color as the sole determinant. Total scores for Color have a theoretical range from 0 to 135.

While subtle distinctions in the different uses of shading as a determinant are usually made in the Rorschach, no such differentiations are made in the Holtzman Inkblot Test. As with Color, the scoring of Shading was based solely upon the apparent primacy of shading as a determinant. Because pure shading responses are so rare, only a three-point scoring system was used, yielding a theoretical range from 0 to 90.

The scoring of movement is linked closely to content in most contemporary scoring systems for the Rorschach. Too frequently such practices lead to highly arbitrary convention as to whether or not movement is scored or how it is scored. In the Klopfer system (24), for example, "airplane" and "bat" present difficult problems. Can you be sure the airplane is flying? Even when an airplane does fly, there is no movement of its parts and no movement relative to any frame of reference unless landscape is added. Is "bat" to be scored FM for animal movement while "airplane" is scored Fm for inanimate movement when both concepts are really precision alternatives rather than uniquely different responses? The resulting picture is often highly confusing from a psychometric point of view. The essential character of the movement response is the energy level or dynamic quality of it, rather than the particular content. Leaning heavily upon Zubin (52), Sells (42), and Wilson (49), a five-point scale was adopted varying from "0" for no movement or potential for movement, through static, casual, and dynamic movement to a weight of "4" for violent movement such as whirling or exploding. Movement Energy Level ranges theoretically from "0" to 180.

Different authorities vary in the extent to which concept elaborations and specifications are confounded with the goodness of fit of the concept to the form of the inkblot. In the Holtzman Inkblot Test, Form Definiteness was defined independently of form level in the usual sense and refers solely to the definiteness or specificity of the form of the concept represented in the response, disregarding completely the characteristics of the inkblot. Working independently with a large number of concepts culled from inkblot responses, five psychologists placed them in rank order with the most form-

definite concept at the top. The independent sets of ranked concepts were then merged to yield an overall rank order for the entire
list. Cutting points were chosen so that five levels of form definiteness could be distinguished. The resulting set of examples served
as a scoring manual, with a weight of "0" for the most indefinite
concepts, such as anatomy drawing, squashed bug, or fire, and a
weight of "4" for the most definite concepts, such as Indian chief,
violin, or knight with a shield. Form Definiteness has a theoretical
range from 0 to 180.

Form Appropriateness, the last of the six major variables, is by
its very nature a subjective variable, requiring extensive preliminary
work to make scoring reasonably objective. And yet, it is this very
subjectivity which gives the variable great theoretical importance.
Beck (3) recognized the likelihood that goodness of fit of the concept
to the form of the inkblot would be closely related to degree of
contact with reality and undertook a major study of form level that
has proved to be one of the most valuable contributions to the
Rorschach. Considerable effort was spent in arriving at acceptable
standards for scoring Form Appropriateness. Different responses
to each inkblot were listed separately for each location and rated
independently by at least three judges. A seven-point scale was
used with "0" representing extremely poor fit. Although there
was good agreement of judges in most cases, a final judgment for
each response was reached only after full discussion in conference.
The resulting manual provides a guide to the scoring of Form Appropriateness on a three-point system with zero for unusually poor
form and "2" for unusually good form. Form Appropriateness can
range theoretically from 0 to 90.

The agreement among independent but well trained scorers for
a sample of 46 records proved in general to be very high: product-
moment correlations of .99 for Location, Form Definiteness, and
Movement Energy Level, .97 for Shading, .95 for Color, and .91
for Form Appropriateness. Good estimates of reliability based upon
internal consistency were obtained by using Gulliksen's matched
random subtest method (18). Correlations ranged from .80 for Form
Appropriateness to .91 for Shading. All six variables proved to be
reasonably normal and continuous in distribution. Studies are now
underway to determine the correlations between Forms A and B
with several time intervals and populations of subjects.

Once the standardization of the Holtzman Inkblot Test is complete, it should be possible to develop specialized multiple-choice
versions of test for measuring variables of particular interest. Sey-

mour Fisher and Sidney Cleveland have already had some success in developing a series of multiple-choice items to be used with 40 of Holtzman's inkblots which yields a measure of their Barrier Score (13). The particular inkblots used were selected on the basis of earlier item-analysis data so that each blot would be accompanied by three fairly acceptable choices, one representing a barrier response (such as "a knight in armor"), one representing a penetration response (such as "x-ray"), and one which was neutral (such as "flower"). The subject was asked to check the one he liked most and place a different mark on the one he liked least, leaving the third choice blank. Both the Group Rorschach and the new multiple-choice test were given to 60 college students by Fisher and Cleveland. The correlation between the two sets of Barrier Scores was .64 [2]. This fairly high correlation, coupled with the fact that the distribution of scores on the multiple-choice test was much greater than on the Rorschach and was more normally shaped, suggests that the multiple-choice Barrier Score would be superior to the measure reported earlier by Fisher and Cleveland (13).

Considerable ground has been covered in this analysis of the more common problems encountered in the objective scoring of projective techniques. The very nature of the projective hypothesis, that an individual will reveal something of his private self in the way in which he responds to ambiguous stimuli, has encouraged an almost unbelievably wide range of assessment techniques under the rubric of projective methods. In focussing upon quantitative methods of analysis and their objectivity as measured by reproducibility, a whole host of important problems concerning the meaning of projective responses has been deliberately side-stepped. Concepts of validity and their empirical determination, examiner-subject interactions, variability of response across different populations of subjects have been dealt with only tangentially if at all.

One cannot help but observe that few, if any, of these many projective devices can serve well two masters at the same time, particularly when their original purpose is exploitation of the projective hypothesis in the clinical diagnosis of personality. While not necessarily incompatible, the assumptions and historical biases inherent in the projective approach on the one hand and those in the psychometric approach on the other are at opposite extremes of a continuum defined roughly in terms of the degree of structure and control of the subject's response that is imposed by the method. An

---

[2] Personal communication from Dr. Sidney E. Cleveland.

unfortunate and bewildering array of inadequate quantification characterizes most projective techniques when there is pressure upon the projectivist to conform to the rigorous statistical standards of psychometric theory without concomitant pressure to revise the technique itself. A major challenge to psychologists interested in the objective assessment of personality is the development of psychometrically sound personality tests from available projective devices, a point made by Thurstone (45) 10 years ago which still stands today.

References

1. Auld, F., Jr., Eron, L. D., and Laffal, J. Application of Guttman's scaling method to the TAT. *Educ. psychol. Measmt.*, 1955, 15, 422-435.
2. Baughman, E. E. A comparative analysis of Rorschach forms with altered stimulus characteristics. *J. proj. Tech.*, 1954, 18, 151-164.
3. Beck, S. J. *Rorschach's test: I. Basic processes.* New York: Grune and Stratton, 1944.
4. Blake, R. R., and Wilson, G. P., Jr. Perceptual selectivity in Rorschach determinants as a function of depressive tendencies. *J. abnorm. soc. Psychol.*, 1950, 45, 459-472.
5. Buhler, C., Buhler, K., and Lefever, D. W. *Rorschach standardization studies.* Published privately by authors, 1948.
6. Cattell, R. B. *Personality: A systematic theoretical and factual study.* New York: McGraw-Hill, 1950.
7. Cronbach, L. J. and Meehl, P. E. Construct validity in psychological tests. *Psychol. Bull.*, 1955, 52, 281-302.
8. Cronbach, L. J. Statistical methods applied to Rorschach scores: A review. *Psychol. Bull.*, 1949, 46, 393-429.
9. Dana, R. H. An application of objective TAT scoring. *J. proj. Tech.*, 1956, 20, 159-163.
10. Dorken, H., Jr. The reliability and validity of spontaneous finger paintings. *J. proj. Tech.*, 1954, 18, 169-182.
11. Elizur, A. Content analysis of the Rorschach with regard to anxiety and hostility. *Rorschach Res. Exch.*, 1949, 13, 247-284.
12. Eron, L. D. Responses of women to the Thematic Apperception Test. *J. consult. Psychol.*, 1953, 17, 269-282.
13. Fisher, S. and Cleveland, S. D. *Body image and personality.* Princeton, N. J.: D. Van Nostrand, 1958.

14. Fiske, D. W. and Baughman, E. E. Relationships between Rorschach scoring categories and the total number of responses. *J. abnorm. soc. Psychol.*, 1953, 48, 25-32.
15. Frank, L. K. Projective methods for the study of personality. *J. Psychol.*, 1939, 8, 389-413.
16. Frank, L. K. *Projective methods.* Springfield, Ill.: C. C. Thomas, 1948.
17. Gibby, R. G. Examiner influence on the Rorschach inquiry. *J. consult. Psychol.*, 1952, 16, 449-455.
18. Gulliksen, H. *Theory of mental tests.* New York: Wiley and Sons, 1950.
19. Haggard, E. A. *Intraclass correlation and analysis of variance.* New York: Dryden Press, 1958.
20. Harrower, M. R. Group techniques for the Rorschach test. In Abt, L. E. and Bellak, L. (eds.) *Projective psychology.* New York: A. A. Knopf, 1950.
21. Hartman, A. A. An experimental examination of the Thematic Apperception Technique in clinical diagnosis. *Psychol. Monogr.*, 1949, 63, No. 303.
22. Holt, R. R. The Thematic Apperception Test. In Anderson, H. H. and Anderson, G. L. (eds.) *An introduction to projective techniques.* New York: Prentice-Hall, 1951.
23. Kinget, G. M. *The Drawing-Completion Test.* New York: Grune & Stratton, 1952.
24. Klopfer, B. and Kelley, D. M. The Rorschach technique. Yonkers-on-Hudson, N. Y.: World Book Company, 1942.
25. Lindner, R. M. The content analysis of the Rorschach protocol. In Abt, L. E. and Bellak, L. (eds.) *Projective psychology.* New York: A. A. Knopf, 1950.
26. McClelland, D., Atkinson, J. W., Clark, R. A., and Lowell, E. L. *The achievement motive.* New York: Appleton-Century-Crofts, 1953.
27. Macfarlane, J. W. and Tuddenham, R. D. Problems in the validation of projective techniques. In Anderson, H. H. and Anderson, G. L. (eds.) *An introduction to projective techniques.* New York: Prentice-Hall, 1951.
28. Machover, K. *Personality projection in the drawing of the human figure.* Springfield, Ill.: C. C. Thomas, 1948.
29. McReynolds, P. Perception of Rorschach concepts as related to personality deviations, *J. abnorm. soc. Psychol.*, 1951, 46, 131-141.
30. Meehl, P. E. Configural scoring. *J. consult. Psychol.*, 1950, 14, 165-171.
31. Morgan, C. D. and Murray, H. A. A method for investigating phantasies: the Thematic Apperception Test. *Arch. Neurol. and Psychiat.*, 1935, 34, 289-306.
32. Munroe, R. L. The inspection technique for the Rorschach protocol.

In Abt, L. E. and Bellak, L. (eds.) *Projective psychology.* New York: A. A. Knopf, 1950.

33. O'Reilly, B. O. The objective Rorschach; a suggested modification of Rorschach technique. *J. clin. Psychol.*, 1956, 12, 27-31.
34. Pascal, G. R. and Suttell, B. J. *The Bender-Gestalt Test.* New York: Grune & Stratton, 1950.
35. Rapaport, D., Gill, M., and Schafter, R. *Diagnostic psychological testing. Vol. II.* Chicago: The Year Book Publishers, 1946.
36. Rosenzweig, S. The picture-association method and its application in a study of reactions to frustration. *J. Pers.*, 1945, 14, 3-23.
37. Rosenzweig, S. Idiodynamics in personality theory with special reference to projective methods. *Psychol. Rev.*, 1951, 58, 213-223.
38. Rotter, J. B. and Willerman, B. The Incomplete Sentence Test as a method of studying personality. *J. consult. Psychol.*, 1947, 11, 43-48.
39. Rotter, J. B. Word association and sentence completion methods. In Anderson, H. H. and Anderson, G. L. (eds.) *An introduction to projective techniques.* New York: Prentice-Hall, 1951.
40. Sarason, S. *The clinical interaction.* New York: Harper & Bros., 1954.
41. Schafer, R. *Psychoanalytic interpretation in Rorschach testing.* New York: Grune and Stratton, 1954.
42. Sells, S. B., Frese, F. J., Jr., and Lancaster, W. H. *Research on the psychiatric selection of flying personnel. II. Progress on development of SAM Group Ink-Blot Test.* Project No. 21-37-002, No. 2, Randolph Field, Texas: USAF School of Aviation Medicine, April, 1952.
43. Shneidman, E. S. *Thematic test analysis.* New York: Grune & Stratton, 1951.
44. Stein, M. I. *The Thematic Apperception Test.* Cambridge, Mass.: Addison-Wesley, 1955.
45. Thurstone, L. L. The Rorschach in psychological science. *J. abnorm. soc. Psychol.*, 1948, 43, 471-475.
46. Tomkins, S. S. *The Thematic Apperception Test.* New York: Grune & Stratton, 1947.
47. Trites, D. K., Holtzman, W. H., Templeton, R. C., and Sells, S. B. *Psychiatric screening of flying personnel: Research on the SAM Sentence Completion Test.* Project No. 21-0202-0007, No. 3, Randolph Field, Texas: USAF School of Aviation Medicine, July, 1953.
48. Trites, D. K. *Psychiatric screening flying personnel: Evaluation of assumptions underlying interpretation of sentence completion tests.* Report No. 55-33. Randolph Field, Texas: USAF School of Aviation Medicine, March, 1955.
49. Wilson, G. P. *Intellectual indicators in the Rorschach test.* Unpubl. doctoral dissertation, The University of Texas, Austin, Texas, 1952.
50. Witkin, H. A., Lewis, H. B., Hertzman, M., Machover, K., Meissner, P. B., and Wapner, S. *Personality through perception.* New York: Harper & Bros., 1954.

51. Young, R. D., Jr. *The effect of the interpreter's personality on the interpretation of TAT protocols.* Unpubl. doctoral dissertation, The University of Texas, Austin, Texas, 1953.
52. Zubin, J. and Eron, L. *Experimental abnormal psychology.* (Preliminary Edition) New York: New York State Psychiatric Institute, 1953.

VIII

An Approach to the Objective Assessment of Successful Leadership *

BERNARD M. BASS
Louisiana State University

"HAD I BEEN PRESENT at the creation," Alphonso the Learned (1221-1284 A.D.) quipped, "I would have given some useful hints for the better ordering of the universe." Alphonso could have made the same comment today about the chaos in leadership theory and research.

The construction of typologies often represents first attempts to bring some order, for understanding of a phenomenon usually can begin only after some of its important elements are guessed. In the field of leadership, we were abundantly blessed with a wealth of guesses. Fisher (27) listed some 19 distinct ways of typing leaders revealed in the literature from 1915 to 1948, for leadership has been a topic covering a wide variety of phenomena, many only remotely related to each other. But these typologies are a mere beginning compared to the one hundred or more available definitions.

One cluster of these defines the leader as an individual in a given office. *Status* is a more useful way to describe variations among individuals in position and in behaviors due to their different positions since it is commonly employed for the purpose by those work-

* This work was aided by funds from the Louisiana State University Council on Research and Contract N7 ONR 35609.

ing in the fields of organization, group behavior, and industrial psychology. A second cluster of definitions emphasize the leader as focus of attention, as representative of the group. Again, there already is available a widely used concept, *esteem*, the value of members to the group regardless of their position.

The leader often is defined simply as anyone who engages in leadership acts. But, what is a leadership act?

LEADERSHIP DEFINED

Agreeing with Bowman (21) and Gibb (33), I consider leadership an interaction between members of a group. Although the groups are usually face-to-face, this is not considered a necessary condition for the occurrence of leadership. It is rather a usual condition. Leadership occurs *when one member's behavior is concerned with changing another member's behavior.*

This definition is close to those of Gurnee (35) and LaPiere and Farnsworth (46) who defined leaders as agents of change; as persons whose acts affect other people more than other people affect them. It also conforms to Smith's (65) conceptualization of controlled interaction, and with those defining leadership as influence and as behavior making a difference among groups.

A may try to change *B's* behavior; this is *attempted* leadership. *B* may actually change his behavior as a consequence of *A's* attempt; this is *successful* leadership. *B's* change may result in *B's* own goal attainment; this is *effective* leadership (38).

This conceptualization differs from Hemphill's (39) mainly in the kinds of changes included in the meaning of leadership. For Hemphill, leadership acts are limited to those concerning alteration of consistent patterns of interaction within the group. Excluded are: signals, task analyses, expressions of attitudes, information giving or asking, requests of suggestions, proposals, and acceptance or rejection of earlier suggestions. I have chosen a much broader definition. Each of these acts excluded by Hemphill generally will be regarded as leadership although it will depend on the function of the specific act.

What are the ways in which *A* can change *B's* behavior? *A* can alter *B's* drives both in strength and direction. Stated in different terms, *A* can change what *B* regards as his goals and the importance of these goals. By pointing out the challenge and rewards of studying law, a professor may arouse or strengthen in a student strong interest in a law career. A Caesar or a football coach may arouse his men to fighting pitch with a speech before battle. For us, these are acts of leadership. Lowering of motivation may also be included. A baseball manager providing strong, fatherly reassurance to his "too-tense" team near the end of the race for the league championship is engaged in a leadership act.

A can strengthen or weaken relatively responses of B to various stimuli. A can change B's behavior by reinforcing certain habits or reducing the strength of these tendencies. Included among these habits are abilities (habits where we evaluate the response in terms of success in goal attainment) and attitudes, faiths, and beliefs (habits where the response is towards what stimulated it). Another way of describing the same phenomenon is to state that A can alter B's abilities to cope with his immediate problem. Concretely, a sales manager who informs his subordinate of the necessity of submitting accurate, clear, daily reports of his activities and then occasionally compliments the salesman on his reports when done well and criticizes items when not presented correctly, is strengthening a habit pattern to submit desired reports. This is leadership. A counselor of a group in therapy who fails to "reward" a neurotic member for his emotional outbursts nor show alarm, may be serving to reduce the strength of a behavioral tendency by the neurotic to exhibit such behavior. Therefore, the counselor is displaying leadership.

ARBITRARY RESTRICTIONS ON THE MEANING OF LEADERSHIP

Changing the immediate needs of B and B's ability to satisfy his motivation are not the only ways of modifying B's behavior. For ex-example, altering the integrity of the central nervous system of the organism, B, via surgery, injury, drugs, etc., will modify B's behavior. Also, B's behavior may be changed by changing the circumstances stimulating B. Alterations of the integrity of an organism's central nervous system, and manipulations of the stimulating situation are arbitrarily excluded, by definition, as leadership acts. Psychosurgery or drug therapy are not leadership acts—by definition. Changing slides projected on a screen, as such, is not a leadership act—by definition. On the other hand, teaching and psychotherapy which are not usually considered leadership processes, must be included in what I have defined as leadership, because they cannot be differentiated by definition from the more general concept, leadership, as defined here. But, leadership, as defined, can be distinguished from a number of related concepts such as behavioral contagion, influence, followership and vicarious experience. Space limitations prohibit discussion here.

Titles and office-holding involve much more than leadership. It is necessary to distinguish between the leadership displayed by the foreman from all the behavior of a foreman, for foremen shuffle papers, compute output figures, check inventories, and operate equipment and so on. If leadership is defined as anything done by one who holds an office or by one who is designated a leader, we would find ourselves trying to develop principles encompassing almost all human behavior.

MEASUREMENT OF SUCCESSFUL LEADERSHIP

Table 1 illustrates many of the possible ways of measuring successful leadership.

TABLE 1

SOME WAYS OF ASSESSING LEADER BEHAVIOR

| | *Assessor* | | |
Mode of Assessment	*Self*	*Other Members of Groups*	*Observations, Records and Instruments*
Historical	Autobio-graphical	Recollection	Historical Documents; Biographies, Case Histories, Interviews
Selective	Announcement of Candidacy	Sociometry Voting	Nominations and Election Results
Job Placement	Usurpation	Cooptation Appointment to Office	Appointments and other Administrative Acts
Ratings and Check Lists	Self	Superior-Buddy-Peer-Subordinates	Observed Roles Played; Frequency of Acts; Test Results
Projective	Projective Sketches	Projective Sketches	Thematic Analysis of Content of Essays
Effect on Others		Example: Satis-faction with Group Effort	Observed Changes in Groups
			Overt Changes in Members and Groups

Historical

Naturalistic case-histories are a common approach employed by many social scientists, such as applied anthropologists, to assess leadership in primitive societies, industrial groups, and volunteer agencies. Often associated with this process is intensive interviewing of present or former members of the group to obtain their recollections and present opinions. Heavy reliance on such methods can be found in the works of Elton Mayo (48) and F. J. Roethlisberger (60) or Burleigh Gardner (32).

Analyses of case histories, as such, were employed by Ackerson (1) and Brown (22). Examination of biographies to assess leadership was exemplified by Cox's study (25) of the biographies of 300 geniuses. Less formal attempts of this sort began with the first historical writing. For example, *Plutarch's Lives* paired Roman and Greek leaders to assess each member of a pair in comparison with the other.

Selective

Stogdill (66) listed 28 major studies assessing leadership by choice of associates suggesting as most exemplary the work of Jennings (44). Many of these actually focused on esteem, not leadership, *per se*. Although given much prominence only in the past two decades by the sociometrists, the procedure is found in Terman's 1904 leadership experiment (70). Nominations by observers outside the group have also been commonly employed (e.g., Burks, (23)).

Studies of election results have been of concern to political scientists, public opinion analysts, and related social scientists. Attention here is often centered on voting behavior rather than on leader behavior stimulating the voting. However, Sanford's (61) work illustrates how political elections are related to the personality needs of the voter and the stimulus properties of the office-seekers.

Job Placement

Coup d'etat, other forms of usurpation, as well as observed and recorded legitimate administrative acts provide further means of assessing successful leadership. Appointment to office and tenure also are guides to identifying and studying leader behavior. Stogdill (66) mentioned 33 psychological studies of persons occupying positions of leadership varying from fraternity presidents or government administrators. But most of these are studies of status, rather than of leadership as I define it.

Ratings and Check Lists

Most common at present is the use of specially developed rating procedures and check lists for studying leader behavior. For example, the work of Stogdill and Coons (67) and associates illustrates the factorial approach to construction of behavior check lists beginning with empirical surveys and concluding with theoretically-oriented, factorially independent scales of leader behavior. These scales have been used to describe leaders by superiors, associates and subordinates as well as by leaders themselves. The widespread use of peer ratings or buddy ratings in the military services are another example of ratings to assess leader behavior (42).

More objective and theoretically-based in their mutual construction are the categorizations of roles by Benne and Sheats (17) and the interaction process analysis of Bales (4). In the same class is Thelen's (71) description of a method of categorizing behavior in groups based on Bion's work-emotionality concepts. In Benne and Sheat's methods, observers note which of many defined roles are played by the various members of the group. For example, successful discussion leaders of initially leaderless discussions reliably have been observed playing the roles of initiator-contributor, opinion-giver, elaborator, compromiser, orienter-evaluator, energizer and encourager (7). Bales' procedures reduce subjectivity further. Each action by a member is categorized in one of twelve types falling into four areas. The frequency each member exhibits each type of behavior can be measured with high observer reliability. Again, leaders in initially leaderless discussions are found to exhibit certain of these behaviors with high frequency particularly those in the areas of attempting answers and positive socio-emotional responses.

Tests

Early attempts to describe leader behavior were characterized by the "armchair" listing of traits found among successful leaders by the leaders themselves, by observers, or by surveyors of the leadership literature. Another similar indirect approach was based on administering personality inventories and other psychological tests to designated leaders inferring leader behavior from the traits found to predominate among the leaders (66).

Projective Techniques

Torrance (73) has presented ambiguous sketches of leader-follower situations to groups. The stories told by the groups appear to provide reliable indices of the overt effectiveness of leadership within the group. Indirect information about leader behavior has also been gathered by administering the Thematic Apperception Test to business executives (40). My Job Contest (26) involving the analyses of themes of essays by workers at General Motors submitted as contest entries represents still another projective approach to studying leadership and behavior in groups.

NEED FOR OBJECTIVE ASSESSMENT

If we are primarily concerned with understanding, predicting, and controlling leader behavior, as such, it becomes desirable to develop ways of "sensing" the behavior itself. On the plane of observables (51) are needed the similar sense impressions corresponding statistically to the constructs. The bridge from the theoretical model to the protocols of the laboratory will be firmest if subjective impressions do not intervene between the theoretical constructs and the "world of facts." The facts about behavior are vague. They are doubly difficult to deal with when gained "secondhand" from observers or group members' reports. We desire operations definite and quantitatively precise if possible; operations repeatable and objective. In order to study leadership experimentally, we should like to anchor our definition in leader behavior measured sufficiently objectively to avoid being tampered with by observers' or participants' biases—unless we want to study biases.

Dangers of Subjectivity

Reliance on observers, participants, or subjects' mediation of the raw data to be examined give rise to dangers. Viteles (76) illustrates the error possible in depending on case history and interview studies. The "Hawthorne" investigators attributed much of the control of behavior in a bankwiring room to an informal organization which demanded conformance to norms or common standards. The workers did not reveal to interviewers their animosity toward management because parts were re-engineered when time studies were in error in favor of the workers, nor did they report their "stretchout" of work which was due to fear of being laid off in the depressed economy.

Even categorizing observed behaviors falls short of desire. Using the same 13 categories of behavior (a modification of Bales' classification), Bell (16) studied leader behavior in 10 groups in a laboratory in a northern university and 10 groups in a southern school of the same size. Significant differences appeared in the categorized behavior of emergent leaders in each location. Some of this may have been due to overt behavior differences, but some of it was probably a function of observers. Again, Borgatta (20) asked subjects to write how they would react to the Rosenzweig Picture Frustration Test; then the subjects showed how they would act; finally, they were placed in the situation. There were no significant correlations among the three methods of response. Similarly, Halpin (36) reported little relationship between a leader's beliefs about what he should do and what his subordinates said he actually did. The picture is complicated further by the observation that members of a group when stating their own opinions tend to compromise what they privately "sense" and what they perceive to be the group opinion on the matter (34). Mencius (372 B.C.-289 B.C.) recognized the difficulties of depending on judgments of leader behavior by their immediate superiors alone. In paraphrase, his advice to heads of state was:

"When all those about you, the ruler, say that a man is talented, do not immediately rush to promote him. Only after his subordinates say so also should you examine him more fully as a candidate for promotion. In the same way, do not rush to demote a man on the evaluation of his superiors alone."

Once we have a rationale for understanding behavior, we must have measurements to promote and communicate our understandings.

. . . . the language of number sometimes provides a certain minimum standard of integrity in communication, without which cooperation of human beings on some kinds of subjects is almost fruitless . . . Lord Kelvin declared, if you can't measure it, you don't know what you are talking about. (78, p. 366, 368).

OBJECTIVE MEASUREMENT OF INFLUENCE

Many of the early social psychology experiments on suggestibility provided objective assessments of leadership. The leader usually was the investigator; the followers, his child subjects. For example, Triplett (74) pretended to throw a ball into the air. Then, he determined the percentage (about 50 per cent) of fourth to eighth grade children who actually saw the ball go up and disappear. Binet (18) assessed the susceptibility to influence by having subjects draw lines indicating their judgment of the length of stimulus lines. The stimuli increased in size up to a certain point. The judgments of the suggestible subjects continued to increase even after the stimuli presented by the leader, Binet, did not increase.

In more recent years, the classic studies by Sherif (63) and Asch (3) are similar illustrations of objective approaches to the study of influence. Sherif showed how subject's reports of the movement of a pinpoint of light (actually stationary) could be altered by his hearing other subjects' judgments of the same autokinetic effect. Asch found that some subjects could be made to declare the shorter of two lines was actually longer, if all other members of their group (all experimental "plants") declared such was the case.

Objectivity in assessment of group products also has been common in social psychology. For example, Mayer (47) and many later investigators such as Weston and English (77), compared the speed and accuracy of performance of children on selected tasks when working alone and in the presence of co-workers, finding that presence of others facilitated performance. In recent years have come comparisons of supervisors of more productive departments with supervisors whose departments are lower in productivity or other objective indices of group performance (45).

Studies of communication nets initiated by Bavelas (15) are another example of the development of objectivity in studying influence and leadership. All communications between members of groups are restricted to the passing of symbols or notes. Objective analyses of who passes what to whom are the basis for testing hypotheses.

Objective Approaches to Measuring Leadership

The possibilities of developing relevant, objective, controlled laboratory operations to study leadership is supported by research evidence in a number of ways. Aikman, Lorge, et al, (2) presented the same problem at four levels of "remoteness from reality." The problem was to plan the movement of five men across a "mined" road. The quality of solutions were equally good at all four levels: verbal description, photographic presentation, miniature scale model not allowing manipulation, and a scale model allowing manipulation.

A review of validity studies of the leaderless group discussion concluded that observed success as a leader in this restricted, artificial, brief situation correlated with the leadership performance of the same persons in real life (6). Flanagan, Levy, et al, (28) among several investigators, showed the possibility of constructing highly reliable situational tests for evaluating success as a noncommissioned officer. The tests were based on critical incidents analyses of the leadership positions and included initially leader-less emergencies, leaderless small job management, as well as combat and reconnaissance leadership where the examinee was designated as leader in the situation. Test performance predicted merit as a noncom ($r = .46$). Specific acts of effective and successful leadership were observed and recorded. The average agreement among observers' reports was .83.

Maximum control of experimental conditions has been achieved where the group, itself, is simulated. Each member is stimulated in the same way while he believes he is behaving as a member of a group. Typical of such studies is one by Raven and Rietsema (58). Members of the simulated groups are separated. Each is told he is performing a different aspect of the task, but all actually do the same job. Standard notes are sent to each subject although he thinks, they come from the other members. Every subject thus receives the same "group" experience.

AN OBJECTIVE APPROACH TO ASSESSING SUCCESSFUL LEADERSHIP

Change in member judgment as a result of interaction with others has been studied on a number of tasks. For example, Jenness (43) examined the changes in the judgment of the number of beans in a bottle. Asch's (3) and Sherif's (63) techniques, mentioned earlier, are similar examples. Timmons (72) appears to be the first to have used the differences in correlations among ranked judgments to quantify the effects of group influence. He found the accuracy in ranking solutions to a problem (as measured by the correlation of subjects' judgments with the correct judgments) was greater among subjects given the opportunity to discuss the problem with others. Preston and Heinz (56) and Hare (37) used the correlations among judgments by members of a group to measure stability of judgment, initial or final agreement among members, and degree of acceptance of the group decision. Talland (64) went one step further, finding that the correlation between a member's initial judgments and the final group decision was higher among those rated as leaders.

These within-subject correlational procedures offer a way of objectively determining the successful leadership of each group member as well as related indices of group behavior. They enable us to find objectively how much each member of a group changed every other's opinion. At Louisiana State University, methods have been standardized as follows: On each of a series of test problems, a group of subjects privately rank order their initial decisions about the true order of familiarity of five words. Or they may be asked to rank five cities according to size of population. Or they may have to decide on the order of merit of solutions to problems in human relations case histories. Then, they carry on a discussion to reach a group decision. Finally, they privately register their own rankings again.

Three measures of successful leadership—public, private, and relative—are derived from the correlations between members in opinion before and after discussion:

Successful public leadership of a member is how much more the group decision correlates with his, rather than other members' initial decisions added to how much the final group decision is like the designated member's final ranking compared to how much he had disagreed with others initially.

Successful private leadership is how much less a member changes his rankings than do other members added to how much more the other members' rankings correlate with his rankings after discussion than before.

Relative success as a leader is how much more the final decisions of other members correlate with the initial decision of a designated member compared with how much the final decision of the designated member correlates with the initial decisions of the other members.

The total amount of absolute public or private leadership turns out to be algebraically equivalent to the coalescence of a group (how much members increase in agreement with each other). Total relative successful leadership of all members combined is always zero.

Methods of Data Processing

Earliest data collection was by paper and pencil (8). Subsequent to these initial analyses, data have been collected either by asking subjects to register their opinions on specially prepared IBM mark sense cards or directly into a specially constructed analog computer (12). The cards are processed on an IBM 650 and auxiliary equipment to yield the required correlations. If the analog computer is used, the experimenter reads the correlations directly from an ammeter immediately following each problem.

MEASUREMENT RELIABILITY

Table 2 shows the results for four analyses of the split-half reliability of the three measures of successful leadership based on performance of 10 or 12 problems, or about an hour of testing.

Motivation of subjects was varied by selecting for the highly motivated sample those rating themselves as strongly interested in entering advanced ROTC, then collecting the leadership measures as part of an entrance screening examination. The samples of 60 subjects of medium and low motivation were selected by the same means. The motivation questionnaire was validated in several ways; for example, by finding that it accurately predicted formal application to advanced ROTC, as well as by a tendency to appear for the examination. The fourth sample of 95 subjects was composed of arbitrarily selected night school students under no particular extrinsic motivation to perform well.

Except for one reversal, a consistent trend emerged. The lower the extrinsic motivation of subjects, the more consistent the leadership measurements. To maximize consistent individual differences in successful leadership, it appears necessary to examine subjects under no extrinsic compulsion to perform well (11). Two or three hours testing would raise reliabilities to where the measures could be used diagnostically.

TABLE 2

CORRECTED SPLIT-HALF RELIABILITIES
OF MEASURES OF LEADERSHIP AS A FUNCTION OF MOTIVATION

Measure	Motivation			
	High	Medium	Low	Low
	N=135	N=60	N=60	N=95
	K=10	K=10	K=10	K=12
Public successful leadership	.32	.50	.59	.55
Private successful leadership	.30	.44	.75	.52
Relative successful leadership	.48	.29	.61	.64

N = number of subjects
K = number of problems administered
For 133 df, $p < .01$ when $r = .22$
For 93 df, $p < .01$ when $r = .26$
For 58 df, $p < .01$ when $r = .33$

MEASUREMENT VALIDITY

This examination will be similar in some respects to an earlier publication reviewing validity studies of the leaderless group discussion technique (6). Again, construct validity will be considered. The construct validity of the three measures purporting to gauge successful leadership will be compared. Logically, theory (7) suggested that:

1. Ability to solve the group's problems should be higher among those with higher assessments of what was purported to be successful leadership.

2. Esteem among associates should be higher among those with higher assessments.

3. Those with higher successful leadership scores should be observed by others as exhibiting more successful leadership.

4. Those who attempt more leadership should exhibit higher assessed successful leadership.

Ability and Successful Leadership

Table 3 shows the correlations between 255 subjects' purported success as leaders and their abilities as assessed by: (1) the American Council on Education Psychological Examination (ACE); a college entrance intelligence test; (2) by their average initial accuracy in judging the familiarity of the words of 10 problems; [1] and (3) the subjects' academic standing through the sophomore year. (The effects of subsample differences in motivation and status were removed by obtaining correlations within subsamples and then averaging the results.)

TABLE 3

CORRELATIONS BETWEEN ABILITY AND THREE OBJECTIVE
MEASURES OF SUCCESSFUL LEADERSHIP

Measures of Ability	Successful Leadership		
	Public	Private	Relative
ACE	.14*	.14*	.29**
Initial Accuracy	.21**	.21**	.36**
Academic Average	.12*	.12*	.19**

** $p < .01$
* $p < .05$

[1] Initial accuracy of a subject was the rank order correlation between his initial rankings of the familiarity of the set of 5 words and the correct rank order of familiarity of the words.

For all 255 subjects, a significant correlation (at the 1 per cent level) was found between the ACE and relative successful leadership. Relations with the other leadership measures also tended to be positive but somewhat less significant. Consistent with the higher reliability of the leadership measures, the correlations (not shown) were higher when subjects were lower in motivation. Intelligence seemed especially important to relative success as a leader among groups where members were more equal in status ($r = .41$).

Average correlations of .21, .21, and .36 between initial accuracy and the three measures of successful leadership—public, private, and relative—were found for the 255 subjects. Again, the correlations were higher (.34, .40, and .46) when motivation was low.

Academic performance showed the same pattern of relationships with successful leadership but the average correlations, although significant because of the large number of cases, were not much above zero.

Generally, the results were consistent with the proposition that ability to solve the group's problems should be higher, (but not too much higher) among those with higher assessments of leadership supporting the contention that the assessments truly were measuring leadership. The relations are strongest between ability and relative successful leadership in contrast to the other two measures of successful leadership.

Esteem and Successful Leadership

Table 4 shows the correlations between the subjects' successful leadership during testing; their esteem as rated by their ROTC Tactical Officers based on observations over a two-year period; and their esteem as measured by their peers during the situational testing.

The members of each group tested rated each other on a five point scale on how much loss to the group's effectiveness would be

TABLE 4

CORRELATIONS BETWEEN ESTEEM AND THREE OBJECTIVE
MEASURES OF SUCCESSFUL LEADERSHIP

Measures of Esteem	Successful Leadership		
	Public	Private	Relative
Tactical Officer's Evaluation	.13*	.14*	.15*
Esteem by Peers	.28**	.31**	.36**

** $p < .01$
* $p < .05$

incurred if a particular member left the group. A member's self-rating provided a measure of his self-esteem. The average rating others in his group assigned him provided the measure of esteem by peers.

Low positive correlations, again higher where members were low in motivation, were found between the three leadership measures and the Tactical Officers' ratings. The correlations were lower than commonly found when observers' ratings of successful leadership in initially leaderless discussions have been compared with Tactical Officers' ratings (6). Part of the difference may be due to the lower reliability of the objective data used here.

Esteem-by-peers was significantly related (.28, .31, and .36) for all 255 subjects to the three measures of successful leadership. They also showed the inverse relation with motivation. Thus, the corresponding correlations (not shown) for only those subjects of low motivation were .32, .42, and .54. The results are consistent with earlier positive correlations between esteem and the objective measures of public and private success in leadership among 95 night school students (10).

Again, the findings suggest that the leadership measures have validity as such. Of the three measures, relative success as a leader seems most valid as judged by its higher relation with esteem-by-others.

Rated vs. Actual Success as a Leader

At the end of the test, each member of a group checked items about whether or not every other member had attempted to motivate others and had not been ignored. The items were: aroused the interest of others; talked about the importance of group success; put others' suggestions into operation; changed desires of others; made others feel free to take part; inspired others; increased general level of activity; encouraged others to participate; and supported others.

These items were intermixed on the check list with a set of items concerning success in initiating structure: made the situation clear to others; gave others the information they wanted; proposed courses of actions others wanted; helped the interactions among others; made plans acceptable to others; coordinated others' activities; and offered new solutions acceptable to others. (See Stogdill and Coons (67) for a detailed discussion of initiating structure).

The average number of motivation items checked by all other

members as descriptive of a subject's behavior provided the subject's subjective score as a motivator. Similarly, the average number of initiation items checked for a subject by the others provided a subjective estimate of the member's success as an initiator. Average correlations of .24, .31, and .28 were obtained between rated success as a motivator and the three measures of actual success as a leader. Average correlations of .25, .33, and .30 were found between rated success as an initiator and the three measures of actual success. High motivation reduced the relation for relative success as a leader but not for the other objective measures.

Attempted vs. Successful Leadership

Attempted leadership, measured by the average time in seconds a subject spent talking during each discussion, exhibited reliabilities of .71, .91, and .92 with decreasing motivation (11). In order to be successful as a leader, a member of a group must attempt leadership. A positive correlation is expected between the two independently obtained measurements if both are truly measuring attempted and successful leadership respectively.

Significant correlations of .17, .15, and .28 were found for the 255 subjects. Again, probably because of higher reliability among those of lower motivation, slightly higher correlations of .19, .19, and .33 were obtained with the 60 subjects of lower motivation.

Construct Validity of Measures of Successful Leadership

Thus, we compared the construct validity of the measures of successful leadership by examining the correlations between the measures and the ability of 255 subjects, their esteem, their rated success as leaders, and their attempted leadership.

The initial accuracy and intelligence of the subjects predicted to some extent their success as leaders, as expected, if the leadership measures were truly measuring leadership. Esteem of members by their peers in the group discussions and by their tactical officers in ROTC were also positively related with the leadership measures, as expected. Rated success correlated significantly with actual success as a leader and as expected, those with higher measured success as leaders, attempted more leadership.

Generally, these correlations were higher when subjects were lower in motivation. This conformed to the fact that the reliability of the leadership measures was higher when motivation was lower. The correlations were also higher generally for relative successful

leadership than for the absolute measures, public and private success as leaders.[2]

Testing Hypotheses About Leadership

The purpose behind developing the objective measures of successful leadership was to test by suitable experiments a variety of
hypotheses about leadership generated by a theory of leadership I
have constructed. Here are some of the results:

The theory suggested and results indicated that more successful
leadership was displayed in 51 groups as problems grew more
difficult regardless of other factors.

According to the theory, ineffective groups should show more
change subsequently in who exhibits successful leadership. A different outcome emerged in an empirical test with these measurements.
All groups became or remained effective as long as they did not
change leaders "in midstream." The results suggest that it may be
more important for groups to reach early agreement on who shall
lead regardless of whom they agree upon.

A third analysis of related data tested the proposition that the
increased effectiveness of a group is related positively to the amount
of successful leadership that occurs. These results emerged mainly
where all members were equal in control and were more motivated.

Our findings in these studies support a variety of other propositions concerning successful leadership. Many of these are well-
documented by other investigators examining the same issues with
different techniques. Others are not. Some are "obvious," "reasonable," "common-sense;" others are not. Some seem immediately
applicable; others are facts to be filed for future reference.

Further Evaluation

Our method for measuring successful leadership is relatively simple
compared to other similar objective techniques. For example, in
one such similar method (75), individuals were measured operating
alone in their response to the autokinetic phenomenon. Then t-
tests were run between successive combinations of paired members
and those found significantly different from each other were tested
in pairs. Leadership occurred if one member did not change, yet
members were significantly apart initially, but were not significantly
apart finally. While the definition of leadership used is almost

[2] For a more detailed report on the construct validity of the three measures, refer
to (31).

identical with the one described in this paper, the method of measurement appears more complex and expensive.

Some other advantages of our method of studying behavior in groups by measuring the correlations of opinion before and after interaction include the fact that the scores relate immediately to definitions of the theory of leadership and the relationships found among the measurements may be used to examine hypotheses generated from this theory. Also, the measures are continuous, and can be defined in algebraic notation. Moreover, each trial, providing a single measure, is short and self-contained, permitting application of repeated measurement designs. Again, the procedure is widely generalized in that the problems presented to the groups can be drawn from almost any type of subject-matter requiring decision-making or the making of ranked judgments. The measurements, in turn, while using widely varying content for problem-solving, will remain directly comparable. Subsequently, the outcome based on the relations among the measures yield generalizations of significance in the study of group phenomena, as such.

The group interaction studied need not necessarily involve oral discussion or even face-to-face contact. All communications among members could be by written messages or by any devised symbol system without any loss of the effectiveness of the technique.

The data lend themselves to both digital and analog high-speed computer analysis. It is possible to proceed directly from the data collection session to actual machine processing without any intermediate clerical work.

Yet, the process is "artificial," or unnatural and restrictive. But for various purposes it may be worth the loss in "naturalness." However, the procedure is not like the Bales' response classifying technique which can be used to study groups operating under "everyday" conditions. The method can only be applied as a testing situation to such natural groups. The natural groups can be studied where the method is introduced to them as a screening examination or a team work test.

References

1. Ackerson, L. Children's behavior problems: Vol. 2. *Relative importance and intercorrelation among traits.* Chicago: U. Chicago Press, 1942.
2. Aikman, L., Lorge, I., Tuckman, J., et al. Differences in the quality of the solution to a practical field problem at various degrees of remoteness from reality. *Amer. Psychol.,* 1953, 8, 311 (a).
3. Asch, S. E. The doctrine of suggestion, prestige and imitation in social psychology. *Psychol. Rev.,* 1948, 55, 250-276.
4. Bales, R. F. *Interaction process analysis.* Cambridge: Addison-Wesley Press, 1950.
5. Bass, B. M. Situational tests: II. Variables of the leaderless group discussion. *Educ. psychol. Measmt.,* 1951, 11, 196-207.
6. Bass, B. M. The leaderless group discussion. *Psychol. Bull.,* 1954, 51, 465-492.
7. Bass, B. M. Outline of a theory of leadership and group behavior. Technical Report 1, Contract N7 ONR 35609, Louisiana State University, Baton Rouge, Louisiana, 1955.
8. Bass, B. M. Consistent differences in the objectively measured performance of members and groups. Technical Report 3. Contract N7 ONR 35609, Louisiana State Univ., Baton Rouge, La., July, 1955.
9. Bass, B. M. Interrelations among measurements of member and group performance. Technical Report 4. Contract N7 ONR 35609, Louisiana State Univ., Baton Rouge, La., August, 1955.
10. Bass, B. M. Interrelations among the measurements of leadership and associated behavior. Technical Report 5. Contract N7 ONR 35609, Louisiana State Univ., Baton Rouge, La., December, 1955.
11. Bass, B. M. Effects of motivation on consistency of performance in groups. Technical Report 16. Contract N7 ONR 35609, Louisiana State Univ., Baton Rouge, La., January, 1958.
12. Bass, B. M., Gaier, E. L., Farese, F. J. and Flint, A. W. An objective method for studying behavior in groups. *Psychol, Rept. Monogr.,* 1957, 3, 265-280.

164

13. Bass, B. M., Pryer, M. W., Gaier, E. L., and Flint, A. W. Interacting effects of control motivation, group practice, and problem difficulty on attempted leadership. *J. abnorm. soc. Psychol.*, 1958, 56, 352-358.
14. Bass, B. M., Wurster, C. R., Doll, P. A., and Clair, D. Situational and personality factors in leadership among sorority women. *Psychol. Monogr.*, 1953, 67, No. 366.
15. Bavelas, A. Communication patterns in task-oriented groups. In Lerner, D. & Lasswell, H. D. (Eds.) *The policy sciences.* Stanford, Calif.: Stanford U. Press, 1951.
16. Bell, G. B. Methodology in leadership research. *Amer. Psychol.*, 1954, 8, 329 (a).
17. Benne, K. D. and Sheats, P. Functional roles of group members. *J. soc. Issues*, 1948, 4, 41-49.
18. Binet, A. *La suggestibilite.* Paris: Schleicher Bros., 1900.
19. Blocksma, D. D. Leader flexibility in group guidance situations. *Educ. psychol. Measmt.*, 1949, 9, 531-535.
20. Borgatta, E. F. An analysis of three levels of response: and approach to some relationships among dimensions of personality. *Sociometry*, 1951, 14, 267-316.
21. Bowman, L. E. Approach to the study of leadership. *J. appl. Psychol.*, 1927, 11, 315-321.
22. Brown, S. C. Some case studies of delinquent girls described as leaders. *Brit. J. Educ. Psychol.*, 1931, 1, 162-179.
23. Burks, F. W. Some factors related to social success in college. *J. soc. Psychol.*, 1938, 9, 125-140.
24. Carter, L. F. Evaluating the performances of individuals as members of small groups. *Personn. Psychol.*, 1954, 7, 477-484.
25. Cox, C. M. The early mental traits of three hundred geniuses. Genetic studies of genius. Vol. II. Stanford: Stanford U. Press, 1926.
26. Evans, C. E., and Laverne, N. L. My Job Contest—an experiment in new employee relations methods. *Personnel Psychol.*, 1949, 2, 1-16.
27. Fisher, L. F. *Philosophy of social leadership according to Thomistic principles.* Washington: Catholic U. Press, 1948.
28. Flanagan, J. C., Levy, J., et al. Development of an objective form of the leaders reaction test. *Amer. Inst. Res.*, Pittsburgh, Pa., 1952.
29. Fleishman, E. A. The description of supervisory behavior. *J. appl. Psychol.*, 1953, 37, 1-6.
30. Flint, A. W. Forecasting leadership potential using an objective method of interaction analysis as a screening test. Unpublished Master's Thesis, Louisiana State Univ., Baton Rouge, La., 1957.
31. Flint, A. W. and Bass, B. M. Comparison of the construct validities of three objective measures of successful leadership. Technical Report 17, Contract N7 ONR 35609, Louisiana State University, Baton Rouge, La., 1958.
32. Gardner, B. B. *Human relations in industry.* Chicago: R. D. Irwin, 1945.

33. Gibbs, C. A. The research background of an interactional theory of leadership. *Australian J. Psychol.*, 1950, 2, 19-42.

34. Gorden, R. L. Interaction between attitude and the definitions of the situation in the expression of opinion. *Amer. sociol. Rev.*, 1952, 17, 50-58.

35. Gurnee, H. *Elements of social psychology.* New York: Farrar & Rinehart, 1936.

36. Halpin, A. W. The observed leader behavior and ideal leader behavior of aircraft commanders and school superintendents. In Stogdill, R. M. & Coons, A. E. (eds.) Leader behavior: *its description and measurement. Bur. Bus. Res. Monogr.* 88, Ohio State U., 1957.

37. Hare, A. P. Small group discussions with participatory and supervisory leadership. *J. abnorm. soc. Psychol.*, 1953, 48, 273-275.

38. Hemphill, J. Leadership in small groups (unpublished manuscript).

39. Hemphill, J. K., Pepinsky, P. M., Shivitz, R. N., Jaynes, W. E. and Christner, C. A. Leadership acts. 1. An investigation of the relation between possession of task relevant information and attempts to lead. *Personn. Res. Ed.* Ohio State U., Columbus, 1954.

40. Henry, W. E. The business executive: the psycho-dynamics of a social role. *Amer. J. Sociol.*, 1949, 54, 286-291.

41. Herrold, K. F. Teachership as leadership. *Teach. Coll. Rec.*, 1947, 48, 515-521.

42. Hollander, E. P. and Webb, W. B. Leadership, followership, and friendship: an analyses of peer nominations. *J. abnorm. soc. Psychol.*, 1955, 50, 163-167.

43. Jenness, A. The role of discussion in changing opinion regarding a matter of fact. *J. abnorm. soc. Psychol.*, 1932-33, 27, 279-296.

44. Jennings, H. H. *Leadership and isolation.* New York: Longmans, 1943.

45. Katz, D., Maccoby, N., Gurin, G. and Floor, L. G. Productivity supervision and morale among railroad workers. Survey Res. Center, U. Michigan, 1951.

46. Lapiere, R. T. & Farnsworth, P. R. *Social psychology.* New York: McGraw-Hill, 1942.

47. Mayer, A. Ueber einzel and Fesamtleistung des Schulkindes. *Arch. f. d. Ges. Psychol.*, 1903, 1, 276-416 (original not seen).

48. Mayo, E. and Lombard, G. F. F. Teamwork and labor turnover in the aircraft industry of southern California. *Harvard Business School*, No. 32, 1944.

49. Metcalf, H. C. and Urwick, L. (eds.) *Dynamics administration. The collected papers of Mary Parker Follett.* Bath. Mgmt. Public Trust, 1941.

50. Miller, D. C. and Philbrick, W. W. The measurements of group learning process by use of the interactional telemeter. *Amer. soc. Rev.*, 1953, 18, 184-191.

51. Morganau, H. Philosophy of physics. Sigma Xi Lecture. Louisiana State Univ., Baton Rouge, La., 1956.
52. Noble, C. The meaning-familiarity relationship. *Psychol. Rev.*, 1953, 60, 89-98.
53. Odier, G. Valeur et valence due chef. *Schweiz. Arch. Neurol. Psychiat.*, 1948, 61, 408-410 (original not seen).
54. Olmsted, D. W. Organizational leadership and social structure. *Amer. J. Sociol.*, 1954, 19, 273-281.
55. Pfiffner, M. M. The supervision of personnel. New York: Prentice-Hall, 1951.
56. Preston, M. G. and Heintz, R. K. Effects of participatory vs. supervisory leadership on group judgment. *J. abnorm. soc. Psychol.*, 1949, 44, 345-355.
57. Pryer, M. W. Effects of feedback on group behavior using a social analog computer. Unpublished M. A. Thesis. Louisiana State Univ., Baton Rouge, La., 1957.
58. Raven, B. H. and Rietsema, J. The effects of varied clarity of group goal and group path upon the individual and his relation to his group. *Amer. Psychol.*, 1956, 11, 360 (a).
59. Ray, W. S. Complex tasks for use in human problem-solving research. *Psychol. Bull.*, 1955, 52, 134-149.
60. Roethlisberger, F. J. and Dickson, W. J. *Management and the worker.* Cambridge: Harvard U. Press, 1943.
61. Sanford, F. H. Leadership identification and acceptance. In Guetzkow, H. (Ed.) I. *Groups, leadership and men.* Pittsburgh: Carnegie, 1951.
62. Sharp, H., Brogden, H., Houston, T. and Reuder, M. Evaluation of interaction chronograph as a predictor of leadership ratings. *PRB Res. Note* 5, 1952.
63. Sherif, M. A study of some social factors in perception. *Archives Psychol.*, 1935, No. 187.
64. Slater, P. E. Role differentiation in small groups. *Amer. sociol. Rev.*, (in press).
65. Smith, M. Control interaction. *J. soc. Psychol.*, 1948, 28, 263-273.
66. Stogdill, R. M. Personal factors associated with leadership: a survey of the literature. *J. Psychol.*, 1948, 25, 35-71.
67. Stogdill, R. and Coons, A. E. *Leader behavior: its description and measurement. Bureau of Bus. Res. Monogr.* 88, Ohio State U., 1957.
68. Talland, G. A. The assessment of group opinion by leaders, and their influence on its formation. *J. abnorm. soc. Psychol.*, 1954, 49, 431-434.
69. Tead, O. *The art of leadership.* New York: McGraw-Hill, 1935.
70. Terman, L. M. A preliminary study of the psychology and pedagogy of leadership. Pedagogical Seminary, 1904, 11, 413-451.
71. Thelen, H. A. (ed.). Methods for studying work and emotionality in group operation. *Dynamics Lab.*, Chicago, 1954.

72. Timmons, W. M. Can the product superiority of discussers be attributed to averaging or majority influences. *J. soc. Psychol.*, 1942, 15, 23-32.
73. Torrance, E. P. Perception of group functioning as a predictor of group performance. *Res. Stud., Wash. State Coll.*, 1953, 21, 262-265.
74. Triplett, N. The psychology of conjuring perceptions. *Amer. J. Psychol.*, 1900, 11, 439-510.
75. Urban Life Research Institute. Ann. Tech, Rept., Contract ONR NONR-475(01), New Orleans, La., March 1, 1953.
76. Viteles, M. *Motivation and morale in industry.* New York: W. W. Norton, 1953.
77. Weston, B. S. and English, H. B. The influence of the group of psychological test scores. *Amer. J. Psychol.*, 1926, 37, 600-601.
78. Wheeler, J. A. A septet of sibyls: aid in the search for truth. *Amer. Sci.*, 1956, 44, 360-377.
79. Wickert, F. (ed.) Psychological research on problems of redistribution *AAF Aviat. Psychol. Program Res. Rep.*, No. 14, Washington: U. S. Gov't. Printing Off., 1947, 298 p.

IX

An Actuarial Approach to Clinical Judgment [*]

WILLIAM A. HUNT

Northwestern University

DURING THE past century the psychological approach to judgment has taken two divergent trends, with the adherents of each often in open conflict. One of these approaches, firmly associated with the experimental tradition, and producing orderly, repetitive data that lend themselves to nomothetic treatment I shall call the *actuarial*. The other, firmly anchored in clinical practice, and producing individual data, highly unique in their nature and lending themselves to idiographic treatment I shall call the *intuitive*. Rather than accept the current view of these as qualitatively different and irreconcilable, I shall take the position that they are merely the opposite poles of a rough continuum, a quantitative continuum marked by the clarity and specificity with which the stimuli are defined, by the degree to which the judgmental setting is standardized through careful control of the known pertinent variables and the elimination of extraneous cues, and by the provision of uniform modes of reporting or response that lend themselves to convenient mathematical treatment.

ACTUARIAL TREND

The *actuarial* trend in the field of judgment arises in the early measurement of sensory mechanisms with Weber, Helmholtz, Fech-

[*] This study derives from a larger project subsidized by the Office of Naval Research under contract 7 onr-450(11) with Northwestern University.

ner, etc., and shortly develops into the full stream of classical psychophysics where today the lawful uniformities of judgment are
being uncovered and investigated. The investigations are no longer
merely in the traditional areas of sensation and perception but in
the complicated fields of affectivity, aesthetics, social attitudes, etc.,
(29) and even in the field of clinical practice as our data to follow
will attest. Information theory, decision theory, and probability
learning have all drawn from this source. Work in this classical
tradition typically involves the use of physical stimuli, about which
years of investigation in the physical sciences have taught us much.
We can accurately specify how much we want of what, and can
reproduce the stimulus conditions subsequently with some accuracy.
I say "some" accuracy because there is always sufficient error variance demonstrable in our data to raise doubts concerning the complete identity of our repeated trials. That this margin of error or
variability is minor and within acceptable limits does not negate
its existence. Note also that as we move from physical materials
to such complex stimuli as art objects, social situations, or schizophrenia verbal responses, the margin of error rises and is reflected
in increasing variability of judgment. Yet our data remain within
limits of communality that make it possible to treat them nomo-
thetically rather than idiographically.

The experimental situations in which psychophysical judgments
are obtained are laboratory ones, highly artificial and with all known
extraneous cues carefully removed. Very explicit and meaningful
instructions are given to the judge or observer to control his reactions. The categories used are clear, understandable, and common, such as "greater" or "less," "heavier" or "lighter," or the simple
numerals of some quantitative scale. Again, we may find variability
in greater or lesser amount as we vary our techniques but it either
lies within acceptable limits or we improve the technique. By
averaging measures, by smoothing curves we arrive at an illusion
of exactness or complete communality that the actual dispersions
or even inversions of the raw data often belie. If we ask ourselves
the question, "Did subsequent trials duplicate the conditions of the
first trial?", our answer must be, "Probably not exactly, but sufficiently so that we may assume the repetitiveness necessary for sequential data upon which to base statistical predictions."

INTUITIVE TREND IN JUDGMENT

The *intuitive* trend in judgment has as long a history as the actuarial trend albeit not as scientifically respectable a one. It comes down to us through the Germanic *Geisteswissenschaftlich* approach, through such cultural historians as Dilthey and Spengler, and through Spranger, the student of personality, and his concept of *Verstehen* or understanding. It culminates today in clinical psychology and psychiatry in what we call clinical intuition, but what I would prefer to label clinical judgment. Here we find the clinician as judge faced with stimuli that are not clearly defined (What is schizophrenia and how much is a lot of it?), that cannot easily be controlled and reproduced, and hence raise questions as to whether the communalities exist between trials that permit us to assume the repetitiveness necessary for sequential data and statistical prediction.

The judgmental situation is difficult to control and extraneous variables intrude as the clinician makes his judgment, at one time of a patient in an open social situation in a hospital ward, at another time in the relatively restricted environment of an examining room or office. Nor are the categories of report clear and specific. They may be in the vague nosological terms of one of our current diagnostic systems, or they may be couched in such general terms as "suicidal risk" or "assaultive." They may even be such general statements as "severe anxiety springing from oedipal problems" or such specific ones as "this patient should not be allowed to view the film, 'The Three Faces of Eve,' at the present stage in her treatment." Yet communalities often may be teased out, and highly complicated stimulus situations may yield sufficiently reliable data for usable predictions, even with the relatively unsatisfactory categories of classical Kraepelinian nomenclature, and a relatively undeveloped (compared to the physical sciences) descriptive psychiatry to aid us in specifying and clarifying the symptomatological behaviors which may serve as stimuli.

At every point where we even approach the exactitude of specificity and control of stimulus, judgmental setting, and categories of report which are typical of experimental psychophysics, communalities appear in our clinical data, and the uniformity and sequential repetitiveness necessary for statistical prediction begins to show itself. There is both logic and data, and I shall report some of this shortly, to support my position that the clinical judgment is qualitatively related to the psychophysical judgment, that the differences are ones of quantity rather than kind, that they are contrasting in amount rather than conflicting in nature, and that the clinical judgment is a culturally and educationally handicapped country cousin of the psychophysical judgment, and not a different species of being.

THE ARGUMENT REVIEWED

The argument so far runs like this: the repetitive or sequential data necessary for establishing probability inferences can be obtained from the clinical situation. Careful examination will show the possibility of locating and controlling communalities in stimulus, setting, and report so that judgments may be repeated under like conditions and sequential data may be obtained. Thus a loose class of symptomatic behaviors in a patient observed by a clinician whose training has some uniformity with that of other clinicians and whose judgments are made in an at least partially controlled observational setting may produce reports in terms of some diagnostic category on the basis of which valid predictions can be made concerning the patient's future behavior. These results can be duplicated on subsequent occasions with the same and even other clinicians. The less possible it is to duplicate the essential conditions (which is another way of saying the more unique each judgmental setting is) the less reliable will be our predictions, but clinical practice contains many judgmental situations in which the common aspects far outweigh the unique ones and in which meaningful sequential data may be obtained.

While agreeing that many clinical settings are marked by common and duplicable elements, one can still argue that genuinely unique situations arise where it is impossible to repeat the situation and hence to establish actuarial weightings to guide our predictions. This is the idiographic position in the idiographic-nomothetic controversy, and it is stoutly maintained by many clinicians who would claim that the major characteristic of clinical practice is that clinicians encounter completely unique patients with completely unique developmental histories in completely unique environments, necessitating a completely unique prediction which, by definition of its uniqueness, is not amenable to actuarial treatment. I doubt the frequency of such occurrences, but let us accept them as possibilities.

With no communalities apparently involved, such a unique situation cannot be approached actuarially. Does this deprive us of all opportunity of deriving probability weightings to guide us in making predictions? Before answering this question let me state that I think any act of human judgment is in part unique, even in psychophysics, although in this latter field we can reduce the uniqueness and diminish the error variance in our measures by careful cultivation and control of communalities of stimulus, task setting, and report. The uniqueness is then minimized and becomes statistically unimportant, but it remains, as any one who has spent hours in making psychophysical observations and in processing psychophysical data can testify. But we have deliberately chosen an example which admits no communality of stimulus, task setting, or report. Are we then deprived of any chance of deriving probability weightings in this admittedly (but probably purely hypothetically) unique situation? By no means. Our solution is to transfer the actuarial locus to the clinician himself.

If the occurrence of such unique situations is as common as the adherents of the idiographic approach would have us believe, the chances of any clinician meeting a *single* one is practically nil. He will meet many of them. Thus, while each prediction may be unique in itself and therefore inaccessible *per se* to probability estimates, the clinician himself furnishes a common repetitive element in the judgmental situation. We can evaluate the success of each individual prediction and arrive at an over-all actuarial expression of how often any clinician has been correct in a past series of unique predictions. The probability weighting which results can then be transferred to any future unique prediction for estimating its probable correctness. If clinician A has been right 9 times out of 10 in 10 past unique predictions, we can then use this "9 out of 10" as a weight to infer the chances that his next individual prediction will be correct. We may then extend our reference class from clinician A, to clinicians A-Z, and even to "all" clinicians, or narrow it to clinician A in one specially defined situation, etc., thus achieving probability weightings of increasing applicability. And as we derive such probability weightings, we shall undoubtedly begin to discover previously unrecognized communalities existing elsewhere in the situation. The actuarial locus may then be shifted to these, once they have been recognized. New diagnostic categories, further understanding of the variable involved in the process of judgment itself, and the development of suitable categories of report will all add predictive power in time. Meanwhile, transfering the actuarial locus to the clinician removes a semantic stumbling block that does much to impede clinical progress today.

THE CLINICIAN AS AN INSTRUMENT

In logical terms what we have done is to set the clinician up as a reference class from which we can derive the sequential observations necessary for an inference of probability. When we apply this probability interpretation to the single case, we are using a "transfer of meaning." Such transfers are justified by expediency for the purpose of action. As Reichenbach says, "The frequency interpretation provides merely a substitute for the probability of a single case; the choice of the substitute depends on our state of knowledge, inasmuch as we have to look for the narrowest reference class for which reliable statistics are available. But these qualifications do not represent any serious obstacles to the frequency interpretation; they merely portray the actual procedure used in all applications of statistics to individual cases" (27).

I was groping toward such a solution in 1946 when I said, "We should consider the individual clinician as a clinical instrument, and study and evaluate his performance exactly as we study and evaluate a test" (11). In 1951 I dealt with the "idiographic dilemma" that rises out of the application of probability theory to a single case and suggested, "The justification of a good clinician depends not upon his success with any single case, but upon his overall batting average over a period of time and with a number of cases, this situation probability theory can handle" (9). In 1955 some of these principles were used in interpreting the rationale of psychiatric selection (8). They have been treated at such length here, not merely to furnish the developmental background for the experimental material to be presented later, but because of the vital importance of the question in the ideological and practical development of clinical psychology. If one accepts a sharp, qualitative distinction between the idiographic and the homothetic on the basis of the inaccessibility of the first to statistical treatment, and then relegates clinical judgment to the idiographic, the scientifically oriented clinician is encouraged to neglect the experimental investigation of a basic clinical phenomenon. The non-scientifically oriented clinician is encouraged in the carefree practice of a happy technique which necessitates no evaluative fore- or after-thought since it lies outside the realm of empirical validation.

Idiographic Versus Nomothetic

The most lucid and inclusive discussion of this idiographic-nomothetic controversy to date appears in Paul E. Meehl's classic monograph of 1954, *Clinical versus Statistical Prediction* (26). As both an accomplished statistician and accomplished clinician Meehl writes with an intensity of feeling that testifies that his book is no dry scholarly exercise but the working through of a vital personal issue. He concludes soundly, roundly, and with convincing logic that clinical prediction should be based upon actuarial procedures. From his logic there would seem to me to be no escape, and it is indeed the position taken in this paper. The only alternative would be a flight into mysticism which would be disastrous for clinical psychology as either a "behavioral science" or a "healing art."

With his logic then, I can find no argument. With some of the content which he builds into his logical structure, I would demur. He could have made his case equally well without buttressing it by what seems at times an unjustified demeaning of the actuarial potentialities of clinical judgment itself. By opposing clinical judgment (intuition if you will) to such well developed actuarial techniques as the MMPI, he at times comes dangerously close to denying any actuarial potentiality for the judgmental approach. As my colleague Dr. Roy Hamlin, a persistent researcher in this field of clinical judgment (and a thoroughly objective one), so pithily remarked during an APA round table discussion, "Meehl not only makes a straw man of the clinician but takes his pants away as well."

It is unfortunate that Meehl has chosen to buttress his case for actuarial procedures by using comparative data between "test" and "clinical" procedures in the selection field. The evaluative criteria in selection are very complex and the simple probability statistic which he applies is not suitable to this complexity. As Cronbach and Gleser (5) have recently pointed out in their "Psychological Tests and Personnel Decisions," the statistics of games or decision theory are more suitable for sophisticated evaluation in this field. I have no doubt that actuarial test procedures, where *adequate* and available *ultimately* would still prove more efficient than clinical ones but the race might well be a closer one were a different evaluative statistic to be applied. To illustrate the problem, we have some data never published in complete form and admittedly involving some inference and extrapolation that suggest that in one situation both methods ran neck-and-neck in the percentage of failures identified, but differed widely in the false positive rate (31). There is no simple technique for equating "hits" and "false positives" in evaluation without the employment of exceedingly complicated decision statistics, which unfortunately were only slowly being understood and adapted at the time.

Moreover, by limiting himself to studies in which both methods are used, while tightening the logical force of his argument, Meehl inevitably neglects any instance in which clinical prediction is used independently with some success. I can think of two such studies from our own work (30, 21). Let me state again, my faith in the actuarial procedure is unshaken. I merely feel that a more sympathetic treatment of clinical procedures might have uncovered evidence that they are more efficient than Meehl would lead his readers to believe.

Finally, there is what seems to me to be a serious flaw in the design of Meehl's comparative study. In most cases he compares selected tests against unselected clinicians. He compares carefully developed actuarial procedures, into whose standardization and validation for the specific situation in which they are applied tremendous effort has gone, with clinicians about whose training and efficiency little or nothing is known and who probably have had little intensive training for the specific predictive task into which they have been thrown. It would be equally fair to compare the predictive performance of a group of highly selected and specially trained clinicians with that of the early Bernreuter Personality Inventory. The results might not be invidious to clinicians.

I often wonder what the results would have been if the time, energy, and financing that have gone into the development of the MMPI, had been put into the training of a group of clinical psychologists or psychiatrists in interviewing toward the goals of a specific predictive situation. These criticisms do not destroy the logic of the actuarial position. They do not invalidate any conclusion that in the specific situations Meehl mentions the current predictive efficiency of actuarial test techniques is greater than that of the clinical techniques used. They do cast some honest doubt on any sweeping conclusion that there is no hope for the future predictive potential of clinical judgment, particularly if it is subjected to actuarial study and development such as this paper proposes.

I doubt if Meehl would raise any serious objection to what I have said. As he himself remarks, "I would defend simultaneously (and, I hope, consistently) the two propositions that (1) there are some behavior phenomena which cannot be best studied in the laboratory, at least with any confidence in one's extrapolations, and (2) until some quantification, at least frequency counts and contingency measures, is applied to clinical evidence, we can have very little confidence in our claims." With this I am in total agreement. Perhaps our difference, if there is one, could be summarized by saying that I feel that Meehl views the exercise of clinical judgment as a necessary evil, whereas I view it as a fascinating phenomenon with a genuine predictive potential.

PRESENT POSITION AND PURPOSE

Were I to state my own position, it would be this:

1. There are some behavioral phenomena which cannot best be studied under the controlled laboratory conditions necessary for the development of sophisticated actuarial techniques such as objective test devices, and consequently such sophisticated actuarial devices are not currently available for use in studying such phenomena.

2. Clinical judgment furnishes a technique for the study of many of these behaviors that is necessary, suitable, and promising.

3. Such clinical judgment must and can be subjected to some actuarial evaluation and developed and improved along actuarial lines.

4. The use of clinical judgment is a necessary and inevitable preliminary step in our technical evolution toward an actuarial goal (10). Again, I suspect that Paul Meehl would be sympathetic with this formulation.

Before presenting data which we currently are obtaining from our actuarial approach to clinical judgment, let me state that the motivation for our program stems not from any *a priori* logical formulation, but from the hard reality of certain experimental findings obtained in our earlier investigation of the efficacy of psychiatric selection in the U. S. Navy in World War II. This program and its rationale has been presented elsewhere (8), but I should like here to review briefly several of the studies from which our interest in clinical judgment arose.

EARLY STUDIES

A large scale validational study of the efficacy of the Navy's neuropsychiatric screening program furnished evidence that it was succesful in reducing subsequent psychiatric attrition during service (19, 18). Since clinical judgment in the form of individual clinical diagnoses and predictions from interview impressions, etc., formed an important part of the screening technique, it was impossible to conceive of how the general program could be valid if such an integral part of it were invalid. In two subsequent studies we investigated clinical prediction specifically. In the first of these a clinician graded a group of 944 seamen suspected of maladjustment. A rough quantitative scale based on the categories *mild*, *moderate*, and *severe* was used, and subsequent attrition in each category confirmed the quantitative judgment of the clinician (30). This was a pre-planned predictive experiment, and not set up as a *post hoc* study. The clinician was selected on the grounds of his general professional competence it is true, but we were not interested in what anyone, irrespective of ability or training, could do but in the performance of a reputable clinician. After all, this is the same kind of selection that is used in choosing the objective tests used in selection experiments.

Encouraged by these results, we then made a study of the predictive value of certain diagnostic categories such as neurosis, schizoid personality, asocial psychopathy, etc., relating the original diagnosis to subsequent behavior during service. Many clinicians furnished the judgments used this time. While the study has never attracted wide attention, it is, I believe, one of the few experimental studies in which actual correlates in common social behavior were shown for the diagnostic categories involved. Neurotics were shown to be less of a disciplinary problem than a normal control group, but to have a preponderant incidence of alcoholic behavior when they did get into trouble. Schizoid personalities showed no incidence of alcoholic difficulty but were a leave and insubordination problem. The psychopaths were, of course, outstanding as a source of disciplinary difficulty, but were particularly noticeable for insubordination (21). Replication confirmed these findings (20). Not only were we encouraged by this evidence of clinical competence, but by the further evidence of some reliability and validity in these common diagnostic categories. The presence of such behaviors promises an objective observational basis on which valid clinical judgments may be based.

FOLLOW-UP AND OBJECTIVES

Two further studies supported our belief that the clinical judgment that we had been working with was a valid, lawful phenomenon. We reasoned that the diagnostic judgment should be easier the more maladjusted the interviewees were; and that, since the basis for the judgments must rest on observable behavior, the more maladjusted the interviewed group was the more symptomatic behaviors the clinician would note during his interview. Both of these hypotheses were confirmed (23, 22). By now we were convinced that clinical judgments could be valid and reliable, that clinical judgment itself was a lawful orderly process open to experimental analysis, and that its study and development offered the promise of supplying a useful clinical technique in those situations where more formal actuarial techniques, such as objective tests, were not available. To be useful, however, we were convinced that it must be approached and developed as an actuarial technique. As a consequence, we began the experimental program I shall now discuss.

To assist in clarifying the objectives of our program, let me say that we envisage it as a combination of basic and applied research, basic in that we wish to understand the nature of clinical judgment, applied in that we hope our understanding will further its useful potential as a tool in clinical practice. In any research sufficiently well planned and executed to merit the name it is difficult to separate "pure" and "applied" aspects. I cannot imagine any basic research which does not have implications for the control and manipulation of man and his environment. A narrow involvement in practicing technique for technique's sake, a type of schizoid, narcissistic laboratory play activity, may and does result in the kind of counting-the-pickets-in-a-picket-fence experimentation which may be temporarily accepted, but whose absurdity sooner or later is recognized. Nor can I imagine any applied problem, carefully analyzed and thoughtfully approached, the practical answer to which does not add something to our knowledge of the fundamental phenomenon involved. There may be experimenters in either situation who refuse to look beyond the immediate significance of their data but this is a human limitation and not one of research methodology.

This blending of basic and applied interest, this cross fertilization and mutual facilitation between approaches, has nowhere been better illustrated than in the flourishing post-war program of military research, where the attempt to answer practical problems has necessitated the furtherance of fundamental knowledge, and where in turn the fundamental knowledge obtained leads to new practical applications. Again, one senses a quantitative rather than qualitative difference, and I have been casting about for some parameters on which this could be expressed if not measured. Two seem to me to be of use in expressing the quantitative relation between the basic and applied approaches. These are the generalization potential of any group of scientific data, and their resistance to scientific obsolescence.

The more widely we can generalize from our specific laboratory situation to other diverse fields and the longer our findings remain useful without fundamental revision (resistance to obsolescence), the more basic our research is. Using a military illustration, it is the difference between spending thousands of dollars to obtain information about the fundamental processes of perception, which can then be applied widely and over a long period of time to many different problems of recognition and decision making; and spending thousands of dollars on a specific recognition problem involving a particular viewing scope, when the results have little implication for other weapons systems, and where rapid technological progress may make the particular weapons system outmoded before the research can even be published. There are many similar problems in training and education, involving both training methods and their evaluation (testing).

METHOD

In our work we have attempted a happy compromise between findings that would have some immediate application in professional practice and yet have some basic value in terms of potential generalization to other situations and some resistance to the obsolescence attributable to foreseeable changes in psychological interest and practice. We have used stimulus materials which are relatively clear, and easily duplicable. The judgmental situation is realistic, convenient, and fairly controllable. Our observers are representative of their class. The categories of response are understandable, easy to use, and lend themselves to mathematical treatment. The total setting attempts some of the experimental rigor of the psychophysical situation, without losing the semblance of actual clinical practice.

The stimuli used were verbal responses to intelligence test items, specifically items from vocabulary and comprehension tests. These can be repeated with exactitude and are easy to present. The evaluation of such materials for qualitative cues of personality disorder is a common experience in clinical practice. The stimuli were presented on mimeographed sheets with space provided for recording the evaluation. The task in essence involves the clinician sitting at his desk and evaluating test responses in a reasonable approximation to normal working conditions. This also frees us from the necessity of calling each clinician into a fixed laboratory situation, thus increasing the number of clinicians available and the geographical range from which they may be drawn. We concentrated on responses to vocabulary items since vocabulary is a brief, easily administered, popular type of test of wide usefulness which has stood up well through the years and promises to be valuable for some years to come. It may be scored objectively for purposes of comparison, and offers a relatively fertile sample of the thinking processes of the subject.

The judges were all well trained clinicians. The original minimal criteria for selection were a Ph.D. and four years of full time professional experience. Most of them were well beyond this minimum. While our 48 judges must remain anonymous, they are recognized, well established professional people, drawn from all over the country, and include many of the leaders in the profession today. Our naive subjects were all drawn from undergraduate students in psychology at Northwestern University. We must remember, however, that their naivete was relative. They are certainly more intelligent and more sophisticated psychologically than the average man.

The judgments were in terms of a 7 or 9 point quantitative scale, running from the minimum to the maximum of the phenomenon being evaluated. Such scales are understandable, easy to handle, and lend themselves to mathematical treatment. We must remember, however, that they are rough ordinal scales and as yet we have made no attempt to meet such problems as equal-interval steps, etc. Standardized instructions were used with every attempt being made to render them clear and unambiguous. We will set forth below the results of our studies in rough chronological order, and then discuss their implications.

First Results

As sometimes happens, our first approach to the problem was overly ambitious and somewhat disastrous. Reasoning that the effects of stimulus context which produce judgmental distortions in classical psychophysics should also appear in clinical judgment, Arnhoff attempted to find anchoring effects in a situation involving ratings of the amount of schizophrenic confusion exhibited in patient responses to vocabulary test items (1). Professional clinicians, graduate students in clinical psychology, and naive undergraduates were used as subjects. Anchoring effects were not demonstrable, the reliability of the clinicians' judgments varied widely, and to our embarrassment reliability as measured by the standard deviation of the mean judgments was inversely related to level of training. This last was particularly upsetting

Fortunately, interviews with some of our subjects and careful inspection of our data indicated that two opposite context effects, contrast and assimilation, might be cancelling one another out in the statistical analysis of our data; and there were indications that our instructions might be too general and allow too much opportunity for individual interpretation by our trained clinicians. As Arnhoff has aptly stated it, "When dealing with experts in a judgmental situation, the task should be well defined and the criteria set forth clearly. Otherwise the riches of knowledge may yield confusion rather than clarity" (1).

Partly as a result of our frustration and partly to illustrate some of the pitfalls inherent in such work, we wrote a brief, humorous note on "Reliability, Chance, and Fantasy in Inter-Judge Agreement among Clinicians" (14), which was intended as a tongue-in-cheek pedagogical device. Fortunately it was accepted as such in amused approval by many of our colleagues, but unfortunately, was taken seriously by others. It taught us a lesson of caution about interjecting subtle humor into the deadly serious business of science.

Despite the discouraging beginning, we remained confident of the promise of our approach, and decided to continue with a less ambitious, better planned, progressively analytic approach to the problem. The first step we deemed necessary was to answer the basic question of the reliability of clinical judgment. If we could establish this, we could then proceed to investigate some of the more complex phenomena of judgment.

Further Work

Accordingly, Arnhoff and I (13) selected 50 of the most reliable vocabulary test responses from a pool standardized for his previous study. To these we added 50 comprehensive test responses also gathered from schizophrenic patients. These were rated by 16 professional clinicians in the Chicago area. A 7-point scale was used, and we wrote improved instructions designed to eliminate the previous ambiguities. Judgment was on the basis of "how schizophrenic each of these responses is." We defined reliability both as agreement of each judge with the group, and as individual consistency upon retesting. The original ratings were repeated after intervals of 3 and 18 months.

Agreement of the judges with the group on vocabulary responses showed r's ranging from .73 to .92 for the first rating, .69 to .95 on the second, and .81 to .92 on the third. For comprehension items these were .64 to .88, .66 to .86, and .71 to .89 respectively. Test-retest r's between the first and second ratings for each clinician ran from .65 to .91 for vocabulary, and .68 to .90 for comprehension. Since all the clinicians were from the Chicago area we ran a cross validational group of 16 other clinicians from all areas of the United States. A single rating only was obtained from this group. The judge-group r's ran from .59 to .92 for vocabulary and .63 to .90 for comprehension. Correlations between the mean values assigned each stimulus by the first group (original rating) and the new group were .93 for vocabulary and .96 for comprehension. These reliabilities are quite high and led us to believe not only that such ratings are reliable for clinical use, but that they can be used for experimental purposes in the further investigation of the nature of judgment.

Arnhoff's finding that reliability, as defined by the standard deviation of the mean stimulus values, was in inverse relation to amount of professional training still bothered us. Consequently with the aid of Nelson Jones and Mrs. Hunt, I made several studies of the judgments given by naive undergraduate students using our new and improved instructions (17). While the mean value was not significantly different from that of the trained clinicians, the standard deviation of the mean was significantly greater indicating that contrary to Arnhoff's original results clinical experience is acting to increase the reliability of the professional clinicians' judgments. The correlation between the mean stimulus values for the groups was .88, however, indicating a high degree of agreement between their ratings.

Increasing the Gap Between Clinicians and Naive Raters

Encouraged by the high reliabilities obtained thus far, Jones and I (15) extended our investigation beyond the simple dimension of "schizophrenic" to include more subtle dimensions or specific aspects of schizophrenic thinking. Our prediction was that the ratings of trained clinicians would diminish in reliability but still be within acceptable limits, while the gap in performance between trained and naive judges would increase as the ratings became more difficult. The stimuli were the 50 vocabulary responses previously used. The new dimensions were potential intelligence (defined not in terms of the correctness of the response, but in terms of the potential intelligence level indicated by it), communicability (a dimension of private-public meaning), and concreteness (the classical concrete-abstract aspect of schizophrenic thinking). The experienced clinicians were 31 of our previous subjects all of whom had rated the words earlier for "schizophrenic." All 31 made ratings of "potential intelligence," 15 of "communicability," and 16 of "concrete-abstract." The naive subjects were a new group of 90 undergraduates, 30 of whom judged on the schizophrenic dimension, 30 on intelligence, and 15 each on communicability and concrete-abstract.

Reliability was defined as each judge's agreement with the group. For the trained clinicians the r's for schizophrenia ranged from .63 to .94 with a median of .88, for potential intelligence from .22 to .83 with a median of .70, for communicability from .70 to .91 with median of .80, for concrete-abstract from .38 to .71 with a median of .55. Reliability dropped but was still within respectable limits. For the undergraduates the r's were: schizophrenia −.50 to .89, median .72; for intelligence .14 to .83, median .61; for communicability .39 to .85, median .75; for concrete-abstract −.54 to .73, median .60. Negative values were contributed by only three subjects. Again, while not quite as reliable, the undergraduates ran fairly close in performance to the clinicians. The r's between the mean value assigned each stimulus by the two groups were .95 for schizophrenia, .83 for intelligence, .94 for communicability, but −.43 for concrete-abstract. The picture of disagreement became sharper where we studied the pattern of interrelationships between our dimensions.

Since we were using the same 50 stimulus words in each judgmental setting it became possible to compare the relation between our four attributes of "schizophrenia," "potential intelligence," "communicability," and "concrete-abstract" through rank order correlations based on the mean value of the stimuli for the four types of ratings. For our experienced clinicians the dimension of schizophrenia was highly negatively correlated with communicability, not related to intelligence, and minimally related to a tendency to concreteness. There was no relation between intelligence and communicability, but a high one between intelligence and abstraction. The r between communicability and abstraction is significant but low. With the possible exception of schizophrenia and communicability it seems obvious that our clinicians are differentiating between the dimensions.

The picture of schizophrenic thinking presented by these findings is in accord with conventional thinking except for the low relation between schizophrenia and the tendency to concreteness. Concrete thinking classically has been attributed to the schizophrenic. Our results, however, are in accord with those of McGaughran and Moran (25) obtained in a sorting experiment where they found a tendency to personal, noncommunicable thinking more typical of the schizophrenic than a tendency either to concreteness or abstraction.

For the naive undergraduates, however, the results are quite different. Everything is highly related, either positively or negatively, to everything else. The evidence would indicate that they are not distinguishing between the scales, and possibly are falling back upon some common denominator as a basis for all their judgments. In any case, the findings confirm the variability picture, and it seems evident that while our naive subjects perform rather well when rating for broad, general aspects of disorder, they fall down when given more subtle dimensions to use. It is at this point that the superiority of our trained clinicians becomes apparent.

Additional Categorization

In our latest investigation, Jones and I (16) have introduced a different category of disorder with a different dimension of judgment and a return to the use of responses on comprehension test items. Using 50 such items drawn from Wechsler-Bellevue materials administered to a group of Naval disciplinary cases, 15 of our pool of clinicians were asked to rate on the basis of the asocial tendency revealed in the responses. The responses were selected to represent a wide range of such tendency. Ratings also were obtained from an undergraduate group.

The findings show the same high reliability obtained with schizophrenic materials. For the clinicians the r's ranged from a high of .92 to a low of .64 with a median of .82. A random splitting of the group gave an r of .94. For the undergraduates the range was from .88 to .51 with a median of .72, again quite high but lower than the clinicians. The split-group r was .93. The agreement between clinicians and undergraduates, based upon the mean values assigned the stimuli, was .91. The difference between the mean values of all the stimuli for the two groups was not significant; nor, contrary to our previous findings, was the difference in standard deviations significant.

The fact that high reliability or good inter-judge agreement continues to appear as we extend our reference groups by adding new dimensions and a new type of disorder indicates some possibility of generalizing about clinical judgment. We cannot, of course, conclude that all clinicians are reliable in all judgmental situations, but within the limits of our rating technique and those situations we have used, clinical judgment begins to emerge as a reliable technique which can be applied in evaluative situations. Incidentally it is of interest to note that what individual differences do appear seem to be limited to specific situations. We find no evidence of consistently "bad" judges appearing among our clinicians.

PRACTICAL APPLICATIONS

Having described our motivation as coming from a blending of basic and applied interests, it is fitting at this point to suggest some of the practical applications that might follow from it. One immediate application is the use of scales as teaching devices. The presenting of clinical materials scaled to show the orderly quantitative progress of the dimension in question would seem to be a better method of pedagogical communication than the disorderly hodgepodge in which such illustrative material is usually presented. We have published such material for schizophrenic thinking as is exhibited in both vocabulary and comprehension responses (12). Our future program envisages further refinement of the above materials plus the production of scales for the other dimensions we have investigated. As yet we have no experimental data on their pedagogical efficacy, but rough observation of their use indicates that they show promise for teaching purposes.

The value of obtaining reliable scaled judgments of significant test behavior which previously was only open to broad, qualitative interpretation is obvious. Through such a technique the previously subjective and non-quantitative becomes objective and quantitative. Not only is communication more clear and more precise, but the possibilities of statistical treatment are increased. It is even possible that future tests and test items might be selected against the criterion of their adaptability to such scaling techniques.

The practicing clinician will think of many possible specific adaptations. One which we hope to test in the near future is the use of judgments of potential intelligence to provide an internal scatter measure with any vocabulary test. The responses on such a test could be scored in two ways: first, with the usual objective stencil or rules for "correct" and "incorrect" to give a measure of functional intelligence; second, with scaled values on the dimension of potential intelligence as we have used it to give a measure of the subject's previous (or potential, if the disorder is thought of as reversible) level of ability. The discrepancy between these two measures should provide some estimate of the current intellectual deficit.

One of the most intriguing possibilities stems from the ability of our naive judges to perform in a fashion closely comparable to our trained clinicians provided we use broad, general dimensions. This confirms what common sense and experience has already demonstrated, that even the man in the street can recognize deviant behavior (and this without the advantages of training on our scales!). If this recognition can be turned into reliable scale judgments, the use of such scales by nursing aids and ancillary ward personnel has possibilities. Such scales might be helpful in the courts, in social work situations, and certainly in the military services. It might even be possible to turn English professors into diagnosticians, as well as scholars!

Present Concerns

As we speak of the future, we reveal one of the great deficiencies of our work at present. We have dealt so far with reliability and have not touched diagnostic validity. Some, I think, can be inferred from our reliabilities, but irrespective of current squabbles concerning the identity or difference of the meanings of the terms reliability and validity, validity does point to a realm of practical diagnostic applicability with which we have not dealt. Particularly pertinent is the fact that the stimuli used to date have been carefully preselected to offer a representative range of patient responses. What will happen to the reliability of judgment when clinicians exercise it on unselected test responses? Will actual, run-of-the-mill tests in themselves offer sufficiently rich materials for such scaling techniques? Our techniques will be improved as our understanding of clinical judgment improves.

In closing, I should like to deal briefly with those studies in which we have explored some of the factors causing distortions of judgment in the hope that through their understanding and control we may improve clinical performance. That there are phenomena common to all acts of judgment has long been a cherished belief of mine (7). The specific area we have chosen to investigate is the effect of the context upon the judged value of the stimulus. Arn-hoff's original study (1) was of anchoring effects, which are part of the general context. His failure to find these effects did not discourage us, and we resolved to return to the problem. Fortunately at this time the interest of my colleague, Professor Donald T. Campbell, was aroused and his collaboration secured. He suggested a more sophisticated design that seemed better suited to our purposes than the one we had been using. With the assistance of Mrs. Nan A. Lewis, we set to work.

The stimuli were our schizophrenic verbal responses which were rated for the amount of schizophrenic thinking involved, using a 9-point scale. Northwestern undergraduates provided our subjects. In essence, our experimental situation consisted of the repeated presentation of stimuli of median value against a limited context of stimuli from either the upper or lower halves of the scale, a transition to the opposite context followed. Context effect was measured by changes in the judged value of the median stimuli. Our hypothesis was confirmed; median stimuli were judged higher when presented in a context of low stimuli and lower when presented in a high stimuli context (2). For reasons not pertinent here, involving some general problems of psychophysical technique, we repeated the problem with tones as stimuli, and confirmed our previous findings (4). We have demonstrated that these effects can be used as a criterion for the evaluation of different types of scales (3).

It was still necessary to bridge the gap between naive undergraduates and trained clinicians, and Jones undertook this problem (24). In an experiment involving 48 professional clinicians, 16 clinical psychology graduate student trainees, and 16 naive undergraduates, Jones was able not only to demonstrate these effects, but also their dependence upon professional experience and previous experience in a similar rating situation. In view of the fact that Jones' design did not involve the repeated stimulation of the study by Campbell, Hunt, and Lewis, it is understandable that the effects were not strong. One of Campbell's students, Dr. Marshall Segall, has since demonstrated that such context effects can be demonstrated with social attitudes (28).

It thus seems fair to conclude not only that clinical judgment in terms of our scaling techniques is sufficiently reliable at present for some practical adaptation, but that further understanding of the judgmental situation will lead to greater possibilities in its control, and hence to more accurate judgments and judges. The importance of training the judge has recently been recognized in psychophysics itself. In an article reflecting much of our own orientation in the clinical field, Engen and Tulunay say, "The use of unpracticed and naive Os as instruments of precision, e.g., in measuring sensory magnitudes on a ratio scale, may not be unlike the use of un-calibrated physical instruments. With such instruments, constant errors, such as those associated with context, may remain unknown. It may, however, be feasible to "calibrate" the human O by giving him experience with the various types of psychophysical judgments and their sources of bias" (6). If such an august discipline as psychophysics can benefit from such a program of improvement, may not the lowly field of clinical psychology aspire to the same goal? At the very least we are in good company!

References

1. Arnhoff, F. N. Some factors influencing the unreliability of clinical judgments. *J. clin. Psychol.*, 1954, 10, 272-275.
2. Campbell, D. T., Hunt, W. A., and Lewis, Nan A. The effects of assimilation and contrast in judgments of clinical materials. *Amer. J. Psychol.*, 1957, 70, 347-360.
3. Campbell, D. T., Hunt, W. A., and Lewis, Nan A. The relative susceptibility of two rating scales to disturbances resulting from shifts in stimulus context. In preparation.
4. Campbell, D. T., Lewis, Nan A., and Hunt, W. A. Context effects found with a judgmental language that is absolute, extensive, and extra-experimentally anchored. *J. exp. Psychol.*, in press.
5. Cronbach, L. J., and Gleser, Goldine C. *Psychological tests and personnel decisions.* Urbana: Univer. Illinois Press, 1957.
6. Engen, T., and Tulunay, U. Some sources of error in half-heaviness judgments. *J. exp. Psychol.*, 1957, 54, 208-212.
7. Hunt, W. A. Anchoring effects in judgment. *Amer. J. Psychol.*, 1941, 54, 395-403.
8. Hunt, W. A. A rationale for psychiatric selection. *Amer. Psychologist*, 1955, 10, 199-204.
9. Hunt, W. A. Clinical psychology—science or superstition. *Amer. Psychologist*, 1951, 6, 683-687.
10. Hunt, W. A. *The clinical psychologist.* Springfield, Ill.: Charles C. Thomas, 1956.
11. Hunt, W. A. The future of diagnostic testing in clinical psychology. *J. clin. Psychol.*, 1946, 2, 311-317.
12. Hunt, W. A., and Arnhoff, F. N. Some standardized scales for disorganization in schizophrenic thinking. *J. consult. Psychol.*, 1955, 19, 171-174.
13. Hunt, W. A., and Arnhoff, F. N. The repeat reliability of clinical judgments of test responses. *J. clin. Psychol.*, 1956, 12, 289-290.
14. Hunt, W. A., Arnhoff, F. N., and Cotton, J. W. Reliability, chance,

and fantasy in inter-judge agreement among clinicians. *J. clin. Psychol.*, 1954, 10, 294-296.

15. Hunt, W. A., and Jones, N. F. Clinical judgment of some aspects of schizophrenic thinking. *J. clin. Psychol.*, in press.

16. Hunt, W. A., and Jones, N. F. The reliability of clinical judgments of asocial tendency. *J. clin. Psychol.*, in press.

17. Hunt, W. A., Jones, N. F., and Hunt, Edna B. Reliability of clinical experience. *J. clin. Psychol.*, 1957, 13, 377-378.

18. Hunt, W. A., Wittson, C. L., and Burton, Henrietta W. A further validation of Naval neuropsychiatric screening. *J. consult. Psychol.*, 1950, 14, 485-488.

19. Hunt, W. A., Wittson, C. L., and Burton, Henrietta W. A validation study of naval neuropsychiatric screening. *J. consult. Psychol.*, 1950, 14, 35-39.

20. Hunt, W. A., Wittson, C. L., and Hunt, Edna B. Hidden costs in the utilization of the psychiatrically marginal man. *J. clin. Psychol.*, 1954, 10, 91-92.

21. Hunt, W. A., Wittson, C. L., and Hunt, Edna B. Military performance of a group of marginal neuropsychiatric cases. *Amer. J. Psychiat.*, 1952, 109, 168-171.

22. Hunt, W. A., Wittson, C. L., and Hunt, Edna B. The relationship between amount of presenting symptomatology and severity of disability. *J. clin. Psychol.*, 1955, 11, 305-306.

23. Hunt, W. A., Wittson, C. L., and Hunt, Edna B. The relationship between definiteness of psychiatric diagnosis and severity of disability. *J. clin. Psychol.*, 1952, 8, 314-315.

24. Jones, N. F. Context effects in judgment as a function of experience. *J. clin. Psychol.*, 1957, 13, 379-382.

25. McGaughran, L. S., and Moran, L. J. "Conceptual level" vs. "conceptual area" analysis of object-sorting behavior of schizophrenic and non-psychiatric groups. *J. abnorm. soc. Psychol.*, 1956, 52, 43-50.

26. Meehl, P. E. *Clinical vs. statistical prediction.* Minneapolis: Univer. Minnesota Press, 1954.

27. Reichenbach, H. Probability methods in social science. In Lerner, D., and Lasswell, H. D. (eds.), *The policy sciences*. Stanford: Stanford Univ. Press, 1951.

28. Segall, M. H. Attitude and adaptation-level: the effect of experience on extremity judgments and on expression of opinions. Unpublished doctoral dissertation, Northwestern Univer., 1957.

29. Volkmann, J. Scales of judgment and their implications for social psychology. In Sherif, M., & Rohrer, J. (Eds.), *Social psychology at the crossroads*. New York: Harper, 1951.

30. Wittson, C. L., and Hunt, W. A. The predictive value of the brief psychiatric interview. *Amer. J. Psychiatr.*, 1951, 107, 582-585.

31. Wittson, C. L., and Hunt, W. A. Three years of naval selection. *War Med.*, 1945, 7, 218-221.

X

Increasing Clinical Efficiency

Starke R. Hathaway
University of Minnesota

THE CHIEF contribution of psychology to clinical efficiency is the use of psychometric devices to more quickly and accurately effect clinical decisions. Efficiency in clinical testing does not very clearly signify anything by way of subject matter; the connotation suggests maximum usefulness for minimum cost and effort. This treatment of that connotative field will be a broad one within two important limiting conditions. One limit is suggested by the word "clinical." The points to follow are intended to apply most clearly to routine work with clients or patients who are tested as part of the evaluation of mental handicap or disorder but exclusive of special research purposes. A more indefinite limit will be the primary concern with personality tests and testing rather than with interests, aptitudes, or intellect.

WHY DO WE USE TESTS?

If one were to go from clinician to clinician conscientiously attempting to estimate the items contributing to the use of tests, many of the most frequently stressed points would not be amenable to statistical or other objective evaluation of test efficiency. For example, some clinical psychologists use tests as a fairly effective starting point to let them participate in the diagnosis or psychodynamic formulation of the problems of the patient. This psychologist, probably fortunately for the development of his science, more often feels a need for a real or seeming instrumentation in contrast to simple opinion from experience, before he can contribute in the team development of formulation.

The Rorschach and other projective devices have probably gained a great deal of their popularity because of their adaptability to the satisfaction of this need. In many cases, a candid psychologist will sum the whole of his value argument for a test by saying that he finds it to be prolific in source material for psychodynamic statements (psychological causes) about patients. These statements are not only valued in the clinical setting in which many psychologists work, but in a majority of cases there is some real criticism by clinical peers if test data are not presented as background for dynamic evaluations. Although these statements rest in some way upon data in the test, they are not usually evoked by objective aspects of the test as the technical requirement of a test is usually stated, and they mostly depend upon professional hearsay or at most upon weak data from validity study. We are often guilty of accepting some halo effect weight to our subjectively derived observations of a patient because the basic observations were made in the course of administration of an objective test. That is, our statements gain in staff creditability and in our own belief in them to the extent that they are associated with other informational items properly termed objective and validated test data.

An allied utility from using tests is the relief of the clinician from the responsibility of making a judgment that cannot be based upon any identifiable procedure or objective datum. The test, even if it were completely invalid for the situation, nevertheless constitutes a decision-making device. The need in the psychologist is comparable to the reason we toss a coin. We try to decide certain ambivalent situations by shifting the responsibility to an outside event. A test indication may have more relationship to the decision than a coin would, but often the real value lies in the provision of a sign used to dissolve indecision. Complicated test utilities such as these are often respectable and real, since they are tools for use in clinical areas that cannot be better handled. Of course, we will give up such props as we develop more appropriate and valid tests.

At the outset it is important to differentiate between the function of a test or test situation when it is being used in accordance with our more formal understanding of the meaning of the word "test" and the quite proper observations that go along with the administration of a test and which are, perhaps, better thought of as resulting from a controlled interview situation. The Rorschach provides a good illustration of this contrast. It is a test when it yields scores and profiles, but it is merely a partially controlled interview when the clinician uses unscored and unstandardized data to describe the patient's personality, no matter how much authority and experience lie behind the interpretations.

CLINICAL VERSUS PSYCHOMETRIC DATA

The confusion of psychometric methods with interviews and with other non-metric methods of gaining information may, in part, have started from an over-reaction that is historically characteristic of psychology. The movement toward acceptance of the use of psychometric data in practical clinical application occurred against a strong tradition in the use of interviews and oral examinations. Psychiatry was deeply involved with these subjective methods and, in general, psychologists found it hard to compete. It was not very effective to pit a test score against the word of the experienced clinical man. The struggle for recognition of the value of psychometrics may have caused over-reaction against subjective clinical evaluations to the point where modern psychologists have neglected the potentialities of the interview and, particularly, the possibility of developing more objective information from the interview by using methods that control the situation.

If the psychometric aspects of Rorschach technique continue to show poor efficiency, we must not over-react again and lose the value of the method for lack of the flexibility to change our concept of the method. Until forced out of the position by pressure to appear more scientific, the best clinicians using the Rorschach depended very little upon formal test methods, such as scoring and the formalizing of clinical signs. The current Q-technique enthusiasm, which illustrates the possibility for measurement derived from subjectively summarized clinical information, is relieving pressure toward the inappropriate use of objective psychometric methods. Similarly promising is the increasing development of validated clinical statements derived from objective test profiles that are considered as complex patterns or codes rather than individual scales. For example, social conformity and continuation in school are related to MMPI codes showing high scale 5 or 4 (5) for children who have the specified profiles. This kind of validity data completes the link between objective test profiles and the signs that are validated from projective devices.

To a certain extent, experienced clinicians have found there is a gain in clinical efficiency from a simultaneous objective test and interview. It is hard to teach this skill, and encouragement of the practice often leads to corruption of the objective test evidence. In summary, it is probable that we are beginning a period of rapid development in efficiency by the development of "cook books" with the scheme exemplified by Meehl (9) and developed by Drake (2). The distinctive character of this movement is the development of clinical generalizations about personality from objective test data that are in some way synthesized. This synthesis may be effected by use of a code (3) or some other clerical system to skim the validity cream from a profile of objective personality scale scores.

WHO SHALL ADMINISTER THE TESTS?

Tests for clinical use can be divided into those that must be administered by a clinical psychologist and those that can be administered by a psychometrist. The psychometrist can have one or two years of graduate training or be an in-service trained person chosen for the ability to get cooperation and observe general rules. Examples of tests that use professional time are the WAIS, the Rorschach, the TAT, and a long list of others including many of the tests for mental deficit. Some of these tests require nearly half a day for administration, scoring, and evaluation. Examples of tests that can be administered by a psychometrist are the Shipley, the MMPI, Sentence Completion, and the Porteus. All of these require skilled interpretation, but the completed profile or answer records are the starting point. The use of these latter tests is much more efficient, at least in terms of professional time investment.

With the shortage of clinical psychologists and with the general resistance of the fully accredited psychologist to doing routine testing, the tests that require skilled professional time in administration or scoring will need to provide much more information or other value than will the second type of test before their use is justifiable. Progress toward efficiency should increasingly recognize this fact as the clinical psychologists feel more responsibility for efficiency in their routines. At present, one rarely sees any mention of the cost in professional time as part of the validity or other value discussion of new or old tests. Some psychologists even seem to feel that the processes of testing should be kept complicated and that the psychologist should base his professional standing upon them.

As is true of most of the other significant factors in the examination of practical test efficiency, it is not easy to place comparative values upon the differences between tests in professional time for administration and scoring. There is a danger that we will go too far, not use individual tests when they should be used, and, even more likely, not give enough time to an interview with the patient when we are provided with the test data by someone else. As a policy, for example, routine MMPI's can be handled in large numbers by one experienced reader who makes a few screening judgments on each profile put before him. But for diagnostic and other significant decisions, an interview with the patient is imperative. For efficiency, such interviews by the clinician should be approached with a maximum of completed test profiles and other test information in hand. They become directed and efficient checks upon the peculiar significance of the test indications as applied to the patient and upon the probable validity of the test data.

It is apparent by now that a great gain in clinical efficiency can be made when we face the fact that psychology must accept leadership in expanding the use of psychometricians. It is inexcusable for a clinic to employ psychologists at the Diplomate level and for these to spend much of their time scoring or administering tests when equal or more information could be obtained by a psychometrician. But when no psychometric or clerical help is available, it is more reprehensible for the clinical psychologist not to use tests if he has been hired as a clinical psychologist to bring his special skills to the clinical team. Acceptance of this position would embarrass many individual psychologists and some large clinical programs when Ph. D. level psychologists are exclusively used with no provision for psychometricians or clerical workers.

Test Efficiency and Test Statistics

Test efficiency has most often been treated by approaches that suggest practical statistical formulations with parameters that can be estimated. The following development briefly reviews the principle factors in such evaluations to suggest that practical clinical efficiency often very loosely relates to orderly statistics.

Cronbach and Meehl (1) have expanded the subject of test validity from the standpoint of research and development of tests. Test validity and reliability of tests are certainly significant items in clinical efficiency. Statistical equations and fairly precise arguments that define test efficiency in terms of estimated parameters depend upon critical items such as the placement of the cutting point, the amount of overlap, and the base rate of occurrence of the critical events.

Treatment of test efficiency, as indicated in a four-fold table of test hits and misses in proper cross validation, is a well recognized procedure. Unfortunately, as Meehl and Rosen (8) repeatedly state, this procedure is rarely presented properly, and the data are not available for it in the case of most of the personality tests. Estimations of the base rate for ordinary applications together with consideration of the data for advantageous cutting points are even rarer in our literature. The clinician usually works with very little of this information even if he is able to state his local problems properly.

On the whole, as Meehl and Rosen show, application of the efficiency formulas where we can estimate the necessary parameters tends toward discouraging conclusions. As methods for desirably changing the predictive probability of statements about patients and their problems, many of the tests we use are impractically weak; some actually lower the predictive accuracy because of their improper cutting scores. We should be much freer to not make statements from test data. Effectively this means that we can administer a test and refuse to use a proportion of the scores because they fall in indeterminate areas. Such a practice will permit strong statements about a few of the persons tested even when a weak test is used. A testing program could sometimes be justified when only one among a hundred scores can be used rationally.

When efficiency of a test is based upon the data in the four-fold table, or overlapping frequency distributions, or upon some relationship of these values to the base rate, one must decide what efficiency weight should be given to every one of the types of test hits, errors, and indeterminacies. The problem is rather simple if only one category is considered significant. For example, one might select true positives as the exclusive measure of efficiency. With a large and stable supply population, that test giving the largest per cent in the true positive cell would be the most efficient. Although some situations approach this simple case, there are probably no completely consistent examples. Some other category such as the false positive cases will always influence the efficiency evaluation in the practical situation. Most often a combination of several test validity categories must be considered. Among these, the per cent of false negatives is especially likely to be critical. For example, we are very unhappy if we fail to identify one patient with a brain tumor because the appropriate test indicator was negative for tumor. We can, however, accept a few more false positive indications. By contrast, if a test is intended to predict which boys will become severely delinquent, the false positive cases can be very embarrassing. People are quite tolerant of favorable predictions (false negatives) even if the prediction is wrong. Efficient evaluations closely depend upon the special demands put upon the test by the applied situation and are difficult to generalize.

Fortunately, the samples on which we usually work are enriched samples; they have a larger base rate than does the general population. Using a test of schizophrenia for hospital patients, we know that the rate of the criterion condition will be higher than among non-patients. Real suicidal intent is rare in general populations, but among hospital patients who look depressed, it is many times more common (10). Our tests are fortunately used so that they operate as successive hurdles in probability. This can help the efficiency by pushing the base rate of the critical event upwards. Arguments such as these mitigate the dismal picture of clinical test efficiency that is suggested by candid consideration of the statistical facts available tends.

In summary, statistically evaluated test efficiencies can be applied when proper parameters are available or can be estimated. These efficiencies must be rationalized for the special test application according to the base rate and the importance of each of the various kinds of hit and error. We should be more hard headed about the significance of these equations and tables, since it can often be demonstrated that no way of treating the data would justify routine use of some of our tests, and in other cases it would become apparent that a test is useful only under restricted conditions.

In the long run, inefficiency in the use of clinical resources is undesirable, and the psychologist should be foremost among those who are concerned. There can be no doubt that a great deal of the published material on tests, and much of the routine application of tests, would appear weak if we choose to be critical. This is true even when more effective cutting points are selected or when other special conditions are favorable for increasing efficiency. Optimal adjustment of cutting points or identification of the sharpest test use can not usually be achieved in ordinary clinical practice.

Why Diagnose?

Clinical psychologists have been the leaders in criticisms of current dynamic formulation and diagnostic systems and have described new factors, tests, and patterns as suggestions for improvement. Neither the new traits and diagnoses they provide nor the new tests have been established as convincing heuristic or predictive devices. One must admit that the diagnoses for functional mental disorders do not have the desirable properties of good medical diagnoses.

The most popular test we use today, as well as our other diagnostic procedures, are devoted to the production of diagnoses that will approximately fit the professional culture. We use the tests that will provide the proper statistics to indicate the rates of the traditional mental illnesses, that show the types of patients handled, or that provide a basis for disability or legal status. There are rarely any crucial elements except these cultural ones involved in deciding whether a patient is schizophrenic or a severe neurotic.

In a practical application we do not always want to predict who would be diagnosed schizophrenic by a clinic. We really want to know which persons will become, or presently are, ill with the so far incompletely defined illness. If there is a morbid unity tending to evoke the diagnosis of schizophrenia, it is obvious that persons with this disorder are often given some other diagnosis or are called normal. This is apparent from the fact that clinicians and clinics do not show high reliability (7). What we may want to identify with a test is the true illness, schizophrenia, and the clinic's diagnostic system can be thought of as another test with less than perfect efficiency. Either the clinical diagnosis or the test could be the better indicator.

For a sophisticated appraisal, we should check both the test and the clinic against multiple symptoms or other items that will permit a relative decision about the efficiencies. We have too much disregarded this aspect of testing efficiency by seeming to assume either that it is good enough for a test to be developed for agreement with clinical diagnoses (which means inevitably limiting the validity), or that some arbitrary amount of disagreement with diagnoses invalidates a test. It seems that, of these two unhappy alternatives, it is better to choose the former unless there is no value in making clinical diagnoses or prognoses.

It is interesting that no one has broken the Kraepelinian system. Good arguments against it are cliches taught to all clinical psychology students. Similarly, good constructive ideas have been developed and partly established in local practice. Apparently no one has had prestige enough or, more likely, no one has really offered a convincingly better system. Even Adolph Meyer and Freud have changed no more than a few small points. The new classifications that have become official are never more than a change of words. Psychologists have tried to hold aloof and unsullied by the use of their tests for supporting a classification that is often exemplified by majority or prestige vote in a case conference; but as clinical psychology accepts more real clinical responsibility, this aloof position is untenable. Undeniably the practicing majority of clinical peers and the common professional language are changing very little. It is in one way understandable enough that psychologists have caused so little change. The psychologists suffer from a plethora of prophets with different theses and these have little in common except the call for a change.

Summarizing the foregoing argument, it could be that some objective clinical tests have been unjustly accused of low validity and efficiency. If present-day clinical practice is largely based upon arbitrary diagnoses and dynamic formulations rather than upon theoretically or scientifically demonstrated indications, test efficiency may now be nearly as high as the predictable upper limit for such arbitrary symptom conglomerates. This thought is a more cheerful one, and the clinical literature is providing some support for it. More and more useful validity items are appearing to support an increasing faith in the objective approaches to personality.

What Is Needed

What we need today is routine practice and what we can now get from our testing and clinical studies is uniformity in the diagnostic reactions of clinicians to the traditional selection of diagnostic symptoms. It is desirable to increase the agreement among clinicians and clinics in applying the accepted diagnostic terms and in making other ordinary clinical decisions. The diagnostic agreement we now achieve is very likely based upon nothing more than training drills that focus attention upon arbitrary symptomatic signs that have no basic meaning. A similar situation exists in psychodynamic formulations. Few of these formulations are validated as indicators of predictively useful behavior sequences or better therapy so as to make one formulation superior to another. Here again, custom and clinical prestige are more involved than is any established fact about the patient's diagnosis or treatment.

If we conclude that the diagnoses and dynamic formulations of present clinical practice derive more from the cultural uniformity of the professional clinician than from the nature of the patient's illness, it becomes reasonable to increase test efficiency by using the test to increase the uniformity of clinical decisions. A reduction of the argument for test use to so low a theoretical level will infuriate some psychologists, but it provides for a real security and useful contribution to those who are clinically operating in the culture. Starting with this point of view, test devices have high efficiency when they provide maximum uniformity and coherence in diagnostic and psychodynamic formulations together with the usual psychometric qualities of objectivity and reliability. In effect, we would gain in efficiency if we abandoned the attempt to validate personality tests by increasing the agreement with diagnoses or clinical estimations beyond a certain point. Advances in validity, once an approximation to criteria of clinical usage is reached, should come more in the form of construct development and in improving the purity of the generalizations from test data.

In this way of thinking, the efficiency of certain tests will steadily rise as the clinical jargon—which develops from the objective data provided in the test signs or scores—becomes more widely used and the universality of patient-descriptive language is advanced by this. This development could make it more possible for different clinics to select more nearly replicable groups of patients for special treatment or study. Objective tests with standard conditions are a necessary prelude to the development of better diagnostic and therapeutic science. Projective devices and expert diagnosticians are not a substitute for this.

A CASE IN POINT

Among numerous illustrations which could be selected, the Pd score of the MMPI provides a good example. The Pd score was originally aimed at producing agreement with clinical staff diagnoses. The criterion groups were made up of various patients diagnosed psychopathic personality. No one has ever thought that this diagnosis signified a constant disease or even a stable pattern of symptoms. But even before the Pd score was derived, it had been suggested, on clinical and psychometric data (4), that there was a smaller group of persons among the psychopaths who were much more similar in symptoms, behavior, and other items. These have gradually emerged as a useful type and today the psychopathic deviate or asocial sociopath is one of the clearest personological constructs. The long suspected defect in emotional function within this sub-group appears to have been substantiated by Lykken's (6) finding of deficient autonomic ("anxiety"?) conditionability. If such new indicators serve to link familiar and useful clinical data to more discriminative psychometric scales, test efficiency will increase although the agreement with the older diagnosis may even decrease.

We would, of course, prefer that decisions from tests should rest upon determined validities and established improvement over base rate predictions. The average clinical situation is far from this ideal at present, and if one insisted upon practicing according to the ideal, one would find it hard to use personality tests.

Many clinical psychologists have a tendency to quit using psychometric data, possibly because they become uncomfortable with the suspicion or evidence that their test data are not improving accuracy of decision. It may also be that they are impressed with the fact that a majority of the psychiatrists, and probably most of the clinical psychologists, in private practice, do not use tests. If laziness is the real reason a psychologist does not use tests, it is hard to prove. When the clinical psychologist does not use tests, he has ceased to identify himself with the scientific future of his profession However, if diagnostic or other contributions of a testing procedure do not sufficiently allay the insecurity of the clinician, do not provide him with useful methods of procedure, or do not protect him from professional danger in proportion to the energy and time that he must invest, he can be expected to abandon the procedure.

We must steadily improve efficiency or lose out in the special field. I wonder what would survive of the present test programs, if the work of the clinical psychologists were evaluated for efficiency by considering the expenditure of professional time and energy in view of the new and useful information provided. I suspect that better than 40 per cent of all the routine clinical testing now done by clinical psychologists would be immediately abandoned. Of course there is comfort in the fact that the field of psychological medicine is full of inefficiency. Even admitting the limitations, testing stands much above most other clinical procedures. If we are in danger of becoming anxiously pessimistic, we need only to review the solid standing of attitude, interest, and ability evaluations. These achievements show the basis for expectation that we will develop more efficiency.

References

1. Cronbach, L. J. and Meehl, P. E. Construct validity in psychological tests. *Psychol. Bull.*, 1955, 52, 281-302.
2. Drake, L. E. Interpretation of MMPI profiles in counseling male clients. *J. counsel. Psychol.*, 1956, 3, 83-88.
3. Hathaway, S. R. A coding system for MMPI profile classification. *J. consult. Psychol.*, 1947, 11, 334-337.
4. Hathaway, S. R. The personality inventory as an aid in the diagnosis of psychopathic inferiors. *J. consult. Psychol.*, 1939, 3, 112-117.
5. Hathaway, S. R. and Monachesi, E. D. The personalities of pre-delinquent boys. *J. Crim. Law, Criminol., and Police Science*, 1957, 48, 149-163.
6. Lykken, D. T. The study of anxiety in sociopathic personality. *J. abnorm. soc. Psychol.*, 1957, 55, 6-10.
7. Meehl, P. E. Wanted—a good cookbook. *Amer. Psychol.*, 1956, 11, 263-272.
8. Meehl, P. E. and Rosen, A. Antecedent probability and the efficiency of psychometric signs, patterns, or cutting scores. *Psychol. Bull.*, 1953, 52, 194-216.
9. Mehlman, B. The reliability of psychiatric diagnoses. *J. abnorm. soc. Psychol.*, 1952, 47, 577-578.
10. Rosen, A. Detection of suicidal patients: an example of some limitations in the prediction of infrequent events. *J. consult. Psychol.*, 1954, 18, 397-403.

XI

Future Impact of Psychological Theory on Personality Assessments *

JAMES G. MILLER
University of Michigan

MICHAEL TODD's moving picture "Around the World in 80 Days" included in addition to the primary stars a number of other outstanding actors, stars in their own right, who consented to play brief vignettes called "cameo parts." And in such a sense we can all say, not "I Am a Camera," but "I Am a Cameo." We are living, behaving systems surrounded by a skin which protrudes into space-time in an engaging variety of patterns. The skin is the boundary which separates us from the environment. This surrounding world is the subject-matter of a number of environmental sciences, most of which are physical or biological. In making their observations these disciplines employ the dimensions of the centimeter-gram-second system and its derivatives, like temperature. In addition they are beginning to employ in some situations a new sort of dimension, the units of information theory.

The various environmental sciences derive a unity from this joint use of dimensions and the classical conceptual system which underlies them. Upon crossing the boundary of the skin, however, things

* Some of the work included in this paper was done in connection with research supported by the Office of the United States Army Surgeon General under Contracts No. DA-49-007-MD-575 and DA-49-007-MD-684, Dr. James G. Miller, Principal Investigator. The opinions expressed in this publication are not necessarily those of the Office of the Surgeon General, Department of the Army.

change. Occasionally the units of the environmental sciences are used, but much more characteristically the dimensions measured in behavioral and personality assessment are entirely different and quite unrelated.

The psychology of personality usually measures traits with names now used technically after having originally been parts of common speech. This fact was dramatized a few years ago when Allport and Odbert (1) went through an ordinary dictionary and compiled a list of words used to describe personality or behavior, hoping thereby to get a full sampling of all possible characteristics.

The way someone trained in physics or engineering would technically describe the action of an automobile and the way a personality psychologist would describe the behavior of a person are strikingly different. The engineer would say that a car has a weight of 3400 pounds and that its previous acceleration at full throttle was 24 ft. per second. Now, however, it has a small pebble of 3/16 inch average diameter in the gasoline feedline of 1/4 inch diameter. As a consequence the rate of gasoline flow at maximum throttle has been diminished from 3 gallons to 1 quart per hour, so the maximal acceleration is now only 6 ft. per second. If the car were a human being, a student of personality would say that, although it had a somatotonic body type, it had formerly rated four on a scale of alertness. This trait was now diminished to a rating of one, and sluggishness had increased from two to five.

This striking difference arises partly from the divergences between the ways we measure the action of human beings and the acts of nonliving systems. A person customarily serves as an observer or rater of the acts of other persons, without intervening objective instruments to quantify the observations. Environmental sciences characteristically use precisely calibrated instruments. To a large degree therefore they eliminate the human error involved in rating.

Some observational activities—for example, pattern recognition —must be done by human beings because as yet we do not have adequate instruments for them. Pattern recognition—of faces, behavior sequences, similar designs—is essential in all science. Content analysis of verbal or written communications is another field in which the human rater must be employed. Continuing efforts should be made to discover ways to replace uncalibrated human beings with more precise instruments in such fields as pattern recognition and content analysis. And as long as human beings are used, the linguistic and other difficulties involved in rating methods should be recognized and everything possible must be done to correct for them. An effort in this direction is "A Glossary of Some Terms Used in the Objective Science of Behavior" by Verplanck (9), compiled admittedly in the Skinnerian frame of reference but broadly valuable for clarifying terminology.

Recently I glanced through a typical personality assessment in what might fairly be called an average well-written clinical case history. It was based on the administration of a large battery of the best-known personality tests. I selected a few of the chief personality traits measured in the evaluation, with titles derived from ordinary English prose. Such dimensions, I believe, should be replaced by more objective variables. Now I will list a few of those words which we have all used or seen in such situations and suggest how they could be made more precise by minimizing opportunity for human error and wherever possible employing centimeter, gram, second units, information units, and derivatives:

Ambivalent. If this trait is demonstrated in overt behavior, a statement concerning the type of physical vacillation between two goal objects, its rate, and duration might well be substituted. If it refers to symbolic behavior, the statement could describe in similar quantitative fashion the amount of vacillation which occurs among various symbol categories identified by content analysis.

Dominant. If this concerns overt behavior, it might be quantified in the way the peck order of animals has been. Dominant symbolic behavior can be measured by some apparatus like the interaction chronograph, which records the number of times in an hour the subject interrupts someone else and the number of seconds of overlap between his speech and that of others with whom he is conversing.

Weak ego. The usual vague clinical impressionism might be replaced by a precise measure of the number of decisions made by the individual for himself as compared with those made for him by others during a standard period of time. The daringness of his decision-making strategies might be evaluated by a test developed in the framework of game theory.

Low need achievement. This could probably be quantified by measuring on a utility scale of some sort (like money) the rewards a person requires to carry out certain standard acts. The more such rewards are required, the lower his need for achievement.

High need aggression. The number of hostile overt or symbolic acts of an individual can be counted during a standard period of time under standard circumstances.

Schizoid. The percentage of characteristically abnormal metaphors or grammatical constructions in a standard sample of talk can be measured. So can the number of times that hallucinations are reported or that the patient appears to be hallucinating.

Moderate word fluency. The number of bits per minute that the individual can read aloud or silently with correct responses concerning comprehension can be measured.

High average performance I.Q. Commonly we measure this by total score from various items or subtests in a test like the Wechsler-Bellevue. The relationships of these subtests one to another are not well understood. Instead we can administer tests involving a known amount of complexity measurable in bits, determining the rates at which a person can solve problems of different known degrees of complexity. Such a method can be applied with equal objectivity to human beings and to lower animals.

There is more or less general agreement among psychiatric clinicians concerning the standard form of diagnostic evaluation; certain published procedures for determining mental status are quite widely followed. But most of the items of such evaluations are qualitative rather than quantitative, or only quantitative in the roughest sense. For example, the number of digits which can be repeated forward and backward, or a series of informational questions of graded difficulty is given as basis for a rough estimate of effective I.Q. Various efforts have been made by Wittenborn, et al (10), Malamud and Sands (4), and others, to develop more quantitative scales of psychiatric status—instruments which can be used not only when the patient is first examined, but repeatedly, to indicate day-to-day changes in some quantitative fashion. Even though these scales are in many ways improvements over the usual clinical method, they suffer from the psychometric shortcomings of other rating scales. These shortcomings include: disagreement from rater to rater concerning the definition of the variable being rated; inter-rater difference in the amount of experience in rating the variable and in the sorts of patients remembered as seen previously (the reference population); lack of a known zero point and of equal intervals between various steps in the scale; nonlinearity of the variable; and lack of orthogonality between variables.

Perhaps the factor analytic method for determining the fundamental psychological dimensions is the best available at the moment. Certainly this procedure has effectively simplified the dimensionalities of the primary mental abilities, of personality, and of semantic meaning. The method, however, cannot rise above the shortcomings of the testing instruments which provide the original scores, including often the limitations of the human being as rater and evaluator. Moreover, the derived factorial dimensions do not have known relationships to the dimensions of the environmental sciences.

I am not necessarily committed to the dimensions of natural science if someone can suggest others which are equally good or better for measuring the interactions of the individual and his environment and consequently for advancing the unity of physical and behavioral science. Lacking such an alternative set of dimensions, we have proceeded to construct a series of tests in which the subject reacts to some electronic or other physical apparatus. We measure his performance, not along classical psychological dimensions, but on the sorts of dimensions that might be used by an electronics engineer if the subject were a component in the electronic system. That is, we determine his personal "transfer function" in this system, using C.G.S. units, derivatives, and information units.

THE DRIVING BATTERY

One set of such test situations is our driving battery (5). These tests have the advantage of face validity, being widely used for measuring driving skills in everyday life. On the other hand, they perhaps do not measure "pure" behavioral variables, certain aspects of the scores really being artifacts of the particular apparatus being used—for example braking time in a driver-trainer is not the same thing as a simple reaction time.

The first piece of equipment in this driving battery is the American Automobile Association's "Auto Trainer." This apparatus consists of two parts: the first includes all the controls of a conventional-shift automobile—starter button, speedometer, steering wheel, gearshift lever, ignition key, and accelerator, brake, and clutch pedals; the second part is a treadmill-like belt about 10 feet long, which extends out from the front of the control unit. The belt, painted to resemble a tortuous roadway, revolves when the controls are in gear, the speed being controlled by the accelerator. In our experiment, however, the apparatus was modified so that the speed could be set by the experimenter's controls at a constant fast rate (equivalent to approximately 20 mph) or a slow rate (approximately 10 mph).

A small model car, the steering mechanism of which is controlled by the steering wheel of the control unit, rests on the belt, its wheels turning as the belt revolves, and the speed of the belt determines its apparent speed. The task of the subject is to steer the car so that it remains in the center of the roadway painted on the belt. A red and a green light are situated at the far end of the belt unit. When the green light is on, the driver is to proceed; when the red light appears, he is to stop the car as rapidly as possible by depressing the brake.

An accuracy counter, a reaction timer, a trial timer, and speed controls face the experimenter at the side of the control unit, out of sight of the subject. A foot switch with which the experimenter can turn on the red light is also connected to the side of the unit. Large staples are embedded in the "roadway" every 3 inches. If the car is kept in the center of the roadway, it makes contact with the staples, completing an electrical circuit and advancing the accuracy counter 1 unit. The reaction timer measures in hundredths of a second the time elapsed between the appearance of the red light and the brake-pressing response.

The subjects are given trials as follows: 20 revolutions of the belt at a fixed slow speed; 20 at a fixed fast speed; and 20 at a speed controlled by the subject. Six reaction-time determinations were interspersed irregularly through each of the 3 trials.

On the driving test, scores are obtained for accuracy at the fixed low speed, at the fixed high speed, and at the variable speed controlled by the subject. The unit of measurement is the number of staples over which the car passes. Since the staples are embedded in the center of the roadway, the subject has to keep the car in the middle of the road to activate the accuracy counter. A time score is obtained, indicating the time required for each trial when the subject is controlling his own speed. During this phase of the test the subject is asked to drive as rapidly and accurately as he can. A derived score is also figured—the ratio of the difference between the accuracy score at low fixed speed and the accuracy score at subject-controlled speed, divided by the time score. This speed-accuracy ratio, which indicates the degree to which speed is sacrificed for accuracy, or vice versa, may be interpreted as a measure of judgment. Reaction times for the brake-pressing response are taken while the car is being driven at low fixed speed, at fast fixed speed, and at variable speed.

The steadiness test is an adaptation of the Whipple Steadiness Test. The test panel contains a series of holes decreasing in size from 7/16 in. to 3/16 in. The subject is asked to insert a round metal stylus 1/8 in. in diameter into each of the holes and to hold it there for 15 seconds without letting it touch the sides of the hole. The apparatus is wired so that a timer is activated whenever the stylus touches the sides of the hole during the 15-second test period. Scores are obtained for three trials on each of the five holes, representing the total amount of time that the stylus touched the rim of the hole.

For the visual tests we employed the master model Ortho-rater constructed by the Bausch and Lomb Optical Company. This device is designed to present slides for testing various visual functions, with distance and illumination controlled. It consists of 2 octagonal slide-holding drums set inside a boxlike apparatus. A binocular eyepiece is located at one end of the box. One of the drums is much closer to the eyepiece than the other and is used for testing near vision; the farther drum is used for testing distant vision. The test slides are fastened to the drum and are easily changed by rotating the drum with an external handle.

Standard Ortho-rater testing procedures are used for seven visual tests. Acuity is determined for both far and near vision; depth perception scores are determined for distant vision only. Vertical and lateral phorias for both near and far vision are also measured.

Precise Measurement of "Pure" Behavioral Variables

We have gone beyond the use of such lifelike measuring situations as the driver trainer, trying to measure "pure" or isolated behavioral variables. On occasion it may be possible to equate functions of known anatomical subsystems with the separate behavioral functions, but perhaps more frequently this is not possible.

In the literature of human experimental psychology are studies with *various* apparatuses—often electronic—designed to measure isolated functions that have a high degree of precision and reliability. We have either adapted existing tests to purposes of personality evaluation under normal or psychopharmaceutical stress conditions or made new tests of our own for special purposes. We have interpreted findings from these testing methods in terms of our general behavior systems theory approach (6). The following are some of the tests which Gerard and I have been using in drug studies.

The Tanner Auditory Perceptual Apparatus. The observer is seated in an individual booth and has in front of him four lights. The first light is a warning flash. The second indicates the signal interval, and may flash one or two times, depending on the experiment. The third light indicates the answer interval during which the observer indicates what signal he heard, or where he heard it. The fourth light is the machine answer light, during which the observer is told the correct answer by another series of lights. The observer wears earphones and through them hears a constant background of noise, which is set at an amplitude of .7 volts. This is turned off only during practice runs. When the actual run has started, the technician lets the observer hear the signal without noise first, then noise is added, and a short practice is allowed. Then 100 presentations are given by the electronic equipment. IBM cards are automatically punched recording the observer's answers on each of the presentations.

The performance is scored in terms of the descision-making theory of signal detection developed by Tanner and Swets (7). It is stated that under given experimental conditions there is one distribution of noise and another distribution of tone plus noise, and these distribution curves overlap somewhat. The quantity d' is defined as the differences between the means of the noise and the tone-plus-noise distribution, divided by the standard deviation of the noise distribution. This d' is measured as a function of the tone-to-noise ratio. Thresholds are obtained when the observer has to rely on his own memory of a previous tone amplitude and circumstances when the previous amplitude with which comparison is made, is presented by the apparatus. In another set of experiments judgments are made as to whether a second tone is lower or higher than the first when the observer has to remember the previous tone and when the previous tone is repeated for him by the apparatus. The threshold for Gaussian noise is also determined. Such measurements have been made by us with subjects under several psychopharmacological drug stresses, and we are studying effects of the drugs on some of the perceptual parameters.

Kristofferson Visual Apparatus. This apparatus (3) employs a four-interval, temporal forced-choice psychophysical method. The subject has a sequence of trials made up of four successive time intervals separated by clearly audible sounds. In every trial a visual target of circular luminescence subtending one degree at the eye is superimposed on a large uniform background of moderate luminescence at one of four time intervals. Which interval is so activated is randomly determined. This target is presented at the fixation point in a location known exactly by the subject. The exposure duration is 0.010 seconds. Fifty successive trials define a unit and require twelve minutes to complete. After one minute's rest the trials can be repeated. Consequently it is possible to derive temporal activity curves as well as dosage curves in this procedure. In work so far carried out we have a definite indication of drug stress effects quantifiable in this situation.

The PSI Apparatus. Members of our group have devoted more effort to the development of this technique and the use of it in a number of different situations, including those involving drugs, than we have to any other single test. The *PSI apparatus* (a contraction of "*Problem Solving Using Information*") permits the combination of a number of elements into various logical relationships. The elements are represented by invariant electronic connections which in the latest version are transistors built into the apparatus. The logical relationships between these elements can be varied by means of a plugboard in the rear of the device. A set of logical relationships between the elements constitutes a problem. The connections determining a particular problem are wired on to a plug which is inserted into the plugboard to constitute each problem.

On the panel is a circular array of lights with corresponding pushbuttons. Each light represents an element and, depending on whether it is on or off, the state of the element. In the center of the panel is a light with no pushbutton, which represents the output of the circular array. A disc that can be placed in the center of the array has arrows drawn on it which show the relationships between the elements. For each problem there is a different disc. All relationships are represented by arrows, and each depicted arrow stands for an existent relationship. The relationships possible are conjunction, disjunction, and negation (hence also implication). The direction of relationships is indicated by the head of the arrows which indicate only the existence and the direction of the relationship, not the kind of relationship. For example, the arrow between lights 5 and 2 might mean a) that if 5 is lit, then 2 will light, or b) that to light 2, it is necessary but not sufficient to light 5, or c) that 5 prevents the lighting of 2. If there is no arrow between two lights, there is no relationship between them; in other words, the null relationship is not presented.

In all problems the task is the same. The central light, representing the output of the network of elements, must be turned on by some combination or sequence of activation of three particular elements, which are referred to as input elements. Any element or combination of elements can be activated by depressing the appropriate pushbuttons. In order to learn how to produce the output of the network—to solve the problem—the subject must analyze the relationships that exist between the input elements.

When an element is activated, the light representing that element on the display panel goes on. Three seconds later, that light goes out and the lights for which the preceding light represents a sufficient condition for activation go on, remain on for three seconds, and in turn go out, activating those elements for which they are sufficient. In this way, an ordered set of consequences of the activation of any combination of elements is presented to the subject. The subject is free to add further activated elements while the consequences of previous button pushes are continuing. He may thus observe sequences of events resulting from the activation of elements and the interaction of multiple sequences. By trying out what happens when various lights or combinations of lights are on, the subject can uniquely determine the nature of all relationships in the network, and thus find out how to solve the problem. Subjects become familiar with the apparatus and situation by means of comprehensive illustrative problems presented in detail by the experimenter, and solve these sample problems before measurement begins. Average time for familiarization and testing on the two problems used most frequently is about two hours altogether.

The raw material for our analysis of the problem-solving process is the sequence of experiments that are performed—that is, the sequences of buttons pushed and the time at which they are pushed. These data are recorded automatically on tape which can be examined and analyzed along many mathematically derived dimensions.

The information content of the network representing any problem can be determined in bits. With the possible exception of Raven's matrices (8) this is the only currently available test of mental abilities made up of problems that increase in complexity in comparable units (bits). It differs from the classical intelligence tests like the Stanford-Binet and Wechsler-Bellevue in which the tasks for various age levels or subtests are entirely different in character, and consequently do not have known commensurability of dimensions. The problems of the PSI apparatus increase in complexity from a one-bit problem (push a certain button and the central light goes on)—the "earthworm floor"—to a very complicated sequence of button-pushes—the "Einstein ceiling?"—by simply adding more bits of comparable character, representing one of the three logical relationships.

By analyzing the nature of the actions carried out during the problem-solving process, taking into account their order, it is possible to relate various aspects of the process to the information gained by the subject up to that point, and also to relate the product of the process, the solution, to the information state. The raw data permit the quantification of a large number of variables, some of which seem to be of reasonable statistical independence. Some of these variables are *power* variables such as the time required for solution, or the number of experiments required for solution. Others are more validly *process* variables, and have consequently been of greater interest to us.

This procedure puts a sort of microscope on cognitive processes, including memory, learning, reasoning, and information processing. We are carrying out factor analytic studies to learn the dimensionality of the domain of 40 or more variables, which are derivative of CGS and information units exclusively. The factor analytic studies are being done both on individuals and on groups. We hope thereby to find ways in which individuals and groups, or normal individuals and individuals under stress, differ in their cognitive processes. We are studying the effects of drugs on such performance, both in diminishing cognitive functions—behavioral toxicity—and also improving it. Horvath, Uhr, Kelly, and Rapaport are involved in various aspects of this work.

Stroud Apparatus. Foster, of our group, has conducted preliminary studies with the Stroud apparatus. This equipment makes it possible to present auditory stimuli at regular intervals whose duration can be varied by the experimenter. There are also two visual stimuli, left and right bulbs which glow at a fixed time after the auditory stimulus. This fixed time can be altered by the experimenter, as can the time between the glowing of the two bulbs. If Stroud's hypothesis is correct, when the two visual stimuli appear in sequence, a certain brief interval after the regular and rapid auditory stimulus the order of the glowing of the two lights will be correctly perceived no better than chance. When they glow about the time the next auditory stimulus is expected, their order will always be correctly perceived. We believe that this time quantum, if it exists, may well be altered by drugs or other stresses.

The Pi Apparatus. This equipment consists of eight translucent plastic knobs 2¾ inches in diameter mounted on 9 x 9 inch squares of black plywood. Each knob contains a light. The eight are arranged in a semicircle around the subject. They can be moved toward or away from the center and are fixed at a distance where the radius of the semicircle is the length of the subject's arm. The subject is seated so that the shoulder of the arm he uses is at the center. Timers control the intervals between the appearance of successive lights, and the duration of the on times for each light.

When a light goes on, the subject is instructed to put it out by hitting the knob. The recording is automatic. Using this equipment Kornblum has been able to find definite drug effects.

Tracking Apparatus. This is a standard task which has been studied extensively for itself alone, but has scarcely been used in evaluating stress effects, although it appears to us to have great promise in this field. The subject's task is to keep a blip on an oscilloscope, the motion of which is controlled by an electronic problem generator, directly on cross-hair lines. He does this by moving a joy-stick. The blip can move at different rates and with differing regularity or randomness. The subject's error in the tracking task can be analyzed into factors due to a) lag in response, b) misperception of spatial distance, c) misperception of speed of motion, and d) misperception of acceleration of motion. Each of these error components can be automatically recorded in digital fashion. It is quite possible that some drugs or other stresses will affect certain of these performance factors, while others will affect other factors, or other functional subsystems.

These are a few of the types of apparatus with which we are now experimenting. It is important, of course, to develop norms for performance on them and to learn all we can about the variables they measure. Many may correlate highly with variables in pencil and paper tests or on rating scales. But we believe that, as there are advances in the use of such instruments, they may provide percision of personality measurement beyond that which at the moment exists.

References

1. Allport, G. W., and Odbert, H. S. Trait-names: a psycho-lexical study. *Psychol. Monogr.* 1936, 47, 1.
2. John, E. R., and Miller, J. G. The acquisition and application of information in the problem solving process. *Behav. Sci.*, 1957, 2, 291-300.
3. Kristofferson, A. B. In Press.
4. Malamud, W., and Sands, S. L. A revision of the psychiatric rating scale. *Amer. J. Psychiat.*, 1947, 104, 231-237.
5. Marquis, D. G., Kelly, E. L., Miller, J. G., Gerard, R. W., and Rapaport, A. Experimental studies of behavioral effects of meprobamate on normal subjects. *Ann. N.Y. Acad. Sci.*, 1957, 67, 701-711.
6. Miller, J. G. Toward a general theory for the behavioral sciences. *Amer. Psychologist,* 1955, 10, 513-531.
7. Quastler, H. (ed.) *Information theory and psychology.* Glencoe, Illinois: Free Press, 1955, 403-413.
8. Raven, J. C. *Progressive Matrices.* London: Lewis, 1938.
9. Verplanck, W. S. A glossary of some terms used in the objective science of behavior. Supplement, *Psychol. Rev.*, 1957.
10. Wittenborn, J. R., Herz, M. I., Kurtz, K. H., Mandell, W., and Tatz, S. The effect of rater differences on symptom rating scale clusters. *J. consult. Psychol.*, 1952, 16, 107-109.

XII

Summary and Conclusions

HAROLD B. PEPINSKY
The Ohio State University

A FRIEND RECENTLY COMMENTED
that psychologists do not listen to other people, because psychologists prefer to tell about what *they* are doing. My friend, who is himself not one of the faithful, had just returned from a conference attended mainly by psychologists, and this was the impression they had given him. If one examines the reference lists appended to the foregoing papers, however, one must infer that this group of psychologists, at least, is well aware of past and current literature on the assessment of human personality. Yet with the exception of Robert Watson, our historian, the symposium participants have run true to my friend's impression. In a very human way, each has made reference to the work of others as a means of justifying what *he* is up to. A brief review of what has been said and some concluding remarks are now in order.

A REVIEW

Robert Watson has traced for us the growing concern of American psychologists for objectivity in the measurement and control of (a) stimulus conditions, (b) the observer, and (c) the responses of the person being observed. At the same time, Watson argues that American psychologists have increased both in their awareness of the complexity of measuring human personality, and in their willingness to tackle complicated problems of measurement. He brings his chapter up to date by reporting on definitions of "objective personality assessment," with which he has been furnished by the other symposium participants.

Performance, projection, and self description approaches are critically reviewed by Donald Super, who comments also, upon the waxing and waning of fads in assessment theory and methods. He concludes that projection (projective) approaches have little practical utility at either the public or private levels of measurement. While Super does not reject the use of performance measures, he cites the higher predictive validity of self description measures, particularly of the biographical (i.e., autobiographical) inventory.

The next participant, Raymond Cattell, does not like scaling methods of assessing personality, preferring instead factor analytic method applied to what he calls "multivariate experiment" in the natural setting. Cattell is armed with an impressive array of rating, questionnaire, and objective test data, which have been digested in large amounts by electronic computers. He argues that multivariate factor analysis is analogous to the clinical method of personality assessment; factor analysis enables the psychologist to remain close to his data as he interprets them and yields information on both known and unknown clinical constructs.

Louis McQuitty, however, thinks that his method of "successive agreement analysis," used to isolate and differentiate personality types, is more flexible than traditional factor analysis. This is because the latter method requires items of invariant validity for all persons sampled, whereas the former assumes items to have differential validity for different groupings of persons. McQuitty's method appears to be a kind of Q technique, in which persons are intercorrelated across a set of items and then, by iterative procedure, grouped into successively larger clusters of like responding persons.

Irwin Berg seriously questions whether item particular content is important in differentiating among "operationally clean" criterion groups of persons and supports this statement by reference to his own and others' research. In his view, it is the characteristic response pattern, or "set," of such a group of persons—measured across widely different kinds of stimulus conditions—that distinguishes the group from other groups (or from people in general). This assumption underlies Berg's "deviation hypothesis," which states that a group that differs from other groups in what Berg has designated as *critical* areas of behavior, will differ also in its *noncritical* behavior.

Such group differences are shown to occur, moreover, in the amount of "favorableness" assigned to personality test items. And this empirical finding is used by Allen Edwards in developing "social desirability" scales. His studies of social desirability exemplify what he refers to as the "construct method" of personality test construction, which he clearly prefers to factor analytic or "criterion group" methods. The idea here is that individuals and groups differ not only in their tendencies to select "True," "False," or "Undecided" responses to items, but in their tendencies to give socially desirable responses to items as well (regardless of whether the socially desirable responses are "True" or "False"). Thus it is considered parsimonious to regard social desirability as being a major contributor to the variance of personality test items. For example, people in general can be expected to regard clinically designated item clusters such as those characterizing "depression" or "schizophrenia" as being socially undesirable, and this expectation is supported by the research of Edwards and his associates. Also, persons who score "high" on these socially undesirable item clusters can be expected to obtain "low" social desirability scores, independently measured, on other tests, which such persons tend to do.

James Miller not only sounds like an electronics engineer in his paper, he makes clear to us that he wants to sound like an electronics engineer in his approach to the problem of personality assessment. Most of the physical and biological sciences, he points out, have common units of observation and measurement (the centimeter-gram-second system) and, more recently, of enumeration (the bit of information) and a classical conceptual system. In stark contrast, psychological language, measurement, and conceptualization is a mess! His compelling argument is that the concepts and methods of general systems theory can be used to advance the unity of physical and behavioral science. First, he suggests how traits frequently used in the description of human personality can be more precisely redefined and measured if the human organism is viewed as a component in an electronic system; second, he describes novel test situations that are being developed at the University of Michigan's Mental Health Research Institute; and third, he shows how such tests can be used to provide precise measures of human personality. As the title of his paper implies, a new and communicable and valid personality theory is in the making; despite present claims of other persons, it is not now available.

Uniquely among the contributors to this symposium, Wayne Holtzman has taken as his assessment model a standard projection device, the Rorschach, and modified it into a test that utilizes more objective stimulus conditions and scoring procedures. In this task, he has sought to combine the qualitative richness of this projective method with the quantitative rigor of psychometric analysis. The result—the Holtzman Inkblot Test—is described following a brief, yet comprehensive review of methodological problems that arise in dealing with projective materials.

Bernard Bass has provided an exceptionally well organized and scholarly background for his discussion of the Louisiana State University leadership studies, including an extensive review of published attempts to assess the leadership variable by objective methods. The maturity of his paper, in an area that has been characterized by procedural sloppiness and sweeping generalization, is a testimonial to the value of a research worker's dedication to a restricted methodology which, in this case, centers on the study of changes of attitudes or preference in groups. Bass's dedication has yielded an enormous supply of empirical data, which he has been able to organize into theoretical propositions that in turn have suggested meaningful and valid predictions. Concurrently, he has developed methods for the rapid processing and analysis of his data, e.g., they are fed directly into an electronic analog computer. Though the yield is "artificial, unnatural, and limited"—to use his own terms, his work has generated a number of hypotheses that can be tested in natural settings, outside of the laboratory.

To the clinician who is fearful that his services are about to be dispensed with, William Hunt's paper on an "actuarial approach to human judgment" will bring reassurance. What Hunt urges, in effect, is that the process of inductive logic, which human organisms are capable of and which electronic computors—to date, at least—are not capable of, be capitalized upon in the assessment of human personality. The process of clinical judgment, like paper and pencil tests, can be standardized in principle, and Hunt has shown in a number of publications, referred to in his paper, that clinicians' interpretations of patients' responses to complex stimulus situations can be highly reliable. He stresses, however, that agreement among judges in such situations demands that the judges be carefully trained for their tasks. Hunt points out that this enterprise is an extension of the search for and uncovering of lawful uniformities of judgment in classical psychophysics.

Finally, Starke Hathaway urges the development of clinical testing procedures that provide a maximum of utility yet require a minimum of cost and effort. Reduction of the "professional time investment" required for test giving and scoring (can a high grade clerk or a technician do it?) illustrates the latter objective; increasing the number of "hits" in predicting from test to criterion data illustrates the former. Hathaway warns, however, against attempts to predict diagnoses or clinical estimations to the exclusion of what he considers a more important kind of validation, i.e., that obtained in the process of construct development. The construction of his own Psychopathic Deviate (Pd) scale, one of the measures yielded by his Minnesota Multiphasic Personality Inventory, is cited as a case in point. Development of this construct, for example, gave rise to the belief that diagnosed Pd's would be relatively deficient in their emotional functioning. A subsequent experiment demonstrated that high Pd's indeed were less susceptible than low Pd's to autonomic conditioning.

Some Concluding Remarks

The symposium participants, as a group, are dissimilar in their conceptions of how personality is to be assessed. Thus, for example, the advocated raw data of assessment range from expressed clinical judgments of patient behavior in the natural setting to subject responses in a controlled laboratory situation that can be fed directly into an electronic computer. On one point, at least, there is overwhelming agreement: whatever assessment data are used must, in principle, be capable of being defined empirically, measured in amount, and recorded as scores in the public domain. It is this kind of belief in "objective" measurement, so obviously a shared conviction of the contributors, that characterizes the present symposium.

On the issue of objectivity versus subjectivity in the assessment of personality, then, there is no quarrel among the participants. But there are other issues on which the participants appear to be in hearty disagreement, or where additional problems of resolution can be expected. This may seem strange, when one stops to consider that a response made by a subject to a defined stimulus condition is, simply, the product of an interaction between subject and stimulus condition. Yet several methodological questions, at least, are suggested by this apparently simple statement: (1) What subject? (2) What stimulus condition? (3) What response? (4) What antecedent events, in respect either to subject or stimulus condition, need to be considered in predicting what a given subject's response will be? An additional methodological question has been barely touched upon by the participants but is nonetheless relevant: (5) In whose view is the stimulus condition to be defined and in whose view is the measured amount of the subject's response to be assessed? Our

Ohio State University research productivity in organizational settings has suggested the importance of maintaining conceptual distinctions here among: (a) the subject, (b) the task-setter who prescribes the stimulus condition, and (c) the observer who reports on and analyzes the subject's response and who may or may not be identical with the subject or the task-setter. Thus, Hunt's clinical judges must be viewed at the same time both as *observers* of patients whose responses are to be predicted, and as themselves *subjects* whose clinical predictions are to be treated as responses. A related methodological question also must be asked: (6) What is the subject's phenomenal view (as a measured response) of the task-setter and the stimulus condition that he prescribes for the subject? It is important to know whether the subject being assessed, e.g., in Bass's laboratory or in a Hathaway hospital setting, regards himself as playing a game as opposed to playing "for keeps," whether the task-setter is regarded as hostile, friendly, or neutral, or whether the task condition has face validity for the subject as something that is important for him to perform.[1]

In retrospect, one could wish that questions of this sort could have been dealt with explicitly by all of the participants in the symposium. Their probable lack of consensus in answering such questions can be inferred, I think, from the participants' lack of specific agreement in defining the term "objective," despite their shared concern for measurement and for scores (see Chapter 1). Lack of consensus, or even of concern, can be inferred, too, from unresolved issues, to some of which we can turn now.

Berg and Cattell, for instance, differ on the issue of item interpretation, Berg implying that particular item content can safely be ignored and Cattell suggesting that subject-item interactions can be interpreted to yield useful clinical constructs. Again, Cattell also differs, e.g., from Super, in respect to the manifest versus the latent content of an item. Super wants the item to have the same meaning for the subject as it has for Super, while Cattell does not want the subject to be able to guess what the item means to Cattell. Then there is the validity issue, with Super arguing for the utility of predictive validity. Edwards and Hathaway expound construct validation, but do not see eye to eye about its purpose. Edwards shows that considerable item-response variance, otherwise attributable to specific clinical syndromes, can be accounted for more

---

[1] This last point is well covered by Joan Criswell. (See Criswell, Joan. The psychologist as perceiver. In R. Tagiuri and L. Petrullo (Eds.), *Person perception and interpersonal relations.* Stanford: Stanford Univ. Press, 1958, pp. 95-109.

parsimoniously in terms of Edwards' social desirability component. Hathaway, a practicing and practical clinician, argues for what works and has utility in the hospital setting, by which criteria the presence or absence of a social desirability loading may be irrelevant to the interpretation of an item.

How item-responses should be analyzed is a third issue, with Cattell preferring factor analysis, McQuitty supporting successive agreement analysis, and Edwards expounding scaling. A fourth issue is that of the laboratory versus a natural setting as the locus of data collection, although even Cattell, the most vigorous exponent of "observation *in situ*," imposes behavioral restrictions on his subjects in the process of obtaining information about them. Hunt's judges, of course, are quite free to observe patients' natural movements in the hospital setting; even here, though, it is assumed that the reliability of predictions among judges is increased by control of the stimuli to which they are exposed. Bass, in contrast, is unashamedly at work in a laboratory, seeking lawful relationships among variables systematically controlled and manipulated.

Strangely enough, none of the authors has stopped to define the term, "personality." Therefore, we cannot know whether this is a definitional problem on which they are at issue. Their chapters indicate, however, that the participants are otherwise impressed with the need for definitional clarity and empirical referents for their variables, and for obtaining reliable scores based on careful observation and measurement of the variables. What emerges from this preoccupation is a kind of stubborn, but highly commendable simplicity in the authors' discussions of their work. We may conclude that the apparent simplicity results precisely because the empirical study on which the chapters are based has been so very painstaking and extensive in every case; each author so obviously knows what he is writing about. On the one hand, the reports give encouragement to the belief that we are closer than ever before to being the proud possessors of psychological laws. On the other hand, the implications of the several chapters are so often at variance with each other that the claim of any of the participants to the possession of knowledge that orders psychological variables into lawful association with each other is somewhat weakened.

Nearly all of the authors give clear indication of their awareness that human life is very complicated and of their humility in pursuing the task of helping us to order and measure the data of human existence. Each takes himself and his work quite seriously and evidences a belief in the validity and urgency of his task. Curiously, what emerges as a dominant theme of the symposium is a pre-occupation with method, instrumentation, and the interpretation of data. For example, the heuristic yield of new methods for the rapid collection and processing of data is taken for granted by several of the authors, who promote the use of electronic gadgetry with great enthusiasm. An implicit and seductive argument that underlies this zeal for a "psychonomy of abundance" is that if we can get *enough* data, we are bound to have *good* data.

Curiously, also—in view of a *Zeitgeist* for interdisciplinary research (e.g., among research fund-granting agencies), Miller is the only member of the group who openly and strongly advocates an interdisciplinary research effort. None of the participants has paid more than passing lip service to the possible contributions that sociologists, anthropologists, or other kinds of social scientists might make to problems of assessing human personality. Is this because other social scientists have nothing to contribute to the symposium topic? One regrets that this question did not become an issue for the symposium.

Despite a few understandable sins of commission and omission, there is much to read in the present series of papers that is rich and satisfying. A new and abundant harvest of ideas and facts and methods of inquiry has been made available for research workers and practitioners alike. The papers give heartening testimony to the fact that one can stay very close to one's data yet, in making sense out of them, manifest considerable imaginativeness and productive originality. Certainly, by comparison with the OSS and VA assessment research of the previous decade, there is ample evidence furnished us here of significant accomplishment in the development of a methodology for the objective assessment of human personality.

Subject Index

Actuarial approach, clinical judgment in, 179 ff., 220

Anxiety, factor analysis and, 56
state and trait pattern of, 56

Behaviorism, objectivity of measurement and, 7 ff.
performance and, 8
personality and, 8 ff.

Clinical data vs. psychometric data, 194 ff.

Clinical diagnosis, use of tests, 220-221

Clinical efficiency, 192 ff.
use of tests, 192 ff.

Clinical judgment, actuarial approach, 169 ff., 176 ff., 179 ff., 220
distortions of, 187
experimental findings, 177 ff.
idiographic-nomothetic controversy, 172 ff., 175 ff.
necessity of, 177
prediction from, 172 ff.

Clinical judgments, scaled, 179 ff.
practical applications, 186 ff.

Clinical study, probability theory and, 172 ff.

Clinical tests, administration, 195 ff.

Clinical uniformity, need for, 200 ff.

Clinician, as an instrument, 174 ff.

Deviant behavior, language usage in, 92

Deviant response patterns, generality of, 87, 95
importance of, 94 ff.

Deviant responses, learning and, 88
physical diseases, 93

Deviation hypothesis, 86 ff., 218
abnormality and, 87-88
bias and, 87-89
critical and noncritical behavior, 87, 91, 94

Diagnosis, purpose of, 198 ff.

Factor analysis, clinical impressions and, 49
dynamic calculation and, 54
interpretation of, 50
personality assessment, 218, 223
personality inventories, 101
psychological dimensions, 207 ff.

Factor analytic findings, 47 ff.

Holtzman Inkblot Test, 137-140

Intelligence, measures of, 4, 5
theories of, 6

Intelligence testing, applications of, 6 ff.
in Britain, 6, 7
in U. S., 6
statistics and, 6, 7

Item content, 218, 222
early personality tests and, 83 ff.
empirical demonstration and, 89
face validity and, 83-85
unimportance of, 83 ff.

Name Index

229

232

232